The Red River
Campaign and Its Toll

The Red River Campaign and Its Toll

69 Bloody Days in Louisiana, March–May 1864

HENRY O. ROBERTSON

McFarland & Company, Inc., Publishers
Jefferson, North Carolina

LIBRARY OF CONGRESS CATALOGUING-IN-PUBLICATION DATA

Names: Robertson, Henry O., 1968– author.
Title: The Red River Campaign and its toll : 69 bloody days in Louisiana, March–May 1864 / Henry O. Robertson.
Description: Jefferson, North Carolina : McFarland & Company, Inc., Publishers, 2016. | Includes bibliographical references and index.
Identifiers: LCCN 2016011806 | ISBN 9781476663784 (softcover : acid free paper) ∞
Subjects: LCSH: Red River Expedition, 1864.
Classification: LCC E476.33 .R63 2016 | DDC 973.7/36—dc23
LC record available at http://lccn.loc.gov/2016011806

BRITISH LIBRARY CATALOGUING DATA ARE AVAILABLE

ISBN (print) 978-1-4766-6378-4
ISBN (ebook) 978-1-4766-2447-1

© 2016 Henry O. Robertson. All rights reserved

No part of this book may be reproduced or transmitted in any form or by any means, electronic or mechanical, including photocopying or recording, or by any information storage and retrieval system, without permission in writing from the publisher.

Front cover: print titled *Battle of Pleasant Hill* (Library of Congress)

Printed in the United States of America

McFarland & Company, Inc., Publishers
Box 611, Jefferson, North Carolina 28640
www.mcfarlandpub.com

For Amy,
Adeline and William

Table of Contents

Acknowledgments   viii
Preface   1
Introduction   7
ONE—The Curtain Rises: The Red River Valley, 1803–1860   23
TWO—The Secession Crisis: Unionists and Confederates, 1860–1861   37
THREE—The Pain of Sacrifice: The Red River Home Front, 1862–1864   55
FOUR—Cotton, Cotton, Cotton: 1863–1864   67
FIVE—The Campaign Begins: January–March 1864   77
SIX—The Most Terrible Charge: The Battle of Mansfield, April 8, 1864   95
SEVEN—The Union Hold at Pleasant Grove: April 8, 1864   108
EIGHT—The Tumult of Pleasant Hill: April 9, 1864   116
NINE—The Old South and Cane River Crossing: April 23, 1864   133
TEN—Gone with the Wind: The Burning of Alexandria and the End of the Campaign, May 13–18, 1864   149

Conclusion   168
Chapter Notes   179
Bibliography   196
Index   207

Acknowledgments

This book would not have been possible without the help and support of many great individuals and fantastic institutions. My thanks go out to all of them.

Louisiana College provided a summer faculty development grant that provided necessary funds for travel, research, and writing. My thanks to the committee, and its able chair, Dr. Wade Warren. Several Vice-Presidents of Academic Affairs provided additional support: Glenn Sumrall, Michael Travers, Timothy Searcy, Travis Wright, and Cheryl Clark. The college presidents, Dr. Joseph Aguillard, and now Dr. Rick Brewer provided release time and encouragement that kept this work going. Director of the Richard Norton Library at the college, Dr. Terry Martin, and the library's many dedicated staff members over the years filled every inter-library loan request, ordered important books for the permeant collection, and maintained a high level of service. I am grateful for everything they do. Timothy Roper, art professor and director at Graphic Services, fulfilled several important orders in a timely manner.

My colleagues over the years, especially Collin Garbarino, Christine Reese, E. Gabrielle Walker, and Gilbert "Buck" Jones, allowed me to be a scholar-teacher and pursue my academic interests near and far. Robin Bunting, executive secretary in the Division of History and Political Science, performed miracles with every book-related task put before her. No one is better at what she does.

Both Terry Jones and Jeff Prushankin, two of the best Civil War scholars in the country, read an early draft of the book and provided excellent peer review suggestions for improvement. I have incorporated their comments where possible and all have made this book better. Kathleen McGinty-Johnston gave the manuscript a through reading.

She is the finest copyeditor I have met and she proved that the pen is mightier than the sword.

More than anyone, Gary D. Joiner, a geographer and historian, listened, encouraged, and shared his wealth of multi-disciplinary knowledge. This book would not have been possible without his faith in my work and his scholarship on Louisiana's past. North Louisiana has no better scholar than Gary. Several other outstanding academics, the late Arthur W. Bergeron, Jr., Susan Dollar, Don S. Frazier, the late James G. Hollandsworth, Jr., T. Michael Parrish, John Sacher, and Elaine Thompson, have all shared their expertise with me.

A number of librarians and archivists went above and beyond in their assistance: Sean Benjamin at Tulane University, Judy Bolton at Louisiana State University, Michelle Riggs at Louisiana State University at Alexandria, Bill Stafford at the state archives in Baton Rouge, Roland R. Stansbury at the Young-Sanders Center, and Mary Linn Wernet at Northwestern State University. Marlea D. Leljedal at the Army Heritage and Education in Carlisle, Pennsylvania, provided invaluable assistance with illustrations. All these individuals preserve, present, and secure some of the most outstanding collections of material related to the Red River campaign. They made sitting alone in an archive reading the letters of dead people a tremendous joy.

The panelists and participants at the 2004 Red River Civil War Symposium at Louisiana State University at Alexandria offered insights that inspired me to begin my own work. Many thanks to Louisiana State University at Alexandria faculty Dr. Jerry Sanson, Dr. Jim Rogers, Dr. Greg Gormanous, and Chancellor Robert Cavanaugh for sponsorship and help with the event.

I presented versions of several chapters of this book at a number of public speaking engagements. The Shreveport Book Festival, Kent Plantation House in Alexandria, the Civil War Roundtable of Central Louisiana, the Baton Rouge Civil War Roundtable, and the 2014 "Defending the Homeland" Symposium at Shreveport all provided great opportunities to share my material.

Enough cannot be said about the director of the Mansfield State Historic Site, Scott Dearman. He answered every question I put to him with the careful eye of a seasoned scholar. Louisiana is blessed with other great museum professionals. Alice Scarborough, director of the Kent Plantation House, Dale Genius, director of the Alexandria History Museum, Don Fontenot, director of the Forts Randolph and Buhlow

State Historic Site gave of their time, offered insights into the campaign, and showed me important artifacts.

Interest in Central Louisiana's Civil War history is kept alive by many knowledgeable community members. Charles Neal in Rapides Parish, Glenn Maxwell in Grant Parish, Steve Mayeaux in Avoyelles, Joe Kutch in Pineville, the late Carl Laurent and Judge Thomas Yeager in Alexandria, and Don Marlar in western Rapides Parish are among the best. My visits to Mansfield, Pleasant Hill, Monett's Ferry, and Fort DeRussy site in Avoyelles Parish gave me invaluable insight into what happened at those places. The U.S. Army Corps of Engineers maintains an excellent museum at Grand Ecore that I have visited with students and on my own. The Cane River Creole National Park is another great site worthy of frequent visits and its dynamic superintendent, Laura Gates, has done an excellent job with interpretation of the area's history.

The 2007 Civil War class at Louisiana College wrote entries for a Red River campaign guide that helped my own thinking on the subject. Those students have graduated and gone on to successful careers. My thanks to each of them and all the others in classes I taught over the years. From time to time, I organized trips to sites associated with the Red River Campaign and other Civil War National Parks in Mississippi, Virginia, Maryland, and Pennsylvania. I hope all my students will return to those battlefields for a second look except this time without their notebook, pens, and anxious looks.

My family, Amy, Adeline, and William, have been a great source of strength over the years. Without their love and affection, this book would not have been possible.

Preface

Almost every school day for ten years, I drove my son and daughter across the Purple Heart Bridge that connects Pineville, Louisiana, and the city of Alexandria. After dropping them off, I crossed the bridge again on my way to Louisiana College where I work as a history professor. Most afternoons I picked the children up. That made four times in a day I crossed the Red River. With trips for dining and shopping, it was not unusual for me to log sixteen crossings a week. While working on this book, I joked to myself that no historian crossed the Red River more than I did. Rare was a day when I did not cross that waterway and think about its Civil War history.

Coming or going, I glanced over the guard rail and took in the whole view—the flat expanse of the river, the trees dotting the shoreline, the levee, the homes behind it, and the expanse of sky arching over it all. At times, I beheld the Red's dark blue surface shimmering in the sunrise. On other occasions the red, orange, and purple of a striking sunset caught my eye. Sometimes the whole scene was shrouded by a thick gray fog. Though tamed by an extensive series of locks and dams, heavy rains still turned the river into a raging torrent of deep, milky red. Spring and summer brought recreational boats plying up and down its course. On one crossing, I witnessed the arrival of the famed *Delta Queen* steamboat, gliding into view with the grandeur of an old Victorian lady. On another, a bald eagle soared overhead just as I topped the bridge.

When March rolled around each year, I recalled that in 1864 Union gunboats appeared around the bend in the river within sight of where the modern bridge was built. Union army commander General Nathaniel Banks joined it, and a major campaign began in Central Louisiana. The invading army and navy pressed northward, aiming for

Shreveport and the conquest of Texas. Their advance halted on April 8 at a farm outside of Mansfield, Louisiana, where a smaller Confederate force commanded by General Richard Taylor delivered a stinging defeat. A follow-up battle took place that evening at Pleasant Grove, and then the next day, eighteen miles south of the first encounter, another fierce struggle ensued around the village of Pleasant Hill. President Abraham Lincoln's army retreated, a beaten force. This was one of the last major victories for the Confederacy.[1]

Realizing the army was in retreat, Admiral David Dixon Porter ordered his flotilla to reverse course. The gunboats had come within sight of Springfield Landing, approximately sixteen road miles from Shreveport.[2] With the army on the run, the river vessels became exposed to enemy fire from the banks and several vessels came under intense attack at Blair's Landing, east of Pleasant Hill. General Tom Green and his Texas cavalry troopers poured on a withering fire in what was surely one of the most unusual of Civil War battles.[3] Green would be nearly decapitated by a shell from one of the boats. His death ended an illustrious military career that included service in the Texas War for Independence and the Mexican War.[4] The gunboats were further harassed on their way back to Alexandria and then became trapped by rock formations exposed as the water level fell. An ingenious officer and Wisconsin lumberman, Lieutenant Colonel Joseph Bailey, came to their rescue with a plan for winged and crib dams that raised the water level just enough to allow the boats to pass. His engineering, along with the prodigious labor of African-American troops and Maine soldiers who had been lumbermen before the war, saved the day. Once free, the navy steamed back down the river only to find Confederate snipers and batteries popping up along the route. At a curve in the river called Egg Bend, located in Avoyelles Parish, the *USS Covington* took so many hits from Confederate artillery that the crew abandoned the vessel and set it ablaze. It blew up, causing a tremendous blast heard for miles around.[5]

The army left Alexandria on May 13. Troops set the town afire; in a few hours, the heart of the city lay in ashes.[6] Confederates clashed with the Union army twice more at Mansura and in a bloody engagement at Yellow Bayou. The Union army reached Simmsport with the intention of crossing over the Atchafalaya River. The Mississippi was running high and fast with the spring rains; it was impossible to lay down pontoon bridges and too dangerous to ferry men to the opposite bank. This time is was the army that was trapped by water. Once again,

Bailey came to the rescue and devised a plan to lash the navy's boats together side by side and create a temporary bridge across the raging divide. By May 20, with the Union army safely across, the campaign came to an end.[7]

From March to May of 1864, Louisiana's Red River campaign would be one of the most destructive of the Civil War. On the advance as well as the retreat, fire consumed cotton, outbuildings, and homes. Alexandria suffered nearly complete destruction. Both armies commandeered supplies and disrupted the spring planting season. Enslaved people all along the Red made dashes for freedom, further destabilizing the region's social and economic conditions. The desperate battles between the Union and Confederate forces were marked by terrible brutality. A localized civil war took place as Jayhawker bandits tormented anyone with their reach. The months of this campaign were among the most trying in the history of Central Louisiana.

How did a region relatively untouched until 1864 become a victim of the cruel hand of war? A number of factors contributed to the tragedy. The rift between Unionists and Secessionists was even deeper and wider in the region than in other parts of the country—a circumstance underestimated by previous historians. Lust for the Red's great commodity, cotton, meant greed and corruption contributed to the degeneration of the war locally. Additionally, the disintegration of a slave-based society was suddenly and violently accelerated by armies fighting nearby. What happened in the Red River Valley in 1864 goes a long way towards explaining the nature of the Civil War itself.

Why another book on the Red River campaign? The "dean" of Red River Campaign studies, Ludwell Johnson, gave readers the first treatment of the subject back in 1958.[8] His pioneering study still serves as the foundation for all modern works on the campaign, including this one. A few years following its publication, during the Centennial of the Civil War, a chapter on the Red River campaign appeared in the monumental tome *The Civil War in Louisiana*, written by professor John Winters.[9] For decades, these were the literature on the campaign, though a few students and Civil War buffs published articles from time to time. The Red River remained one of the least known of the Civil War campaigns.

In 1974, the legendary historian Shelby Foote stoked interest by including a narrative about the campaign in one of his popular volumes.[10] Still, throughout the 1970s and 1980s, the Red River campaign did not receive the attention that was being paid to the war in

Virginia, Tennessee or Georgia. One recent scholar commented that Civil War historians had contracted a case of "Virginia disease," for their disproportionate attention given to the fighting there. What happened west of the Mississippi River, another scholar opined, was nothing more than "needless violence."[11] Trans-Mississippi Civil War history would have to wait a bit longer.

In the waning decade of the 20th century, the principal generals of the campaign—Richard Taylor, son of a U.S. president, and Nathaniel Banks, a presidential hopeful—received excellent biographies.[12] In the first years of the 21th century, ground-breaking research appeared by historian and cartographer Gary D. Joiner. I met Gary in 2004 at a symposium for the 140th anniversary of the campaign that I organized at Louisiana State University at Alexandria. I sensed then that a new field of scholarship centered on the campaign was emerging. That forum brought together other scholars, Civil War buffs who were writing their histories themselves, and the late Arthur W. Bergeron, Jr., for one of his spellbinding presentations.

The year before the conference, Joiner's book *One Damn Blunder from Beginning to End* (the title taken from General William T. Sherman's blunt assessment of events along the Red River) made him the new dean of Red River studies.[13] The biggest question Gary tackled was the mysterious fall of the Red River's water level—in springtime, when it should have been rising—that suddenly trapped Union gunboats at Alexandria. Ludwell Johnson and all who followed him attributed the drop to a fickle river. Through meticulous research in archives of engineers and obscure officers, Joiner found it was no accident. An ingenious engineering project allowed Confederate forces to lower the river's volume on purpose. Kept quiet at the time, this tactical feat was forgotten over the years. Any book on the campaign published before 2003 missed these key findings.[14] Joiner went on to compile another book of primary sources from the campaign's participants, an expanded study of what he found in his first book, and he found time to lead the preservation effort for the campaign's battlefields and historic sites.[15]

Another participant at the LSU-Alexandria forum breathed new life into an old yet still significant issue: the infamous command squabble between Confederate generals Edmund Kirby Smith, who was over the department where the action took place, and Richard Taylor, the field commander, was the subject of Jeff Prushankin's fine monograph in 2005. An extraordinary military historian, Prushankin gave us what I hope is the last word on that dispute, which raged on in print during the post-war years. In addition to his work, a number of popular histories on the subject have appeared in print. Most of these are narratives that take their lead from the advances made by Joiner or Prushankin.[16]

My own work began at the time of the 2004 symposium and has progressed for the past eleven years. I approach the subject via the social history route because it has been less travelled by the military historians who have studied the campaign. I have been aided by a rich collection of letters and diaries that have surfaced through recent scholarship, many of which have never been brought into works on the subject. At the same time, the internet has made source material much more accessible. My research included the regimental histories, diaries, and manuscript letters—many digitized and others still tucked away in archives across the country. Most helpful to me has been teaching students about the campaign. I have visited all the sites associated with the campaign, both on my own and with students in tow. I now add my own work to the rising sea of academic and popular ink.

Because so much great work has been done recently, my focus is on the meaning, the *why* of the campaign. I have sought out the historical actors who played key roles in the campaign and those lesser known ones who best illustrate the history's salient features. Soldiers from both sides figure prominently. These were ordinary men from the bayous and woods of Louisiana, the prairies of Texas, the towns of the American Northeast, New England, and the farmland of the Midwest. The participants were in units from more than fifteen states, armies and navy representing a microcosm of America. Many were veterans who had seen tough campaigns before but were still moved by what they witnessed along the Red. I discovered Unionists in Central Louisiana who were not in favor of secession or the Confederate war effort; many joined the Union army when it arrived. Then there were the masters and slaves of this rich plantation society who became as important as the soldiers in the drama. Their world had been built by a prosperous agricultural economy, and was thrown headlong into turmoil. Most fascinating are the lesser known human interest accounts of people who became caught up in this important episode in state and national history.

This is not an uplifting story. For three months, the darkest and most destructive tendencies of the war came out in Louisiana. The Red River campaign may not have been a turning point of the war but it was a turning point for those caught up in its horrors, who saw fighting of an intensity and desperation not seen in the state up to that time. Hundreds died and communities tumbled into chaos as both belligerents burned or confiscated private property. My perspective on these events has been greatly influenced by Louisiana State University professor Charles Royster and his book *The Destructive War*, published when I was a graduate student taking classes with him.[17] He found, as I did, that both sides contributed something to the ferocity of the war. More recently, the writings of Civil War historian Daniel Sutherland have outlined the incredible brutality and wrenching tragedy of the war.[18] Sutherland emphasized the ruthless, irregular nature of the fighting across Arkansas and other parts of the South. In Louisiana's Red River country, I see much resemblance to the world Sutherland described so well. The Civil War turned a corner in the Red River campaign that spring of 1864, and although other places had experienced equally sanguine moments, the fighting along the Red exhibited a high degree of pathos not found elsewhere. Months before total war was seen in Virginia and Georgia, before Union generals Grant and Sherman had even hit their stride, the fighting in Louisiana had reached a violent fever pitch.

Introduction

"On the 2d of April, we arrived at Natchitoches," a Union soldier wrote. The place he found, a small village steeped in French culture, sat in the heart of the Red River Valley. The oldest settlement in Louisiana, it had at one time stood proudly on the Red River. In a cruel twist of fate, the clearing of the Great Red River Raft during the 1830s, intended to open the log-jammed waterway for navigation, shifted the river's course and by 1840 the village became landlocked. The soldier and his unit found anything but a warm reception.

> During our stay here, one of the soldiers of the 24th Iowa was killed in sight of camp by the rebels. He, with two of our Regiment, Pavy and McCune, of Company D, were just outside the lines, foraging, when they were surprised in a barn by two armed rebels and captured. Being unarmed, they made no resistance. After tying them loosely together, they were marched back some distance and seated on a log, when the rebels decided to shoot them, and began tying them more securely. The Iowa soldier, who was in the middle, attempted to release himself; whereupon one of their captors fired, killing him instantly. At this Pavy broke loose and ran for camp, with one of his captors after him, while McCune was knocked down with a musket by the other, who then turned and watched the race. McCune, in the meantime, recovering, untied himself from his dead comrade, and made good his escape, as did also Pavy, who came into camp almost exhausted. A force of cavalry was sent out and the body of the dead soldier was brought in, and the house and barn burnt. The two rebels were afterward captured, but claimed they were Confederate soldiers, at home on a furlough. The rebels threatened retaliation if they were executed, so they were afterwards exchanged.[1]

This eye-opening description of ambush, murder, arson, and retribution illustrated the terrible nature of the Red River campaign. Why did both sides act with this degree of savagery? Like so many things about the state's history, the Civil War has a different story in Louisiana than elsewhere.

Louisiana had been purchased in 1803 from France and became

a state in 1812. With rich agricultural land and a temperate climate with long growing seasons, it quickly became a place sought by white settlers. The geography of its great rivers played a large part in this migration. The Mississippi River formed the eastern boundary of the state and then made its winding way to the Gulf of Mexico. American settlers interested in making new farming communities came down and across this great river. They moved along the dozens of other major waterways and the narrow roads that connected them. In the decades after the 1803 purchase, tens of thousands of Anglo-settlers spread their culture across every corner of the state. The great colonial city, New Orleans, founded by the French in 1718 and influenced greatly by the Spanish who owned it for forty years, expanded into the South's largest port and only major metropolitan center. Along with the newcomers, there remained families of French ancestry, large numbers of slaves with their African customs, and immigrant Irish who crowded into the city's expanding wards. Louisiana's culture and people created a multi-ethnic and religiously diverse state of Catholic, Protestant, European, African, and American customs. This place was distinctive.[2]

The state's economy depended heavily upon the sugar and cotton plantations that emerged along the rivers and bayous. Large concentrations of African-Americans could be found in south Louisiana since colonial times, and thousands more were moving into the cotton fields extending from the state capital at Baton Rouge north and westward. Their labors made the state's planters among the richest men in America. The nabobs owned spacious mansions and city town homes in New Orleans, Natchitoches, Natchez, or Vicksburg. Louisiana developed an economy that firmly planted it in the Deep South.[3]

Even with its strong French culture, a stronger slaveholder's ethos developed and united whites in America's sectional politics. By the late 1850s, the ideas of State's Rights and the pro-slavery Democratic Party triumphed over their political rivals. Louisiana aligned against the North, abolitionists, and the new Republican Party. With the election of Abraham Lincoln, the Deep South states left the Union. In January 1861, a state convention brought Louisiana out as well. A wave of enthusiasm carried volunteers into military companies, and Louisianans participated in the first clashes of the war from Manassas in Virginia to Wilson's Creek in Southwest Missouri. Louisiana itself became a part of the Trans-Mississippi Theater of the war. This vast area that included Arkansas, Missouri, and Texas remained distant from the capital of the Confederacy at Richmond, Virginia, and the Union's at Washington.

Louisiana in the Trans-Mississippi (MODERN PARISH BOUNDARIES)

0 miles 50

Hal Jespersen

Almost a year went by before war came to the Pelican state. In April 1862, a Union fleet steamed up the Mississippi River from the Gulf of Mexico. The intended target of the ships commanded by Admiral David Farragut: the South's largest port, New Orleans. Despite resistance by forts Jackson and St. Phillip, the city returned to Union hands on April 26, 1862. Its docks and public buildings became a base for Union operations, and the war department placed the headquarters of the Department of the Gulf within its boundaries.[4]

From that spring onward, Union gunboats patrolled the Mississippi with impunity, except where the fortifications at Vicksburg overlooked the river. A bombardment of the city in the summer of 1862 failed to prompt surrender. In Louisiana, Baton Rouge fell easily. The state government moved first to Opelousas, then to Shreveport. At Donaldsonville, between Baton Rouge and New Orleans, snipers took aim at the passing boats and shot at anything in their sights. On August 9, 1862, the Union navy bombarded the town and burned a number of hiding places that had housed the Confederates. That put a stop to the shooting. This action on the west bank of Ascension Parish became the first step in what would be a long line of destruction across the state during the war.[5]

Earlier, in late July of 1862, a Confederate force of 2,600 men assembled at Camp Moore, a training ground in the pine woods north of Lake Pontchartrain. Under the command of former Vice-President John Breckinridge, the small army's objective was the recapture of Baton Rouge. The soldiers began a sixty-mile trek on July 28 and immediately faced the worst heat of the summer, with too few sources of clean water along the way. Their brutal march took a great toll on the ranks and the men faltered again when they lost the element of surprise. Union intelligence had picked up their movement and pickets spotted the advance guard outside the city on August 4. The Confederate assault in a thick fog bank early the next morning made progress at first but halted suddenly as fierce fighting by the 2,500 defenders and concentrated shelling from heavy guns aboard the Union's Mississippi River flotilla drove them back. A Confederate vessel, the *Arkansas*, failed to distract the gunboats long enough to draw away their fire. Following the disappointing battle, Confederates retreated north to Port Hudson and fortified the bluffs there against further upriver encroachments.[6]

That August of 1862, a Confederate officer slipped quietly over the Mississippi River and made his way back into Louisiana. General Richard Taylor had been leading Louisiana troops under Stonewall Jackson in the Army of Northern Virginia. Now he left the East and came home where he assumed command of the field army in West Louisiana, a district of the vast Trans-Mississippi Department.[7] Before the war, he had been a businessman growing sugar cane at his "Fashion" plantation along the Mississippi River outside of New Orleans.

His father, the late, great General Zachary Taylor, had been a Mexican war hero and president of the United States. His late sister, buried in Louisiana soil, had been the first wife of Confederate President Jefferson Davis. Born in 1826, the younger Taylor travelled with his father to his various posts as an army brat. At seventeen, he went to Yale University and studied the humanities rather than attending West Point.

His background gave him a strong intellect and an aristocratic air. He dabbled in politics, gambled, drank, and loved cigars, which he puffed on while watching his troops deploy into lines of battle.[8]

As an officer, Taylor became a soldier's soldier.[9] He supported his troops and subordinates alike with a fierce loyalty and worked tirelessly for his army's success. At other times, he could be a prima donna and throw curses upon slow-moving teamsters who drove the army's supply wagons. His postwar memoirs were a carefully worded justification for everything he did.[10] To his credit, Taylor directed a large theater of command

General Richard Taylor was the son of a U.S. President and one of the most successful non–West Pointers in the Confederate army (Library of Congress).

that included all of the state west of the Mississippi River. In this huge geographic area, Confederate forces remained small in number, scattered widely and plagued by chronic supply problems. With such limited resources, he met each Union incursion into the state with imaginative genius that prompted Governor Thomas O. Moore to declare, "We owe it to him that the State is not now entirely overrun and occupied by the enemy."[11]

In December of 1862, a new Union commander, Nathaniel P. Banks, took hold of the reins of the Department of the Gulf. From its base at New Orleans, the department encompassed the Gulf coast from Florida to Texas and into the interior of adjacent states. Banks replaced Benjamin Butler, another political general who had become unpopular with the locals. Similar to Butler, Banks had been a Massachusetts politician. He, however, went on to Congress before the war and became Speaker of the U.S. House of Representatives. In spring 1861, he became a Major General.[12] No skill was necessary to obtain his high military position—only connections. Banks had been an early member of the Republican Party, and the president needed New England support for the war. By date of commission, Banks out-ranked William T. Sherman, a seasoned West Pointer who spent nearly a lifetime in the regular army.

For his first major offensive, Banks ordered his army up from the Gulf of Mexico and into the Bayou Teche sugar country west of New Orleans. From a landing site on Berwick Bay (now at Morgan City, Louisiana), he marched north in March of 1863 and after a short delay broke through several fortifications below the town of Franklin. He then devised a complicated maneuver involving two forces that would surround and trap General Richard Taylor's army. Taylor commanded approximately 4,000 men, and Banks placed at least three times that number in front of him. Another division of 5,000 made the flanking move.[13] At the flat fields between the turns in Bayou Teche know as Irish Bend, a battle took place on April 14, 1863.[14] Taylor put up a great demonstration and then escaped before being surrounded completely.

Undaunted, Banks then advanced through Acadiana, an area settled by the Cajun people in the late 18th century, and drove his divisions over 100 miles past Vermillionville (now Lafayette) and Opelousas until he reached Alexandria on the Red River. Without sufficient numbers to make any opposition, Taylor's men fled before him. Banks paused at the gateway to the Red River and pondered his next move. It was now May, and he could either go up the Red or over to assist General Grant who was

For Major General Nathaniel P. Banks, a Speaker of the U.S. House of Representatives, the Red River Campaign was his last disaster of the War (Library of Congress).

working against Vicksburg. He had orders asking him to help Grant. Banks desired his own glory and there was one operation that could assist Grant and at the same time award him his own laurels. That task would be reducing Port Hudson, the fortified bastion on the Mississippi River. Here he could achieve a victory that might build a reputation as a leader of prowess.[15]

Banks crossed the Mississippi River with his army at Bayou Sara, a point approximately fourteen miles north of the main fortifications. Another column marched up from Baton Rouge, and it clashed with Confederates in a sharp engagement at Plains Store south of Port Hudson. The two Union forces met up and by double envelopment surrounded the Confederate position on the Mississippi. In what was probably his most successful operation, Banks had tightened a noose around the neck of the defenders. Several frontal assaults on the well-entrenched positions failed to dislodge the defenders. An attack by the African-American Louisiana Native Guards faltered, yet their courage in the face of the long odds won for them much needed respect and acclaim in the Northern press. Following a siege of forty-eight days, Confederate General Franklin Gardner surrendered on July 9, five days after Vicksburg fell. His side had lost 900 men killed and wounded, the remaining 6,500 became prisoners, and 5,000 Union soldiers died in combat or were wounded. An additional 4,000 more succumbed to the ravages of disease. Banks achieved success, yet it came at a very heavy price. With Grant and Banks victorious, the whole Mississippi River passed into Union hands. The key to the continent slipped into Lincoln's pocket, and with it an enormous strategic victory.[16]

During late summer 1863, General Banks planned another campaign for the Department of the Gulf. This time he set his sights on Texas. Operations began with a few preliminary strikes along the state's coast and then an amphibious invasion at the Texas-Louisiana border. A naval armada and several troop transports were turned back by shore batteries at the September 8 Battle of Sabine Pass. Stymied by sea, the next month he implemented the land phase of his plans, an overland march into western Louisiana with the intention of turning west and capturing Texas. The "Yankee Autumn," or Texas Overland campaign of 1863, proved to be a dismal failure. The army got off to a slow start, and near Opelousas, General Richard Taylor massed his forces and struck the lead elements of the Union army. The engagement at Bayou Bourbeux discouraged the commanders from continuing out into an unknown route with angry Confederates all around them. The Union army retreated back towards the coast, and that ended the year's campaigns.[17]

In the winter of 1863 to 1864, as planning for major offenses in Virginia and Georgia entered the planning stages, the Washington, D.C., military advisor to the President, General Henry Halleck, promoted a third major action. This one would be launched in the Gulf region. The target remained up for debate. The question became whether or not a combined effort against Mobile, Alabama or a Red River expedition with Texas as the big prize. General Ulysses S. Grant, and initially General Banks favored Mobile for its port capacity and machine shops. Halleck and President Lincoln disagreed with their generals and wanted all of Louisiana and Texas under Union control. As historian Gary D. Joiner wrote, "Halleck's letter to Grant was forceful in explaining that President Lincoln believed a Red River expedition was more politically important than the capture of Mobile."[18] Political considerations connected with Lincoln's reconstruction policies drove this option. Since capturing New Orleans in 1862, Lincoln wished to control a large portion of north Louisiana in hopes that a unified, "reconstructed" government could operate before the fall 1864 elections. This feat would strike a huge moral blow to the Confederacy while alleviating some of the political pressure on Lincoln. With the war now in its fourth year and the country not yet unified, he needed to produce results.[19]

In addition, General Nathaniel Banks, the department commander and the man who would lead the campaign, possessed the right political qualifications for the job. Like many officers during the Civil War, Banks struggled because he had not been a career soldier; in fact, he learned far more about compromise than command. He had started his career as Democrat yet changed parties in the 1850s to become a new member of the Republican Party. It is thought that a major reason Banks came aboard for the Red River Campaign rested in his desire to build credentials for a presidential bid sometime in the future. Whatever the case, Union military actions in Louisiana, as elsewhere, remained heavily influenced by political considerations.

In the Department of the Gulf, Banks had an army ready and waiting. The North had assembled a formidable force consisting of the 19th Corps and two divisions of the 13th Corps. Soldiers from sixteen states filled the ranks of the regiments. To boost these divisions, part of William T. Sherman's 16th and 17th Corps were loaned to the Gulf. These men, 10,000 veterans strong, remained critical to Sherman's up-coming campaign in Georgia. They left quarters at Vicksburg with one big stipulation. They had to be returned to Sherman no later than April 15.²⁰ To supplement these troops, Admiral David Dixon Porter assembled the largest inland fleet in United States history. A graduate of the Naval Academy and dedicated fighter, Porter possessed daring and an exaggerated sense of self. Upwards of ninety vessels and their seasoned crews took to the shallow waters of the Red. The fleet included three monitors, ten ironclads, eleven tinclads, one timberclad, and dozens of other support boats. The narrow and often winding stretches of the waterway would pose many difficult challenges. The navy would not be able to overcome them all and as a result Porter's fleet suffered major losses on what became an ill-fated errand into the wilderness.²¹

The Union strategy called for Banks to move up Bayou Teche and arrive at Alexandria with his army by mid–March of 1864 where they would join Sherman's men and Porter's armada. The 16th and 17th Corps travelled by transport with the navy from Vicksburg to the Red River. From a rendezvous at Alexandria, the combined forces would march north toward Shreveport. In Arkansas, another prong to this offensive fell into place not long after the Louisiana portion began. General Frederick Steele with his nearly 14,000 men received orders to march on Shreveport from the Union base at Little Rock. While the plan for two armies to converge looked promising on paper, the execution of it would be very difficult. Operations

Admiral David Dixon Porter's operations on the Mississippi River helped win the war for the North. The Red River Expedition did not go as well (Library of Congress).

between two forces in two different states separated by hundreds of miles proved too much to bear. From the beginning communication and coordination broke down and instead of one united effort, the desired plan degenerated into two distinct operations.[22]

The Confederate defense of the Red River fell to General Edmund Kirby Smith, who assumed command for the Department of the Trans-Mississippi a year earlier on March 7, 1863.[23] He oversaw operations in Missouri, Arkansas, Louisiana, Texas, Oklahoma, and the Arizona territories. After the Union army captured Alexandria in May 1863, he made his headquarters at Shreveport. Smith hailed from St. Augustine, Florida, where he was born in 1824. His parents, both New Englanders, had moved south. Smith returned northward for education in Virginia and then the United States Military Academy at West Point where he graduated in 1845. The next year he went off to the Mexican War where he won brevets for bravery at Cerro Gordo and Contreras. By the time of the Civil War, he become a career army officer, doing time as an instructor at West Point and performing duties at various posts across the American West. In 1861, he joined the Southern side and participated at the very first major land battle of the war across the rolling hills near Manassas, Virginia. He brought in reinforcements from Joseph E. Johnston's command late in the afternoon and helped stay the Union advance. Smith placed himself at the center of the action and was wounded leading his men at the front lines. The next year, he moved west to join General Braxton Bragg's Army of Tennessee. General Smith participated in the 1862 Confederate invasion of Kentucky, and unlike his commander who faltered at Perryville, Smith directed the Battle of Richmond and achieved a resounding victory.[24]

Smith had earned a promotion when he left Tennessee for the Trans-Mississippi Department. Due to the severing of communication between the Confederate capital at Richmond, Virginia, and that department in July 1863 with the Union capture of the Mississippi River, Smith gained a great degree of command latitude. One recent scholar has written that his powers that included both military and civil authority without any avenues of appeal made him the only true dictator in American history.[25] Smith himself admitted in his characteristic laconic style, "My power in the Trans-Mississippi Department was almost absolute."[26] With that power firmly in hand, he never hesitated to exercise it, even when faced with controversial decisions. General Smith clashed with several state governors, including two in Louisiana, over conscription, confiscation, cotton policy, and use of slaves for the war effort. All along, Smith believed that war measures trumped civilian rights. On at least one occasion, an agitated Governor Henry Watkins Allen of Louisiana stormed into Smith's Shreveport headquarters. There he argued loudly "in his ardent, vehement style," for the return of a suspected traitor who had been arrested and exiled from the state without any legal proceedings.[27] Smith's biggest clash came, however, with his own field commander, Richard Taylor. The two of them, so different in personality and outlook, differed on how to meet the Union army's threat.[28]

From his years of training at West Point and prewar army experience, Smith believed in a strategy of obstruction that would wear down a larger Union invasion force and make the most of his meager resources. Forts, trenches, river obstructions, a naval presence on the upper Red, and artillery positions commanding important points on the river became key components of his plans. Smith relied especially on his staff of engineers, especially David French Boyd and Richard M. Venable. These officers were to map, plan, and oversee a large number of construction projects. Additionally, because Smith was given responsibilities for an entire department, he decided to spread out the small number of troops under his command and then concentrate forces to meet foes, often at multiple points of incursion. This strategy would be challenging, given that he described North Louisiana as "a country destitute of supplies and with limited means of transportation."[29] Smith held steady to his plan,

General Edmund Kirby Smith was an able administrator over a vast territory and a source of General Richard Taylor's consternation (Library of Congress).

and when he and Taylor were at odds, Smith placated Louisiana's soldier prince, often to his own chagrin.[30]

Taylor believed that only a highly mobile field army could defeat a Union army on the move. Smith's shovel and spade approach miffed him because he preferred to stop advances with rifles and bayonets. Maneuver rather than mud banks should rule the day, he believed. Rather than blindly follow his superior, Taylor filtered orders that came down from headquarters and took the initiative despite what Smith wanted done. As the son of a president and brother-in-law to the Confederate president, Taylor could afford to be a loose cannon. With victory in mind, Taylor overcame the army's constant supply problems by establishing stockpiles of food and forage at various points out in the open countryside.

With Taylor going one way and Smith the other, the defense of the Red appeared "schizophrenic," as Gary Joiner has written.[31] It was not as if either man could not see the value in what the other proposed. General Smith appreciated the ability to mass forces and strike just as Taylor reluctantly ordered his divisions to put down their weapons and dig fortifications. The two men just did not see eye-to-eye on how best to prosecute the war. Each played the game of give and take, and only when Union forces arrived did their differences become magnified by the urgency of the situation.

Because Smith was higher in rank and held the department purse strings, his plans held sway. He decided to strengthen fortifications along the Red. The first defenses built along the river from its confluence with the Mississippi River came at a strategic bend in Avoyelles Parish. An elaborate earthen installation named Fort DeRussy, already in use, was given high earthen walls to provide a platform to deter gunboats that might proceed up the river.[32] Early in 1863, it had been under construction when a Union boat, *Queen of the West*, arrived, ran aground, and was captured there.[33] Later that spring, Union gunboats coordinating with the army's advance to Alexandria captured the fort. They left after only a brief stay as operations moved east to Port Hudson located on the Mississippi River. In the fall and winter, Confederates strengthened what had been started there and added a strong water battery next to the Red reinforced with a layer of iron covering the walls. A large chain obstruction placed across the river complimented it all. The works at Fort DeRussy provided a classic example of interlocking fields of fire and defense in depth. The fort's plans showed the strong influence of skills taught at West Point and European military schools.[34]

Next, the chief engineer of the Trans-Mississippi department, William R. Boggs, turned his attention to an innovative plan that would stop Union gunboats from approaching Shreveport. The large cannons aboard such vessels had brought down forts guarding New Orleans and could do the same on the upper Red. They had to be stopped from even approaching the city. Boggs noticed that Tone's Bayou, located below the city, held an interesting geographic feature. The bayou, actually a man-made shunt, connected the Red and Bayou Pierre. It had been created in 1851 by a planter, James Gilmer, who professed a grand vision. Gilmer had employed dozens of slaves who dug the 5,100 foot ditch in an attempt to divert the river's flow so the town he created and named, Red Bluff, might end up on the main waterway and eclipse Shreveport. His settlement would become the primary commercial hub on the upper Red, and Shreveport would suffer the same fate as Natchitoches in the 1830s. His dream of dominance never materialized because, while he might lord over his laborers, he could not master the river. Only in high water did the natural flow spill over into the bayou, making it serviceable. In 1863, Boggs realized that if one constructed a temporary dam near the mouth of Tone's Bayou, stopping the Red River's flow into it, then removed the dam with explosives, river water could be suddenly diverted into the bayou. This ingenious drainage plan called for no less than lowering the Red River. If successful, the Boggs design would quickly drop the water level by feet. Gunboats that required several feet of draft to operate would run aground.[35]

When the damn was blown not long after the Union gunboats entered the Red, the surprise was complete. Lieutenant Colonel Lucius F. Hubbard of the 5th Minnesota described what happened:

> Predicting probabilities upon the experience of previous years, it was assumed that the channel of the river at that season would afford a depth of water sufficient to enable the fleet to move to Shreveport, without difficulty. Instead of meeting a rise in the water as the fleet proceeded up the river, as was expected, a reverse condition was encountered, the depth of the channel steadily shrinking from the time the boats entered the river.[36]

As a final measure to ensure that no vessel would ever reach Shreveport, the Confederates placed the *New Falls City*, a 300 foot, 880 ton vessel, below Tone's Bayou with the intent of sinking it to block passage above it. When the Union forces appeared on the lower river, the order read:

> The lieutenant-general commanding [Kirby Smith] thinks it may be necessary to have the steamer New Falls City (now lying near Coushatta Chute) sunk in

Red River just at the foot of Scopern's Cut-off. He directs that you proceed without delay with the steamer Osceola to the point where the New Falls City is lying. You will put a crew on board and take her up to cut-off, where you will hold her in readiness to be sunk on the approach of the enemy. When it becomes necessary to sink her any assistance that you may require will be furnished by the officer in command of the steamer *Missouri,* that will be stationed near you.[37]

The last layer of defense would be outside of Shreveport itself. The city would be ringed with earthworks. Chief Engineer William Boggs put together an extensive master plan for the defenses. Seventeen forts and dozens of cannon emplacements appeared on a map.[38] The major roads leading in and out had to be protected as well as the approaches directly across the river at what is now Bossier City. The works had to be strong fortifications capable of withstanding a Union army if it showed up at the doorstep. A prolonged siege deep in Louisiana might exhaust a Federal army's supply line, if the Red River had been lowered and could not be serviced by the navy anymore. Perhaps the Union army would give up rather than endure another Vicksburg or Port Hudson.

In 1863, work crews began moving earth for the elaborate plan. Slaves were pulled off plantations and soldiers put down rifles and took up shovels. Sections of the lines began to take shape. The defenses incorporated natural terrain features such as hills and ridges for extra strength. While grand in design, the works faltered because of a lack of manpower for construction. Not enough earth could be moved to complete everything fully. The scarcity of heavy artillery for sweeping fields of fire doomed its effectiveness. Boggs and his engineers made many compromises. Some batteries held field pieces rather than large caliber artillery. Other emplacements employed the ruse of "Quaker" guns, carved out of tree trunks and painted black to look intimidating. Fort Turnbull, dubbed Fort Humbug, now the site of a National Guard armory on Youree Drive, stood as the most notable of these clever compensations.[39]

Down at Shreveport's riverside, an ambitious naval building program attempted to construct boats for service on the Red. One ironclad, the *CSS Missouri,* had been prepared for use, and the steamboat, *Webb,* required workers for a large re-fitting of that craft. Several steamers were also armed and placed in Confederate service. Most intriguing were shadowy reports from Unionist spies that submarines were being built at the naval yard there. With only vague references, it is hard to confirm their type, numbers, or possible uses. 1999 and 2006 searches

Introduction 21

of Cross Bayou by the same institute that located the Confederate submarine, *Hunley*, off Charleston, S.C., turned up nothing.[40] The dark waters of the Red and the Tone's Bayou plan to drain the river make the use of submarines in the Red impractical. The ironclad *Missouri* possessed danger for its enemies and was thus another story. Admiral David Porter, who remembered how deadly the *CSS Arkansas* had been around Vicksburg in 1862, geared up for any possibility. Because he obtained spy reports confirming the presence of an ironclad at Shreveport, he brought the largest of his gunboats, the *USS Eastport*, into the Red. At 280 feet in length, armor plated, mounting eight guns—two of them capable of throwing one hundred-pound ordinance—his paddlewheel monster could meet any threat. Historian Gary D. Joiner called the craft "an ironclad killer."[41]

When the campaign opened in March 1864, General Smith did not have nearly enough troops to provide the garrison forces necessary for his extensive river defense or Shreveport's earthworks. He barely had enough men for a sizable field army. This lack of manpower plagued Louisiana's Confederates for the duration of the war. The commanders never possessed enough men to fight. Both Smith and Taylor made the best of the situation by reaching out to find troops everywhere. In the parole camps near Pineville, Louisiana, Taylor grabbed men; across the prairies of Texas the word went out for available units to hurry over even after the campaign had started. From points on the Texas Gulf Coast near Houston, Smith freed up available volunteers. He ordered a division of Arkansas and Missouri regiments to begin a long journey south after hearing of the Union's advance. Still, the Confederates assembled only 10,000 to 15,000 men to face General Nathaniel Banks, who put 30,000 soldiers in motion. Admiral Porter's naval expedition of ninety boats started their ascent up the river. These numbers painted a grim picture of the long odds against the Confederates, yet Taylor promised a subordinate, "I will fight Banks if he has a million men."[42]

One

The Curtain Rises
The Red River Valley, 1803–1860

In the decades before the Civil War, the Red River Valley became a grand example of American achievement. Along with other western territories, it had been purchased and settled in only a few decades. The region prospered and became an important part of a growing national economy. This particular piece of the American continent yielded agricultural riches derived from layer upon layer of distinctive red soil. Every year for eons, milky crimson nutrients had settled on the landscape at the end of a long journey from the iron oxide Permian Hills of Texas and Oklahoma. The color became most visible when storms churned up the water into an angry rushing torrent. Entering Louisiana near the angle formed by the Texas and Arkansas borders, the Red runs southeast across the state on its way to the Mississippi. At times, the Red could be swift flowing, and in other seasons slowed to a trickle. In the oppressively hot and humid summers, the bed dried up in places, reduced to the consistency of mud cakes.[1]

Debris from brush and whole trees that fell in from the erosion of its soft banks choked the river for miles. The Red's famous raft of obstructions often gave the appearance of a drainage ditch gasping for life. One soldier from New York State put it well when he called the river "a compromise between Earth and water," describing it as "a dirty, sluggish stream, about the eighth of a mile wide, flowing in an extremely, crooked channel. Its bends and curves are so exaggerated that they seem almost unnatural."[2]

From its entrance in the northwest corner of the state to its confluence with the Mississippi, the course of the Red twisted and turned over 200 tortuous miles. The waterway itself cut through dense forests of cypress, tupelo, gum, oak, and pine. On either side of its banks were large oxbow lakes marking ancient paths cut off when the river shifted direction. Additionally, a number of tributaries fed it, among them Loggy Bayou, Pierre Bayou, Cane River, Bayou Rapides, and the Black River.[3] In the 19th century, an observer noted, "All the bayous of this river, that are very numerous, branching off in every direction, and intersecting every part of this luxuriant valley, partake of the fertilizing character of the main stream."[4]

After 1803, thousands of eager Americans flocked to its banks. From Georgia, Alabama, and the Carolinas, Southerners crowded the routes leading to the parishes (counties) along the Red. In 1836, the new arrival Thomas O. Moore remarked, "Emigration to our country is immense. Every boat is crowded with families for the upper part of the Red River."[5] Three of the parishes along the Red: Caddo, Natchitoches, and Avoyelles had been named for the Indian peoples. In 1723, French explorers came upon rock formations in the Red that caused falls at low water and the word *rapides* became noted on maps. A large area of Central Louisiana was ever after known as Rapides Parish. To the east and west of these river parishes, a host of other newer parishes sprang to life as the number of settlers making this place home increased exponentially.[6]

The people who arrived brought with them a model for success perfected in nearby Southern states. Nearly all brought slaves and started cotton farms and plantations. These men and women arrived from the rolling hills of the Piedmont back east, or from other river valleys, and knew the art of cultivation. Day after day, clearing of the land commenced as acres and acres of productive soil had to be readied for planting. Settlers lit fires to eliminate underbrush and chop down pine trees in an age-old technique of slash and burn. Charred landscapes and smoke-filled skies often marked the first steps towards success. Doing what it took with one's bare hands and sweat of one's brow could be daunting. For one, the climate of the Red River delivered sweltering summers, wet winters, violent storms, and periodic floods. Drought might come other years. Then disease and pests might strike a crop with little or no warning. Added to this already long list of potential dangers were accidents and deadly pathogens that took down man and beast. Settlers learned survival, and if successful, they could reap large profits.[7]

The cotton plant began its Red River reign as an aspiring, adolescent prince. The production of the crop commenced in the years immediately after the Louisiana Purchase. In those early days, the end of season meant bulky bales had to be loaded on flat boats. Only with the advent of the steamboat did transportation become much easier. The labor-intensive cultivation of the crop spread up the banks of the river valley and reached out into all of Northwest Louisiana. By the late teens, the links via the river to New Orleans and its growing port made this part of the state expand rapidly. Favorable market conditions prevailed for the most part, with only a brief interruption by the 1819 national panic, fueled by the yearly cycle of planting, tending, and harvest. Another big land boom, even larger than the initial rush, commenced in the 1830s. The Red and its tributaries became sought-after spots, one promoter wrote about Rapides Parish: "Bayou Rapid[es], that gives its name to the parish though that it runs, intersects one of the most beautiful tracts in the state, that is laid out, on both sides of the bayou, through the whole length of its course, into the finest cotton plantations."[8]

Prices for this cotton started climbing at New Orleans in the 1830s and peaked during the 1836–37 crop year, when sixteen cents a pound could be fetched. Then, almost without warning, the bubble burst. A national panic and subsequent downturn struck markets in spring 1837. Cotton's price over the next years plummeted to its lowest recorded level to date, four cents a pound. One company in Alexandria, opened by the Biossat brothers, advertised to try and attract new customers to their "spacious Warehouse for the storing of Cotton with Business on as favorable terms as anyone else."[9] Following years of hard times, the market turned around in the 1850s and growers witnessed another dramatic expansion that exceeded that of the 1830s. New Orleans prices climbed steadily through the decade and remained between eleven to fifteen cents a pound. The tremendously good year in 1860–61 placed more cotton on the market than ever before and the price tumbled a bit. Still, the market remained at nine to thirteen cents a pound.[10]

Table 1: Number of Cotton Bales Produced 1850–1860

Parish	1850	1860	% Increase
Avoyelles	3538	20068	467
Caddo	4819	9385	95
Desoto	2205	16554	651
Natchitoches	15574	36887	137
Rapides	14190	49168	246

In 1850, at the start of the boom, the U.S. Census reported that the parishes along the Red produced 40, 326 bales of cotton (a bale being 400 pounds).[11] Over the next ten years, more acreage was cleared for cotton production up and down the Red. A newspaper reporter noticed the growth in surrounding parishes as well.[12] In 1860, the U.S. Census counted the bales again; this time an astounding 132,060 were ready for shipment from Avoyelles, Natchitoches, Rapides, Desoto, and Caddo parishes.[13] That number stood over three times what had been available in 1850 (see Table 1). Some parishes recorded growth of three, five, and as much as seven times more bales than produced in 1850. A Confederate general who visited Bayou De Glaize in Avoyelles parish attested to a major transformation there. The impenetrable canebrake where he had come as a youth to hunt had become "opened and improved with large cotton plantations—level and beautiful for their order and regularity of cultivation."[14] His superior, Confederate General Richard Taylor, described the Red River Valley as a "population of large slaveholders engaged in the cultivation of cotton."[15]

By the time of the Civil War, the Red had become nothing less than a smaller version of the Mississippi. By its nature, however, the Red presented a more challenging environment. The struggle to master this land and endure changing market conditions bred strong families.

Cotton Press at Magnolia Plantation, Natchitoches Parish (Historic American Buildings Survey, Library of Congress).

Rapides planter Charles Mulholland, who had lived in Mississippi, moved to Louisiana and found even harder conditions. He reflected on the stark realities in August 1850, jotting down in a record book, "thermostat standing from 3 o'clock to half past 5 o'clock at 97 in the shade—stock suffering for water & the late corn, it is now thought will not make nothing." His sour mood changed at some point because he returned to the journal and crossed through "nothing" with a thick dark line. Then he wrote beside it, "Notwithstanding the long drought & intense heat, the country is remarkably healthy."[16]

In the 1830s, Rapides planter and future secession governor Thomas O. Moore settled in the Red River Valley. He arrived from North Carolina and searched for suitable slaves to make his fields pay. He needed a quality work force in good numbers. "Negroes are remarkable scarce," he wrote, "particularly such as will suit me, I have bought four men at five hundred dollars each, two women, 2 boys, 3 girls, and three children."[17] Moore's purchases allowed him to get started, and with this investment, and their continued hard work, he became successful. In 1836, he reported, "my cotton crop was a little better than my neighbors. I made 236 bales." He netted $12,500 for the season, a tidy sum in those days.[18] All had been possible because of land and slavery. He boasted, "I think Red River is destined to be one of the finest countries in the world."[19]

Since colonial settlement in the 1720s, slavery had grown steadily along the Red, and its brutality flourished with the American expansion of the cotton kingdom. The agricultural historian Lewis Gray calculated the median slave holding on the eve of the Civil War in Moore's Rapides Parish at an astonishing 125. Of all the selected cotton regions Gray examined across the South, no figure was higher—not even Concordia Parish along the Mississippi, a place noted time and again for its large slave population. The familiar *Gone with the Wind* image of gangs of slaves toiling in the hot sun across acres and acres of cotton fields may not have been true everywhere in the South, but it was accurate in the Red River Valley. Gray calculated the median slave holding on the upper Red River parishes, such as Caddo, at a more modest 44. Without question, the numbers bear out that an incredible amount of slave labor had been brought to bear along the Red to make it profitable.[20]

Solomon Northup, a free man who was kidnapped into slavery and brought to Rapides and Avoyelles parishes, communicated to the readers of his popular book the harshness of the slave's daily routine.

Slave quarters at Magnolia Plantation, Natchitoches Parish (Historic American Buildings Survey, Library of Congress).

His memoir, *Twelve Years A Slave*, lately made into an Academy Award-winning motion picture, transmitted in a matter-of-fact style the incredible hardships from day one on a plantation. Along with the huge physical demands on the body, the psychological toll provided an equally cruel condition. Take for example the nervous apprehension that gripped each field hand towards the end of a day. "No matter how fatigued and weary he may be—no matter how much he longs for sleep and rest—a slave never approaches the gin-house with his basket of cotton but with fear," Northup explained.[21]

What took place next determined whether corporal punishment was to follow. All the cotton a slave picked in a day was measured against a quota of what was expected on a typical day or each slave's own standard output. If the cotton brought in failed to meet the benchmark, there was going to be trouble. Northup explained that whippings always followed the weighing of cotton.[22] The world he lived in was a place where slaves were pushed, and pushed hard, to make the land deliver more and more. This new Egypt, the Red River valley, became hell on earth for a very large enslaved population.

The harsh working conditions and punishments meted out, often in sadistic fashion, made some whites apprehensive of what slaves might do if not supervised closely. A woman traveling through Sabine Parish remarked how the mere sight of a runaway slave set off nervous apprehension for her and her traveling companions.[23] Concern did not spring from a sense of guilt about the slave's condition but rather from a fear that conditions might easily breed rebellion. Even with a strong slave code in place that dated back to colonial times and slave patrols walking the neighborhoods, whites could never be certain that they were secure from retaliation. Periodically, rumors of slave rebellion swept the plantation communities. Once, in the mid–1830s, hysteria gripped Red River communities and only subsided when it proved to be a hoax. Other episodes, more localized in nature, became just as intense. In the aftermath of the 1860 presidential election, a Louisiana militia general wrote to the governor's office about the availability and condition of weapons if men had to be dispatched to "curb any disposition on the part of the servile population."[24]

White power secured in mechanisms of control allowed planters to achieve incredible gains from slavery's ugly consequences. Old families such as the Prudhommes, whose history went back to French colonial times in Natchitoches Parish, were a great example. They achieved truly amazing results. From only a few hundred acres in the 1700s, the family advanced their wealth over four generations to own, by the time of the Civil War, 3,400 acres and dozens of slaves. The master of Oakland Plantation, the showplace of the family, Pierre Phanor Prudhomme, enjoyed an education in France and sent his sons out of state to the University of Virginia and Georgetown University. The large number of wine bottles still sitting in his garden to this day attest to his legendary parties. All he accomplished had been done because of cotton and slavery.[25]

Alongside the Prudhommes rose a number of American newcomers who very rapidly approached and surpassed their wealth and status. In the 1840s, Henry Marshall brought his family, money, and over 100 slaves to Desoto Parish from South Carolina. The place where he began cotton cultivation near the border of Texas had not been farmed before. His plantation, "Land's End," seemed at the very edge of American settlement before travelers reached the Sabine River. By 1850, he possessed 5,000 acres and produced 100 bales of cotton, the highest amount of land and greatest cotton production in the entire parish. His farm was valued at $10,000, a tremendous sum for that time period.[26] With capital to pour into his enterprise, cotton that would grow well in the soil, and slaves to work it all, he leaped into the same economic and social bracket as the Prudhommes in far less than the four generations it took them to get there. His ancestors back east had given him a push, and although his roots in Louisiana were not deep at all, they were strong and growing.[27]

The owners of the Goldpoint and Hurricane plantations proved the pinnacle of what could be accumulated in the Red River Valley. These two enormously productive estates sat across the River from Caddo Parish, technically within the new parish of Bossier. They ended up in probate court records because they were inherited by James Pickett, Jr. This lad, just twenty-three years old in 1857, obtained a vast fortune when the two plantations became his and his alone. Through marriage and deaths, the Gilmer and Pickett family lines became linked together with James as the sole heir. The two families had been planting since the 1830s and bequeathed to him hundreds of improved acres and a slave force of ninety-three at one place and sixty-eight slaves at the other. The value of the slaves alone was assessed by the court for tax purposes in excess of $100,000. The land at both places was pegged at another $100,000. The total inheritance of land and slaves equaled at least $200,000. Today this sum might be equated to tens of millions of dollars in value. The probate record remained one of the largest ever executed in the region before the war.[28]

Undeniably, those planters at the top did well, yet all of those under them did not do so badly either. Smaller farmers and petty planters found their own successes. The New Yorker who described the Red River so well mentioned seeing "several little clearings, graced with the meanest construction of log and mud houses."[29] Out in the vast pine tree forests on either side of the Red there were many people working for their own advancement. The records of the general store owner Ezra Bennett contained entries from many average people who lived at such places. The Bennett family of southern Rapides Parish provided credit to those farmers and planters who lived in the close-knit agricultural community near Bayou Boeuf. Their account books chronicled every transaction down to the exact dollar and cent.[30]

These Bennett store owners prospered because they built relationships with farmers who sold only a little cotton at a time and who also required simple loans of capital and extensions of credit. Additional help for growers arrived from simple yet significant internal improvements. During the 1830s, Ralph Smith constructed a small scale railroad line from White's Landing on Bayou Boeuf sixteen miles north and west to the levee at Alexandria. Then at a point near the Bennett store, an ingenious lock and gate, authorized in 1857 and built of brick, regulated water levels in Bayou Lamourie to allow year-round water transportation. The store and others like it through the valley and internal improvements meant more cotton could be brought out to market more easily. Conditions for upward mobility of farmers and planters improved because the focus of public and private efforts remained on making business conditions better.[31]

Legend has it that among the more famous customers at the Bennett store were James and Rezin Bowie, the brothers who invented a distinctive knife that still bears their name. The two of them dabbled in land speculation in Central and South Louisiana. Jim Bowie survived the melee that followed the infamous Sandbar duel on September 19, 1827. A short time later, he moved on to glory at the Alamo.[32] He would be followed by a greater number of families who left their own homes in the South behind for the fertile prairies and river valleys under the Texas sun. The Red River extended westward across the northern woods and prairies of the Lone Star state, and it became a natural route for settlers heading into Texas. The soil there proved ideal for cotton cultivation too, and plenty of newcomers swelled the population of a place that had been virtually vacant at the time of Texas independence. Most of these families who arrived, some with slaves and some without, could not boast that they were born Texans, but under the light of big sky country became Texans by the grace of God.

Among this number were Augustus Ball and his wife Argent. This young couple made their way there from southwest Georgia. Seeking a better life, the two newlyweds made their first home together not far from the Louisiana border. In 1861, the year of their arrival, the locals had named the place Bowie County after the famous Alamo hero. Their neighbors raised some cotton, tended cattle, and exhibited an independent mind-set. The Balls had barely put their things away from the move when war engulfed the nation. Instead of a quiet country practice of house visits along the rural roads of east Texas, Dr. Ball found that the young Texas boys entering the Confederate army needed someone to look them over, patch them up, and send them back into the fight. Available doctors for the army were few and far between. Off he went into Confederate service. By 1864, he had more experience than in a whole lifetime of country practice.[33]

In Louisiana, two crossroads hamlets named Mansfield and Pleasant Hill stood as shining examples of what Texas was to be. These communities sprang to life as part and parcel of the cotton boom of the 1840s and 1850s. These two new towns were in Desoto and Sabine parishes, respectively, located one on top of the other. Mansfield with its crossroads radiating north, south, east, and west held an advantage over Pleasant Hill that contained fewer important roads leading in and out of it. Both emerged twenty miles west of the steamboat landings on the Red River and only about Eighteen miles apart. Newspaper man J.W. Dorr from New Orleans visited both places in July 1860. He did not notice much at his first stop, Pleasant Hill. Once at Mansfield, the parish seat of Desoto, he found a community "rural and retired, on elevated ground, and it is a well-built town of some twelve hundred inhabitants." He admired Mansfield Female College with its 130 students and noted a brand new brick courthouse standing proudly. Both the college and churches signaled to him permanence and refinement. The Episcopalians, Methodists, Baptists, and Campbellite Baptists welcomed the faithful at their four separate buildings. Two hotels, the Planters and Globe establishments, opened their doors to weary travelers, and several stores sold dry goods. These measures of civilization emerged due to cotton fields and slavery. Dorr counted forty-nine prominent planters at the head of society; each produced over two hundred bales a year and claimed dozens of slaves as their primary workforce.[34]

In 1860, the planters were still bringing in more slaves and clearing larger sections of land. That year, the U.S. Census counted 8,507 slaves in Desoto and 4,777 whites.[35] These numbers, where slaves outnumbered whites by almost two to one, indicated a strong plantation culture. The big difference between the neighborhoods here and those along the Red itself came down to the productivity of the soil. Desoto's acres were not nearly as bountiful as those along the Red. One contemporary estimate stated that 500 pounds of cotton per acre could be expected on farms situated on the upper Red in Caddo Parish. By contrast, between 300 and 400 pounds per acre might be achieved from Desoto.[36] The other critical difference between the Red and the outlying parishes had everything to do with location. Desoto growers pressed their cotton into bales and hauled them over long distances to market. River planters enjoyed closer connections to the landings where steamboats arrived to carry the goods to New Orleans. Although disadvantaged by soil and location, the cotton producers of Desoto made the best of their situation and achieved phenomenal success with the number of bales increasing by over 650 percent (See Table 1).

Pleasant Hill, the place Dorr ignored on his way to Mansfield, did not possess the development and refinement of its closest neighbor. The best site description can be found in the writings of a historian who had been born there in 1893: "The village occupied part of a plateau a mile wide from east to west, along the Mansfield–Fort Jessup Road. The highest ground was College Hill on the west." There on the hill, the Methodists had constructed two brick buildings in hopes of one day opening a learning institution called Pierce and Payne College. A farm here and there broke the otherwise vast pine forest around the site. Nearby the village stood a single big mansion, the Childers residence, and beyond a short distance twelve to fifteen buildings sat next to the road. These included a Baptist and a Methodist meeting house. Otherwise Pleasant Hill offered little.[37]

The economic lifeline for Mansfield and Pleasant Hill remained the Red River. A big boost that assisted the region in using that river arrived in the 1830s courtesy of the federal government. Ever since scientific and military explorers probed the wilderness in the early 1800s, there had been interest in mitigating the treacherous conditions of the Red and making the natural resource more navigable. As far up as Alexandria, steamboats could visit all year round. As early as 1807, the town became the headway of navigation. The falls on the river there, which were really two outcroppings of sandstone rock created a temporary hindrance when the water level became extraordinarily low. The biggest and one far more challenging, the Great River Raft, extended for miles north of Alexandria and blocked passage, in Natchitoches Parish, and in large sections above it. The raft, a terrible logjam of fallen debris and silting of the center channel over centuries completely closed sections for years at a time. The U.S. Congress debated river improvements for the nation in the 1820s and appropriated funds for improvements on the Red. The plan called for clearing approximately 150 miles of the river's twisting and turning length. Starting in 1833, and with additional Congressional appropriations over the years, Captain Henry Shreve directed a process of eliminating the Great Red River Raft. He used innovative saws and cutting techniques on his steamboats that succeeded in opening and keeping open a large passageway. He made navigation possible above Alexandria for at least one hundred miles or more. The tedious and time-consuming chore gave an unexpected benefit as well. The river changed course and drained some areas that had been wet opening new lands.[38]

Thousands of whites and their slaves poured into places not

previously accessible or located near a steamboat landing. The determination of Captain Shreve and the federal dollars touched off a land bonanza. Settler claims boomed on the upper river well into the 1850s, and a town at the northern end in Caddo Parish was named appropriately, Shreveport. Even more apropos, the town's fathers named the three main streets Cotton, Market, and Texas. The dusty village that had been for years a traveler's stop on the way to Texas turned into a thriving market town practically overnight. Its frontier atmosphere remained vibrant even as signs of refinement emerged alongside the bars, taverns, brothels, and gambling dens.[39] New steamboat landings for cotton, warehouses for storage, and docks sprouted along the riverfront named Commerce Street. Trade with Texas farmers at Jefferson and Marshall increased each year. Plans for a railroad linking Shreveport with points in Texas and the Mississippi River rolled out in the 1850s. The federal government's investment in the river had paved the way, and all were ready to take the next steps. If the Red River could be harnessed for economic gain, so could the iron horse.[40]

An equally important development critical to the history of the region took place at the southern end of the river. As dramatic as what happened with the birth of Shreveport, the introduction of a brand new crop not previously cultivated in the valley changed the agricultural history. The planting of sugar cane along the lower Red began during the early 1840s and spread during the 1850s. The river's easy outlet to market from Ralph Smith's cotton rail line and other improvements in southern Rapides Parish provided attractive incentives. A labor force of slaves were already there in large numbers and a frost resistant variety made growing at the more northerly latitude in the state feasible for the first time. Other technological improvements, mainly in steam-powered processing equipment, provided the industry with legs in the Red's lower reaches. A business that had made South Louisiana planters the richest men in the United States now came to the Red River. The results were nothing short of impressive.[41]

The cotton planter and future secession governor, Thomas O. Moore, became among the first to enter into the new industry. In 1850, rather early in the expansion, he constructed a sugar house and mill at a cost of $14,000. This huge investment showed his determination and desire to accept a big risk. He did not possess long-term data because there was no proven track record in Rapides Parish. During the crop year 1859–60, thirty-eight sugar planters lived outside Alexandria, Lecompte, and Cheneyville. Collectively, they delivered to market

12,878 hogsheads of sugar. Over ninety percent of them used the most advanced steam apparatus at their plantations. Moore produced one of the largest yields, reaching 1,085 hogsheads.[42]

A neighbor of Moore's, the French planter Gervais Baillio, produced a typical yield for the parish at 367. Wellswood, the plantation of Monfort and Thomas Jefferson Wells, reported 815 hogsheads. Their work exceeded by far other sugar growers who remained in the category of under 200. The next crop year, 1860–61, production fell off for everyone. Only 8,493 hogsheads, or approximately 4,385 fewer units than in the previous reporting period came off the plantations. Among the reasons for the reduction, a drought in the summer months and violent storms damaged the stalks parish wide. Baillio, Moore, and the Wells family, who had led the pack for ten years, all reported smaller yields.[43]

The fall 1861 grinding or harvest season became clouded by the start of the Civil War the previous spring. Only thirty-two Rapides planters reported a yield that season. Despite a slightly lesser number of producers, the sugar masters of Rapides Parish produced 19,159 hogsheads that exceeded by six thousand the hogsheads produced in the banner year of 1859–60. The major producers posted very impressive gains. Their accomplishments stood at a peak because the results would be the last before war took a major toll on the sugar economy. Beginning in fall 1861, the blockade of the Mississippi River by the Union fleet took effect. The loss of New Orleans the next spring then completely closed off the regular outlet for sugar hogsheads. No one knew when commerce might resume again. The firm of Champomier and Bouchereau who had so diligently visited all the operating plantations across the state each and every year did not issue another report until 1869.[44]

This snapshot of the infant sugar industry along the Red shared the same history as the rest of the region, albeit in a shorter time frame: birth, expansion, and growth. The Red River Valley became a dynamic agricultural region. Through the hard work of all, the region's economy became a vital component of Louisiana's success. For three decades, it held out the promise of opportunity. The maturing cotton cultivation, the emergence of Shreveport, an infant sugar industry, and the growth of towns such as Mansfield and Pleasant Hill held out good tidings for the future. With fertile land all around, slaves in steady supply, a few technological improvements, and old-fashioned sweet equity, families had every reason to look forward to the future. The Red's politicians who faced the sectional rift in the late 1850s stood in front of phenomenal growth and wanted to preserve and continue it on the same upward pathway. None of them could have imagined that they might suffer an unimaginable reversal of fortune. Even fewer of them would have believed that the destruction was indeed imminent. Such thinking ran counter to their history and the dogged accomplishment of all who called it home, yet it was coming.

Two

The Secession Crisis
Unionists and Confederates, 1860–1861

The night of April 19, 1861, proved to be one of the most momentous for the Civil War. At Arlington, a stately home overlooking the Potomac River, within sight of the unfinished dome of the nation's capital building, Robert E. Lee had to make a decision. He had been offered command of the entire Union army. Under the shadow of the bulging ionic columns, the "marble man"—as one historian has called him—drew his pen and changed the course of history. He declined the honor of leading the Union, and then in a second missive, dated April 20, he gave a one-sentence resignation as colonel of the 1st U.S. Cavalry. Lee chose to serve his native Virginia and the Confederacy. On the 22nd, he joined the governor's emissary, Judge John Robertson, and together they took a train ride south to Richmond. At the Virginia House of Delegates, before the assembled legislature, Lee accepted a commission in the state forces. A life-size bronze statue adorns the very spot where this moment took place. Although not memorialized in bronze or marble, many Southerners struggled with their own momentous decisions that spring.[1]

That same day Lee left on his southward journey, and hundreds of miles west, another Southerner made up his mind. At Shreveport, Louisiana, David Pierson felt compelled to write his father why he too was joining the Confederate side. The town where he wrote his heartfelt letter had been inundated with recruits following the exciting news of the surrender of Fort Sumter on April 14, 1861. The *Shreveport Weekly News* explained, "Men of all ages, and occupations, have flocked in from the country, and neighboring Parishes; having heard that recruits were in demand."[2] Pierson wrote that he joined the crowds "in defense of our Common Country and homes...." Similar to Lee, he chose his state over the Union. This choice had not come easily; he admitted, "I was opposed to secession, it is true."[3]

Before the war, Pierson had established a thriving law practice in Winn Parish. Small farmers outnumbered large plantation owners there. Less cotton came out of that piney wooded, hilly parish, and it has often been noted that the only thing grown in abundance there was dissent. A sizable group of men there opposed secession and, in future decades, both the Populists and the parish's most famous native son, Huey Long, would find succor among its people.[4] Pierson entered the secession crisis as a Unionist. He had been elected as a delegate to the state's secession convention where he cast a negative vote against withdrawal from the Union. He spoke against Governor Thomas O. Moore's seizure of federal property that happened even before the assembled delegates opted for severing ties with the Northern states.[5]

It appears that Lincoln's call for volunteers following the firing of Fort Sumter convinced Pierson he could "either take up arms against the South or in her defense." Given those two prospects, "I am not slow to choose." As an attorney, so his reasoning went, he could not advocate the rights of clients and not be willing to stand under arms for those same principles of justice he thought the North threatened with an invading army. He promised that he could bear the hardships of a soldier's life, rebuild his law practice after the war, and ultimately, "if I perish it will be but a sacrifice that duty impels every patriot to make upon the altar of his Country's Glory."[6] Pierson's romantic flourish illustrated how strongly these emotions surged in his mind.

Louisiana's secession crisis had its foundation in the long and drawn out irrepressible conflict that one historian has called the nation's sectional conundrum.[7] A divide between North and South that had opened as early as the colonial period grew as slavery drove a wedge between the states. During the 1850s, partisans inflamed passions even more, and that separated the nation sharply into North and South. Nearly every political matter of that decade became a bitterly argued contest. The November 1860 presidential election became the final straw in the long line of degeneration. During the political wrangling that fall, the old fulcrum of Louisiana's politics remained alive and well. The question of who was best suited to defend the state's economic, social, and political interests drove discourse and framed that election.[8]

At first glance the 1860 contest did not appear to tell a story of a great rivalry. Multiple candidates ran nationwide, and Louisiana settled on John Breckinridge, the sitting vice-president from Kentucky and the most overtly pro–Southern candidate. Abraham Lincoln, the nominee of the Republican Party, counted on support from Northern allies. Without sponsorship, he did not get on the ballot and was never a consideration across the entire South. Two other candidates contended for votes. The Unionist peace candidate John Bell of Tennessee and Northern Democrat Stephen Douglas of Illinois attracted votes across the country. When the election ended and the votes were tallied across Central Louisiana, Breckinridge won. The Bell and Douglas tickets lost every parish (see Table 2). The lone exception would be David Pierson's home parish, Winn, where Breckinridge captured only a plurality of the vote.[9]

Table 2: Parishes

	Avoyelles	Rapides	Natchitoches	Caddo	1860 Totals	1861 Totals
Breckinridge	750	1036	754	648	3188	
Secession	605	772	547	751		2675
Bell	290	620	534	545	1989	
Douglas	7	98	106	57	268	
Cooperation	162	416	625	123		1326

	Desoto	Sabine	Winn		1860 Totals	1861 Totals
Breckinridge	634	420	354		1408	
Secession	666	149	88			903
Bell	364	227	257		848	
Douglas	2	45	241		288	
Cooperation	50	421	507			978

In the plantation realm of Rapides, as well as Avoyelles, Breckinridge did his best. The seasoned politician racked up a commanding 400–vote margin in both parishes. For years the story has been that the Red's parishes were greatly in favor of Breckinridge, case closed. A close examination of the 25 precincts in Rapides Parish revealed a much more divided contest. The overall parish result masked remarkable fault lines (see Table 3). At Alexandria, the parish seat, he prevailed by only two votes more than what Bell and Douglas got at that town's polling place. He lost by twenty-two votes at Pineville just across the river. The results show that the parish's townsfolk came out in large numbers for Bell or Douglas. Along Bayou Rapides and Bayou Robert, the oldest cotton growing areas of the parish, Bell managed to squeeze a few more votes than Breckinridge. The sugar planters at Lecompte and Cheneyville also gave more of their support to Bell rather than Breckinridge. These six important locations, tied as they were into the national web of economic relations by the Red River and its connections to New Orleans, harbored more moderate thinking men than pro–Southern Democrats.[10]

Table 3: 1860 Presidential Election Returns Rapides Parish

	Breckinridge	Bell	Douglas	Bell Douglas Win
Alexandria	184	137	49	x
Pineville	36	57	1	x
Lacroix's & Union	46	78	5	x
Mill Creek & Spring Hill	61	68	3	x
Lecompte & Cheneyville	51	72	1	x
Bayou Rapides & Latanier	26	29	5	x
Whiskachita	4	22	4	x
Goree's & Comrade	50	36	0	
Wiley, Simm's & Saddle Bayou	85	26	3	
Plaisance, Cotile & Lamourie	170	36	9	
Calcasieu, Burton's & Ellis	116	35	14	
Stanley's	54	6	0	
Neal's	131	17	4	
Anacoco & Latanier	32	18	1	

In all the rural precincts, Bell and Douglas carried enough weight, surprisingly, that eleven of the twenty-five total precincts went for them. This was not quite half of them but was more than one might have imagined given how far ahead Breckinridge's total votes were at the end of the voting. Breckinridge counted his most ardent supporters in the south and western precincts of the parish. Two Breckinridge strongholds, named Neal's and Stanley's for the family homes where the voting took place, delivered overwhelming numbers. There, among piney woods plain folk and established planters south of Alexandria, the Democratic Party had dominated elections since the 1850s. Breckinridge enjoyed 185 votes, compared to the paltry twenty-seven handed to both Bell and Douglas. These two strongholds provided the heavy weight that swung the election. The farm owners and poorer rural folk found more to like in the pro-slavery and pro–Southern positions of Breckinridge, while moderates remained steadfast among those with business interests.

Table 4: 1860 Presdential Election Returns Natchitoches Parish

	Breckinridge	Bell	Douglas	Bell Douglas Win
Natchitoches	188	159	59	x
Campti, Bayou Bourbon & Graff's Bluff	122	57	24	
Coushatta, Nine Mile Spring & Terre Blanche	180	131	10	
Bayou des Mares	14	29	0	x
Cloutierville	53	55	3	x
Kistachie Black Lake & Williams	79	42	10	
Isle Breville, McGees & Nichols	79	41	3	
Unity & McNeely	40	18	2	

Farther north in Desoto and Sabine parishes, Breckinridge's supporters delivered good vote totals. Because those parishes contained smaller populations, the Southern Democratic margin fell off to a 200–vote lead or half of what it had been in places along the Red. In Caddo and Natchitoches, the oldest parishes, both directly on the Red River, the Breckinridge lead narrowed to only 100 votes out of over 1,000 votes cast in each of those parishes.[11] Of the fifteen balloting places in Natchitoches, only three of them showed more votes for Bell-Douglas than Breckinridge (See Table 4). Once again, it appeared that Breckinridge won big. End of story, right? No, not exactly, because at each of the twelve boxes where the Southern Democrat emerged triumphant it had been a tight race. Only twenty to forty votes separated victor from vanquished. If a few people here and there changed their mind at the polling place, the parish would have gone for the moderate candidates.

In the town of Natchitoches where the largest number of votes in the parish could be found, Breckinridge lost this urban location by thirty votes. Again, a town ballot box, more commercial in orientation, favored Bell and Douglas. There was also an ethnic factor in Natchitoches Parish absent elsewhere. Bell defeated Breckinridge at two communities named Cloutierville and Bayou des Mares. A large population of ethnically French Creole planters, who were white with colonial ancestry, farmed along the Cane River in these places. The voters had favored the Whig party before the war and aligned themselves against the Democrats at every race. Their party had always supported national Union over individual rights and class conflict. Bell had been a member of the Whigs in the previous decade, and the persistence of support from fellow party members proved significant there and across the region.[12]

From what may appear like a solid victory across the Red River region, Breckinridge stood upon a honeycomb rather than a solid base. He did not hold as unanimous an endorsement as the total results might lead one to believe. The other two candidates, especially John Bell, could count on significant vote totals in important places. What any analysis of the election numbers must tell us is that while support for Breckinridge stood strong, and he won the race, there were plenty of commercial-minded planters, ethnic French Creoles, and town folk who preferred Bell, or to a lesser extent Douglas. Those who voted for Bell were more sympathetic towards the Union and against rash moves that might tear it asunder. The men who voted for the moderates in the race would be tested when talk of secession began following the election of Abraham Lincoln.

Men in the Red River Valley split on the question of how best to address the election of Lincoln. His victory triggered other Deep South states to consider secession because the Republican Party platform contained restrictions to the expansion of slavery. Its members included outright abolitionists, and these facts angered the radical fire-eaters who eschewed compromise. The defense of their property, the Constitution, and their whole way of life became jeopardized, as many saw it. Five days before Christmas, South Carolina did not wait to see what might happen in a Lincoln administration. Its hot-headed politicians stepped out of the Union first. The governor of Louisiana had assured the governor of South Carolin, in a private letter written weeks before the election, that if Lincoln won, he would issue a call for a secession convention.[13]

In contrast to Louisiana's governor, other men in Rapides Parish valued the Union enough to not be so hasty. Similar to what took place elsewhere in the South, Louisiana's secession became a complex political event rather than a single victorious dramatic moment. Significant opposition to secession existed in the Red River Valley.[14] Who exactly were these Unionist voters? Two retired U.S. army officers living in the parish expressed distress that the country they sacrificed for would be broken apart by secession.[15] Others worried about the true consequences of the action for their community. Unionists turned to organized political activity. One of the largest planters in the state, Meredith Calhoun, owner of over 700 slaves and 15,000 acres in north Rapides Parish, threw his considerable influence into the ring. He purchased a newspaper, and with the assistance of two educators, Luther F. Parker and Michael Ryan, he reached out for local support. James Madison Wells, who became a vocal critic of the state's direction, embraced the Unionist cause. The 1860–1861 campaign against secession, while sincere, never gained traction.[16]

During the 1860 campaign, Rapides resident Charles Boyce had been the most effective voice for the Unionist cause. He was the son of Judge Henry Boyce, an immigrant from Ireland, judge, and plantation owner who lived near Cotile Landing along the Red River north of Alexandria. His home became a landmark for travelers in northern Rapides Parish, and when the railroad came in the 1880s, a town would be named after his family.[17] Both father and son had been involved with the antebellum Whig party before it ceased to function on the national level. Charles lived a big white house set just behind the river in Pineville. He enjoyed a grand view of the river and the wooden storefronts of Alexandria's downtown just across its banks. In 1857, he became the editor of the *Red River American,* a newspaper issued from one of those buildings in Alexandria, the parish seat. Similar to other newspapers that sprang into existence at the time, its pages pledged support to the short-lived "Know Nothing" movement.[18]

In 1856–57, a cadre of former Whigs gained national attention by pressing nativist resistance against immigrants. The leaders targeted the Irish, who had arrived destitute in Northern cities and New Orleans by the thousands each year starting in the 1840s. Typical jabs at them included deep doses of ugly anti–Catholicism, which still resonated among American Protestants. Cheap appeals to base prejudice did little but unite opponents of the Democrats, who welcomed the Irish into their party. In Louisiana, the Know Nothings became a weigh station for Whigs moving away from a party that had disappeared as an organized entity on the national level. What is most interesting is that, although born in Massachusetts and of Irish extraction, Boyce became a Whig proponent of Unionism rather than a Democrat, the party affiliation of most Irish families.[19]

Many details about Boyce's life, his politics, and the newspaper he edited remain unknown. In 1860, he was thirty-two, stood nearly six feet tall, with blue eyes and a full head of dark brown hair. More information comes from a fellow newspaperman, J.W. Dorr, who proved observant and diligent in writing down what he gathered as he traveled the state. The two journalists enjoyed a one-on-one conversation at Boyce's Alexandria newspaper office. Apparently, Boyce possessed a gregarious personality and spritely wit, which Dorr noted, along with his outspoken Unionism. Boyce never held back and had gained quite a reputation around town. The superintendent of the Louisiana Seminary and Military Academy in Pineville, future Union General William T. Sherman, recorded that he knew "Charley Boyce" to be a solid Union man, not unlike himself.[20]

Boyce's newspaper editorials assailed Democrats and abolitionists alike, and galvanized like-minded men to his viewpoint. "They have never for a moment hesitated to change belief to meet the breeze of popular favor," he once wrote of the Democrats.[21] Dorr asked about Boyce's local allies for the Bell presidential campaign. These men included George Mason Graham, who had been essential to the founding of Louisiana State Seminary of Learning and Military Academy in Pineville.[22] Dorr mentioned how Thomas Jefferson Wells' name had come up—a brother of James Madison Wells. The Wells brothers, Dorr found out, were organizing a "meeting for the appointment of 'anti-secession' delegates" to an upcoming New Orleans convention. Then there was Leroy A. Stafford who unlike the Wells brothers had been a life-long Democrat and now a Bell supporter. Dorr labeled Boyce's readers as the "Union Democracy" men of Rapides Parish. All were prominent planters and important community leaders.[23]

As part of his strategy for the election that fall, Boyce ended the *American* newspaper sheet and took up the political battle for John Bell with a new publication. He called it *Constitutional* and the paper began life with a Latin motto emblazoned on its masthead when translated meant "Union forever." Boyce dedicated himself to getting Bell into office. Similar to Bell, he supported slavery yet could not stand for the Breckinridge candidacy or talk of secession. There in the middle of an expanding cotton kingdom, Boyce produced a mouthpiece for Southern Unionists.[24]

On October 22, an unnamed Shreveport correspondent wrote in to the *Constitutional* about a journey he had taken overland through Natchitoches, Bienville, Bossier, and Caddo parishes. Stopping at nearly every community to speak with the locals, the writer learned the prevailing political opinions all along his route. With the exception of Campti, a community in northeast Natchitoches Parish, every place he visited favored Bell for president. "I do believe the Union cause is steadily gaining ground," he wrote.[25]

The biggest opponent, the writer believed, was not John Breckinridge but the passage of time. He thought Unionists did not have the weeks needed to explain their position and energize enough voters. When he wrote the piece, the election stood two weeks distant. Given another month, partisanship could be defeated with a healthy dose of reason and Bell might prevail. There just was not enough time left in the race. The traveler expressed in the clearest terms that most men he spoke with recoiled at the possibility of Lincoln's election and, to them at least, it would be the worst calamity of all. The Union would not survive it. The most fascinating thing about this letter, which Boyce himself might have fabricated to build support for Bell, was that the informant sounded credible. Unionist sentiment did exist along the Red River and it was not insignificant. Unionists communicated, connected through a paper, and were supported by a feisty, determined editor.[26]

Boyce had much work to do. The state's Democratic Party counted Rapides, and the whole of North Louisiana, as one of its staunchest strongholds. It had been that way at least since the 1840s, when the "Red River Democracy" allied with Senator John Slidell and his political machine, cobbled together from the working class wards of New Orleans.[27] The Rapides Democrats included Thomas Overton Moore, a North Carolinian and 1829 arrival to the area. Through marriage and success as a planter, he accumulated extensive lands in the southern part of the parish, where he grew cotton and sugar cane. Moore became governor in 1859 when he carried forty-six of the state's forty-eight parishes. His opponent had been a neighbor of his, Thomas Jefferson Wells.[28]

Moore and his supporters communicated with each other through the Alexandria *Louisiana Democrat*. Founded in 1845, its interests had always been in favor of westward expansion, known as Manifest Destiny, and Southern principles. Edited by E.W. Halsey, and with attorney Mercer Canfield as its business manager in 1860, its pages praised

Breckinridge. They counted on support from Lewis E. Texada, a planter from along Bayou Rapides, and the planter/businessmen, John K. Elgee and Robert A. Hunter. The learned jurist Thomas C. Manning, another arrival from North Carolina, became their staunchest ally. He advised Governor Moore and remained a chief confidant during the secession crisis and in various capacities in the wartime state government. The traveling newspaperman, J.W. Dorr, paid the *Democrat* office a visit too. He mentioned that the newsroom had become a hotbed of fire-eating, secessionist sentiment. The contrast he painted between the *Constitutional* and *Democrat* could not have been greater.[29]

A glimpse into the thinking of the Rapides Parish Democrats came in a September 1860 letter from a rising star in Texas politics, Louis Wigfall. He wrote to Manning and Governor Moore because a committee they were on had invited him to speak. The letter expressed regret that he could not visit Louisiana for the engagement. This Lone Star fire-eater then expounded on the principles he thought all Southerners should hold dear: "The equality of the states & protection of Southern property" must be "brightly blazoned" on the banner of the Democrats, he told the invitation committee. "In the support of those principles you have my warmest sympathy."[30]

As it turns out, Wigfall was preaching to the choir. Later that same month Moore contacted Manning, and he expressed the same sentiments while expressing hope that Breckinridge might win the presidential contest. Louisiana's Democratic senator and elections manager extraordinaire, John Slidell, had assured him that Southern principles would prevail. Breckinridge would win by a large majority in Louisiana's parishes. "Bell will be badly beaten in this state," Governor Moore repeated to Manning.[31]

In November, Breckinridge won Louisiana yet lost the election to Lincoln. Breckinridge did not carry a single state above the Mason-Dixon Line and lost in many upper-South states. The electoral-rich Northern states tilted towards the Republican candidate. Lincoln's victory came with only Northern states in tow. Rather than wait and see what might happen next, South Carolina acted boldly and left the Union on December 20, 1860. That month, Louisiana Governor Thomas O. Moore sent a special message to the legislature. He explained, "The large majorities given in most of these States for the Electors favorable to Lincoln, is an evidence of the universality of this feeling of hostility to our institutions." He advised, "I do not think it comports with the honor and self-respect of Louisiana, as a slaveholding State, to live under the Government of a Black Republican President."[32] He set a special election for delegates to a secession convention. The Breckinridge men had become the chief advocates for secession.

The men who ran for delegate in that special election fell into two categories: those who favored immediate secession (fast becoming the most popular stance), and those who hoped for cooperation between Southern states in the crisis. The latter proved to be the place where Unionists might congregate. On January 7, 1861, voters went to the polls for the second time in three months. When the returns arrived, the numbers provided further evidence of the divide between Unionists and Democrats now supporting secession.[33] A significant characteristic of this election happened to be the noticeable fall in voter turnout when compared to the 1860 presidential race (see Table 2). About 13,000 voters who had voted statewide did not return to the polls for the secession election.

Only two months and one day separated the two elections. In between came a holiday season, and the first cold weather blew into the state. These facts alone do not account for the decrease. In Rapides Parish, for example, 656 fewer votes were cast. When compared to the 1859 governor's race, the closest statewide non-presidential contest to this one, the turnout was still 406 votes fewer than just two months before.[34] In Natchitoches Parish, the reduction was over 200 votes and the numbers appeared the same across the region. Without solid documentary evidence pointing otherwise, the only plausible explanation is that many men deliberately stayed home. Perhaps they held the belief that Louisiana's secession was a foregone conclusion. One historian who studied the election suggested this scenario.[35] It is also possible a number were Unionists disheartened by the turn of events and they remained at home for that reason.

An examination of the precinct vote for the secession election in Rapides and Natchitoches Parishes revealed that nearly all the places that were in favor of Bell or Douglas for president returned larger numbers for cooperationist delegates (see tables 2, 3 and 4). Secessionist candidates, such as Thomas C. Manning, did best in places that had always been Democratic Party strongholds. Neal's and Stanley's, in Rapides Parish, had given strong support to Moore in 1859 and Breckinridge in 1860, now provided large majorities for Manning and his cohorts. Not a single vote came in for cooperationists at Neal's, for example. At Stanley's, a meager twenty-nine of several hundred votes cast could be counted for them. These results emphasize how the Democrats had become the party set on implementing secession, while Bell's partisans held to their Unionist principles.[36]

The Secessionists swept both Avoyelles and Rapides parishes by large margins, as had been the case with Breckinridge's win back in November, yet the vote for secession was not as robust. Even with fewer participants in the election, Breckinridge's 400-vote lead from the fall contest fell to only a 300-vote margin for the Secessionists in the heart of their stronghold. The same trend emerged in Caddo and Desoto. Both parishes had voted for secession and then voters did not come out as strongly for secession. Three other places flipped or came out strongly against secession: Sabine, Natchitoches, and Winn, by at least three to one favored anything other than immediate secession. Natchitoches showed a closer divide between the two sides. Less than 100 votes of over 1,000 cast separated the victorious Secessionists from their opponents. In a few precincts, notably Cloutierville, where ethnic French lived in large numbers, the vote turned strongly against secession. Dr. S.O. Scruggs organized a Union club in the area that touted the parish's cooperationist candidates. When the totals came in, Cloutierville voted against immediate secession by over 100 votes.[37]

Across the Red River Valley, Unionists and moderates had registered their views at the election. They lost and did not prevent secession delegates from taking a majority at the convention. It convened in Baton Rouge at the gothic capitol building, and by a vote of 113–17, Louisiana left the Union on January 26, 1861.[38] The Unionists would not be reconciled to the loss. An anti–Secessionist delegate, James G. Taliaferro, a planter living in Catahoula Parish (adjacent and east of Rapides), expressed his objection:

> I am unable to see that higher and grander position that gentlemen say Louisiana is to assume by the act of secession. Clouds and darkness rather, are before me. The dimness of age, perhaps, prevents me from penetrating the gloom and seeing the bright skies and green fields beyond. In the exercise of my best judgment, and under my honest convictions of the ruinous tendency of this measure, I must pronounce it an act of madness and of folly. Sir, I vote Nay.[39]

When the statewide election returns from the January election were made public in the newspapers following the convention, that the Secessionists were reluctant to do until after the convention had voted their way, alterations in the vote totals had been made by officials. The tabulations had been inflated to show a greater Secessionist lead. The numbers made it appear that the state was less divided (47.3 percent of the people in the unaltered results had taken the moderate route statewide), and larger numbers were in favor of secession.[40] The Secessionists desired a united front as their alteration of the numbers and censorship of Taliaferro showed. If they could not win over complete agreement, then the next step was to eliminate opposition.

When war broke out in April 1861, Secessionists became Confederates, and they added the police powers of the state to their arsenal. Military means would be brought to bear against Unionists who refused to accept the results of secession. Matters heated up in early 1862 when the state adjutant general, over all state militia forces, learned of activities in two parishes: "secret meetings of disloyal citizens in Natchitoches and Sabine" he warned Governor Moore.[41] The governor had been getting his own independent reports about activity in Rapides and Avoyelles parishes. Then a Shreveport newspaper picked up news from Winn Parish where, the editor thought, residents talked openly of resisting service in the Confederate army. By the summer of 1862, Unionists went from being political adversaries to sworn enemies. Part of the reason for the strong reaction that summer was because the political climate had changed greatly. The fall of New Orleans to Union naval forces in April and the presence of a Union army and navy on Louisiana soil created a siege mentality. Much in the same way that word of slave unrest generated a strong reaction, the Union presence touched the same nerve. The existing 1860 to 1861 political dispute became transformed into a conflict of friendly forces versus enemies. Politics and war became entangled together into an especially lethal brew.

Governor Thomas O. Moore, commander of state forces, took aim at Unionists by dispatching an official request to none other than Confederate President Jefferson Davis, asking him to suspend *habeas corpus* in three Louisiana parishes. In blunt terms the governor assessed the situation: "Traitors have sprung up on Red River." He demanded that martial law be declared so that suspects could be taken and detained at will. "In my own parish and Natchitoches and Avoyelles," Moore reported, "it is wanted at present." President Davis granted the request. In turn, the governor issued Executive Orders 681 and 682, which allowed local militias to arrest anyone who gave "aid and comfort to the enemy" or "against whom good grounds of suspicion exist." This language meant that guilt by association became the rule.[42] A July 31, 1862, order from the Alexandria Provost Marshall's office printed in the pages of the once Secessionist *Louisiana Democrat* newspaper explained the situation: "Martial Law having been proclaimed in this parish by the request of the citizens thereof, to protect them against lawless violence, as well as the treasonable schemes of disaffected persons, it becomes the duty of all good citizens to co-operate with the Martial as well as the Civil Authorities."[43]

The Unionists stood undeterred by Governor Moore and his militia. Rapides planter James Madison Wells became a leader of the Union men.[44] He had been a Whig in the pre-war years and had supported the Stephen Douglas ticket in 1860. His Unionist views did not sit well with local Confederates. A band of guerrillas attempted to either kidnap or kill him. Because he received a warning, he took off from his plantation, "Sunnyside," for nearby swamps. He moved south by roads and rivers for the cover of the stars and stripes in Union-occupied New Orleans. Two associates of his, Alphonse Cazabat and William Hyman from Alexandria, suffered similarly.[45] The Unionist emigre then worked his way into the good graces of the authorities. A Customs House official composed an introduction letter for him to the Lincoln administration. The 1863 missive described Wells as "thoroughly loyal without conditions and is willing to give up his slave property to promote the cause of the Union."[46]

Lincoln's reconstruction plans needed men such as Wells. To create a new political order, Wells and the Unionists would fill offices of a loyal state government. In the process, Wells might settle old scores against rivals by wielding patronage which he and others had not been able to possess during the Democratic dominated pre-war years. This

Governor Thomas O. Moore, 1860s (William Emerson Strong Photographic Album, David M. Rubenstein Rare Book & Manuscript Library, Duke University).

James Madison Wells was a Rapides Parish Unionist and a loyalist Lt. Governor and Reconstruction Governor of Louisiana (Library of Congress).

chance to dole out offices became an attractive element to the Unionists who might be able to navigate the uncertainty of economic and social change with these promises of a fixed income.[47] Lincoln's reconstruction plans promised change. His policy had set up already experimental plantations where black labor would be paid and that alone promised a future where Red River plantations would not operate the same as in the past. The very foundation of the valley's economy would be altered dramatically. For Confederates, these facts confirmed their worst fears. Slavery was at stake in the war, and in politics the Unionists had not been beaten, despite elections and war. They had found new champions in blue. Confederates found the prospects of so great a change so dangerous and unacceptable, their army lashed out at any living, breathing Unionist. The long-standing political disputes of the past now infused military matters with a deeply disturbing tenor.[48]

The Red River Valley stood as the last wealthy and influential region of the state not under Union control. It had to be subdued and brought into the president's reconstruction plans. General Nathaniel Banks, head of the Department of the Gulf, had been a Republican Speaker of the U.S. House of Representatives. When it came to politics, he knew what he was doing. The job of transforming the valley into a loyal stronghold fell to him and it fit perfectly with his ambitions. By

1864, the Pelican State had become an important proving ground for President Lincoln's new reconstruction policies. The chance to advance those plans and take credit for their success could not be missed. Issues relevant to politics and war thus became intermingled.[49]

In late February, Banks supervised elections in New Orleans, and other areas under federal control as part of a plan to install a loyalist governor and lieutenant governor. James Madison Wells won election as lieutenant governor. He took office only days before the Union's Red River military effort began and had the mettle to accompany the Union army as it marched into his home parish. The chief of staff of the Union army reported how on the 23rd of March, "Lieutenant-Governor Wells arrived" at Alexandria. The officer relayed somewhat optimistically that the dignitary was "pleasantly welcomed by the people here."[50]

One Unionist, A. P. Dudley, contacted Banks in February and volunteered to recruit scouts for a forthcoming Red River expedition. Banks wrote him back quickly, the very the next day in fact, and asked for 200 mounted men. The volunteers would have to provide their own arms and horses. The army offered fair prices for use of the mounts.[51] By the 23rd of March, as the Union army reached Alexandria, Dudley proved reliable even if he had only twenty men to show for it. His efforts had fallen far short of the 200 desired, yet he managed to find sixty additional recruits as his men scoured northern St. Landry and southern Rapides parishes. "The men know the country and its routes and its resources perfectly," the chief of staff to Banks, Charles Stone, explained. "All enter the service joyfully under the flag of the nation."[52]

A newspaper reporter who arrived with the army noticed a large number of Unionists who came into the town to take an oath of alliance. He explained, "The people remaining [in Alexandria] are Union men, and are anxious to take the oath of allegiance. The rebel Conscript Act has been enforced here with iron rigor. Almost every able-bodied man has been forced into the rebel army, and the unpopularity of that act and its enforcement, has turned the popular tide against the Richmond Government." The reporter thought, "There never was a measure so detestable as is the rebel Conscript Act to the people here. Men liable to conscription have fled before it, and have been pursued, hunted, and dealt with in a most cruel and despotic manner." A soldier on the scene agreed, "Quite a number of the citizens of Alexandria want us to stay here. They don't like the Southern Conscription, and Seem very fond of Green Backs."[53]

Another Unionist writing to General Banks explained how in

Rapides there had been people "loyal from the beginning" and those of "Southern Sympathy but who have not taken active part against our army." The economic difficulties of both had mounted and "the losses of both classes have been great." He asked that these people be allowed to sell their produce to the Union so long as they had not taken up arms and were willing to take the December of 1863 oath of allegiance. He argued that "The possession of our U.S Currency will tend to keep them loyal."[54]

Out of the communities of Rapides and surrounding parishes, these men now risked their lives for a chance to reverse a course the secessionists had charted three years earlier. Approximately 5,000 white Louisiana residents have been confirmed as supporters of the Union military cause.[55] Their contributions, especially those made in the Red River parishes, became a great asset for an invading force. The appearance of Wells back at the home he fled and the flocking of local Unionists to the flag of the United States were overt and significant public acts, duly noted at the time. A *Harper's Weekly* reporter believed as soon as the army secured the outlying neighborhoods, more Unionists would come forward and throw wholehearted support behind the cause:

> The moment the old flag was restored hundreds of citizens seem to have come forward rejoicing to testify their devotion to the cause it symbolizes. Many who had been exiled from their homes hastened to resume their old places, and aid in the necessary work of social and civil reconstruction; all animated, according to the newspaper accounts, by an intense hostility, not only to the rebellion, but to slavery, as its great cause and principal source of strength. Thus Freedom is everywhere achieving its own revenges.[56]

The expressly political nature of the military campaign and the elections planned for Alexandria and other points where the army went confirmed Confederate fears. In January 1864, the Confederate portion of the state had sworn in their own new officials at Shreveport. The new legislature wasted no time and blasted the Union side with sharply-worded proclamations condemning the reconstruction plans and especially freedom for slaves. The visceral rhetoric attacked the new loyalist government even before it was installed at New Orleans calling it a "wicked and nefarious scheme." The legislators urged citizens to remain true and "preserve their fidelity to the cause of their country and spurn the deceitful invitations of a foe who aims at the destruction of the liberty and rights of the people of Louisiana."[57]

The new governor Henry Watkins Allen, a former Confederate officer

Wounded at the Battle of Baton Rouge, Governor Henry Watkins Allen was a fierce advocate for Louisiana's white citizens (Andrew D. Lytle Collection, Mss. 893, 1254, Louisiana and Lower Mississippi Valley Collections, LSU Libraries, Baton Rouge).

who had been wounded severely at the battle of Baton Rouge, labeled the recent developments the world of tyrants. Similar to the legislature he used the strongest wording possible when he reminded constituents that freeing slaves would upset the South's traditional white social hierarchy. He implored the public, "I warn you not to participate in the proposed election, nor to hold office by and under virtue of the same, nor to attempt by any means to set up or organize a government against the legitimate and regularly constituted authorities of the State." He explained, "If you do you will be the only rebels and will be liable to all the pains and penalties of treason."[58]

The reality of a localized civil war in Louisiana between Unionists and Confederates, within the greater Civil War itself, has not received the attention it deserves in military histories of the Red River campaign.[59] If war is politics by other means, then the Civil War in Central Louisiana became the extension of earlier political contests. The deteriorating nature of the war during the Red River campaign received a great push from the influx of bitter politics into the military realm. Unionists and Confederates traded their booming voices for the crashing sound of rifles and cannons. The marching of competing armies into the region in 1864 energized the festering divisions, tore open old wounds, and contributed to a breakdown of law and order that made the war much worse that it might have been otherwise. Similar to Bleeding Kansas in the 1850s, politics created a bleeding Red River.

Three

The Pain of Sacrifice
The Red River Home Front, 1862–1864

Once war came to Louisiana, white and black, affluent and modest, Confederate and Unionist all began to suffer losses. The pain of sacrifice took a heavy toll on the families in the Red River Valley. Since the outbreak of war in 1861, North Louisiana had sent thousands of soldiers to fight in the Southern armies. Men had died on distant battlefields in Virginia, Tennessee, and Missouri.[1] Approximately 1,000 soldiers mustered and left Avoyelles Parish. At least 100 or 10 percent of all those who had enlisted died in combat. Many more died of disease.[2] On average, the parish suffered approximately two deaths a month for the whole duration of the war. Fathers, brothers, uncles, and sons were not coming home again. If these tragedies were not enough to bear, a whole host of other war-related calamities mounted each year.

The first sign that the Civil War would change the antebellum world of the Red River came when the Union imposed a blockade on the Southern coastline. Markets for cotton and sugar cane dried up. Then the loss of New Orleans on April 26, 1862, delivered a huge military defeat and psychological blow to the Confederate cause. The Crescent City, the South's biggest commercial port, stayed under Union control for the remainder of the war. From the docks at the city, Union gunboats began plying navigable rivers and bayous throughout the state. Their presence made the threat of invasion imminent for the first time, causing families to consider tough choices. A young diarist, Kate Stone, a planter's daughter living with her family along the Mississippi in Northeast Louisiana, mentioned that a neighbor had to convince his wife that they must pack up and leave their beloved home. Kate wrote,

"Dr. Lily and Robert have at last persuaded her to leave the river ... until the war is over, for fear of the Yankees raiding the places when they come down the river."[3] In the spring of 1863, Kate's family did the same. Similar to others who possessed the means, they fled to Texas. Louisiana's waterways, which had been a key to pre-war success, had turned into terrible liabilities.

The Bringier family, who owned hundreds of acres and several grand homes in South Louisiana, decided that they must leave too. With most of their men off to war and with hulking gunboats looming beyond the levee right outside their doors, the women of the plantation departed for North Louisiana. The matriarch of the household became a refugee and the stress became palpable. A daughter in-law reported, "I saw the poor old lady's tears course down her cheeks time and again. She worries over her children, not knowing where they are now or when she will ever hear from them." She went to stay in Natchitoches, a supposedly safe place, until the 1864 Red River campaign brought competing armies to her new doorstep. Any remaining tolerance had reached its limits. Unionist relatives of hers arrived from New Orleans and carried her back through the lines to the city. A grandson who visited her following the whole ordeal described a different women than he remembered. "She is terribly changed," he wrote.[4]

At Bayou Cocodrie, near Cheneyville in southern Rapides Parish, the Newell family recorded a number of terrible fates that befell them.

A refugee family on the move (*Heritage of Valor*, Louisiana State Archives).

In the summer of 1863, one of their family members, Thomas Newell, "was wounded at Pennsylvania and he had not been seen since." The family "supposed that he was taken prisoner" at a country market town named Gettysburg. Without confirmation, they were left to wonder what had happened to him, or if they would ever see him again. An older relative of his was thankful that his advanced age kept him from Confederate conscription. Another family member was not so certain. "Mr. Newell thinks he is smart enough to keep out of the army ... they might get him yet," he wrote pointedly. That family also suffered when a Confederate regiment camped nearby their homestead. "Our own men has done a great deal of damage to the country they are stealing horses every day," one letter related with frustration. A passing Texas cavalry regiment passed by looked "more like baboons mounted on goats than anything else." Finally a neighbor's disturbing report of a violent home invasion rounded out the long list of apprehensions. "Jayhawkers or negros" tied the man's "hands behind his back" and "carried him in another room" and "laid him on the floor" before they "stole every thing ... clothing and money."[5]

Food shortages became a serious problem across the region. The Union blockade stopped imports, and the absence of men from their farms meant that produce dwindled over time. Common household goods such as flour, coffee, and meat became rare and expensive. The Natchitoches Parish Police Jury, as early as March of 1862, recognized that families of servicemen needed help. The jurors passed a resolution reading in part, "The President stated that the object of the special meeting of the Police Jury: 'To take such steps as would be most advisable to afford relief to the destitute families of families of our volunteers enlisted in the Confederate States army.'"[6] In neighboring Sabine Parish, a drought struck in 1862 and ruined the food crops of many farmers. The next year, parish authorities drew out $30,000 in relief funds from the state. Service benefits awarded Army wives and mothers $7 a month with $2 additional for each child living in the household. Records of these payments showed that the number of women getting the benefit doubled from 1862 to 1863. These cash payments were supplemented by the Police Jury establishing free corn distribution for those in need at steamboat landings on the Red River.[7]

The families of the Red River region experienced all these tragedies because, as the war developed, the Red straddled Union and Confederate lines. Historian Stephen V. Ash has developed terminology classifying the geographic areas in the Civil War South.[8] He identified

A refugee camp (*Heritage of Valor*, Louisiana State Archives).

Confederate strongholds and, as the Union army and navy captured territory and cities, areas that became Union strongholds. A third distinct region, the border frontier, developed as a no-man's land between the two sides. By 1863, Louisiana contained all three distinct sectors. A definite Confederate stronghold or gray zone emerged in the Northwest part of the state, where the state capital had been moved.[9] Supplies and men from Texas and southern Arkansas could sustain resistance from there. Almost overnight, Shreveport became a fortified city with trenches, redoubts, and forts guarding all approaches. The town doubled in population and became a mini-industrial center and an important military headquarters.[10]

The Union stronghold originated at New Orleans and extended north up the Mississippi. Following the capture of Vicksburg and Port Hudson in 1863, the entire river and miles of territory on either side fell into Union hands. The blue zone then extended up from the Gulf of Mexico to the town of New Iberia. With a navy to assist them, the Union army advanced across the state. In 1862 and 1863 campaigns, the army struck deep into Acadiana and advanced all the way to the Red River. Confederate raids in the latter part of 1863 made gains into the blue zone in Bayou country but these were lost again when the Union army and navy reasserted control.[11]

The third region, the border frontier, included Point Coupee Parish on the Mississippi River north of Baton Rouge, extending westward to the steamboat landing at the town of Washington on Bayou Teche in St. Landry Parish. From there the border ran westward again but closer to the coast leaving Lake Charles in Confederate hands. The very northern limits touched the lower Red River Valley and southward the frontier extended all the way through Acadiana to New Iberia. The presence of Confederate military units in Avoyelles and Rapides parishes for most of the war meant that the lower Red stood on the front lines of defense. Invasions by the Union army in the springs of 1863 and 1864 made the region more unstable. This middle zone suffered as people fled the countryside and moved into the nearest towns or across the border in Texas. Abandoned farmsteads dotted the landscape and lawlessness blanketed the area.

Next to the loss of territory and struggle to keep order in the frontier zone, Confederate authorities found the most vexing issue in Louisiana came from their effort to get a handle on manpower. The *Natchitoches Union* newspaper on December 11, 1862 called for more volunteers to serve at Vicksburg, the fortress on the Mississippi River. At the time of the plea, a major Union advance was expected at Chickasaw Bluffs north of the city. "We have heard from various sources [and reliable ones, too] that you have a fair proportion of men in your midst fully capable of military service," the editor wrote. All of them needed to be under arms. "It is a burning shame; a stain on the fair name of Natchitoches" that they were not. Laggards needed to step up and do their duty for family, sweetheart, and liberty, the paper explained. Patriotism was being evoked, yet it was a scolding brand that hinted that men in the community possessed some reluctance in flocking to the Confederate colors.[12]

Historian John Sacher has done the most research on the rise of Louisianans' resistance to Confederate service.[13] He pegged the number of discontented Southern men across the Red River valley as much higher than previously thought. Hundreds and perhaps even thousands roamed Northwest Louisiana. Governor Henry Watkins Allen estimated that 8,000 deserters had fled to the southwestern part of the state. While this figure may be exaggerated, he was convinced that the numbers were large. Sacher cited reports from Confederate officers that gave more specific wartime estimates. One put 200 men hiding out in the woods of Sabine Parish. Far from the plantations along the Red and in the piney backwoods, Sabine voters had not been enthusiastic for secession in 1861. A clear sign that serious opposition had formed there came when the parish's conscription officer, E. W. Morgan, was shot to death on May 30 of 1864. The incident prompted Governor Allen to offer a $2,000 reward for those persons or person responsible for what he labeled a "flagrant murder."[14]

A visceral opposition to the draft that led to these instances of violence bubbled up from deeply held beliefs in personal liberty. The idea that freedom meant being shielded from arbitrary government action had been a touchstone of antebellum Democratic politics. This prevailing mood ran head long into the Confederate need for manpower. The Southern war effort required soldiers and in large numbers. When military authorities enforced conscription or other strict war measures to obtain them, Louisiana's governors stood between their citizens and the military raising strong opposition to the means and methods. In his last address to the legislature, Governor Thomas O. Moore boasted, "I have had occasion to bring to the notice of these Generals," violations and they have "been promptly redressed, and I invite citizens who have been impaired by such unauthorized conduct of Confederate officers to report the particulars properly authenticated."[15]

Additionally, class distinctions played a role in resistance to conscription. The Red River contained a large planter class and thousands of slaves. Poor farmers who owned a few or no slaves resented being conscripted while the law exempted rich planters who owned 20 or more. The *Shreveport News* complained that a "broad and degrading line of distinction between the rich slave owner and the poor white man" emerged because of the conscription act.[16] Resentments of poor whites could be serious business. One Louisianan explained how General Alfred Mouton, one of Taylor's best generals, expressed reluctance to order an execution for a man who had evaded conscription. The Cajun general feared that the harsh punishment might have a negative impact on his own political future. The Democratic Party relied upon the common man for votes, especially in the Red River region. To enforce conscription strictly might jeopardize the general's ability to win votes among a core constituency.[17]

An additional aggravating factor that made conscription resistance a complicated matter, and one that Sacher did not neglect to mention, was the terrain of the Red River Valley. Thousands of acres of pine forests far away from the main roads and the backwater swamps provided excellent space for hideouts. Men might slip away and stay for months on end without detection. Hunting them down required tremendous effort through impenetrable forests. A fierce war developed as draft dodgers, conscription agents, and regular Confederate soldiers played deadly games of cat and mouse. The encounters degenerated into a warfare that went outside the bounds of civilized conduct. Most famously, the Catahoula swamps east of the Red and the pine hills of Winn Parish became known for gangs of deserters and Unionist opponents of the Southern war effort. One resident wrote General Taylor on the eve of the Red River campaign in 1864 to complain about the "very troublesome" Jayhawkers between Pineville and the Little River bordering on Catahoula Parrish. In February, a detachment of Louisiana state troops moved into that area north of the Red with orders to shoot anyone who put up armed resistance.[18]

Historian Donald S. Frazier examined guerrilla warfare in Louisiana and found that the state became an especially good "incubator" for savagery, as class distinctions, topography and wartime policies bred a bitterness that sparked irregular fighting. Once Union armies began marching into the border region between the Union and Confederate strongholds in 1863 and 1864, a new terrible phase commenced as both sides consolidated gains and attempted to roll back losses. When compared to other Trans-Mississippi regions, Frazier argued, conditions in Louisiana were outside the boundaries of so-called civilized warfare. Bushwhacking, murder, and looting became common. A deep internal war increased destruction across the Red River parishes and left residents in the middle of a "bitter and bloody struggle."[19]

Avoyelles Parish provided a great example of how terrible the war became. Late in 1863, a company of Confederate soldiers hunting deserters or "recusant conscripts" confronted a party of armed men believed to be suspects. In the tense confrontation that followed, a soldier fired and killed one of the men. The parish sheriff sought out the shooter and arrested him. The parish charged him with murder. "Some excitement prevails in the parish of Avoyelles against the accused, many of the inhabitants being either themselves recusant conscripts or friends & relatives of the few that the authorities are endeavoring to bring to their appropriate places in the army," an officer on General Taylor's staff related.[20] That correspondent was asking Thomas Manning, the Secessionist and aide to the governor, to take the soldier's case. The thorny subject pitted the military and civilian authorities against one another. Although the outcome of the case cannot be determined, the episode illustrated the serious nature of the internal struggle.

Two petitions sent to Governor Moore from the border region

further describe the throes of uncivilized conflict. The first, written anonymously in August of 1862 and signed by "a soldier's sister," came from Bayou Chicot, a community in what was then southwestern Rapides Parish. The writer complained how "outrages of the deepest dye are daily committed in our midst." Jayhawkers had entered the neighborhood and were robbing the inhabitants leaving "no corner untouched." She thought "rope" the appropriate remedy for these criminals.[21] A second, undated petition to the governor by more than forty people—mostly poor farmer's wives who could not sign their names and instead made their mark—expressed desperation. All of them lived in the heavily Democratic Stanley's precinct in Rapides Parish. The conscription act, they explained, threatened to remove all their able-bodied men. The women worried about what might happen to their families if those who tended the crops and did the other vital work were not around. The petitioners demanded that the governor grant an exemption for at least five men who might stay and assist "to furnish supplies for the indigent and destitute families in the precinct."[22]

The most shocking evidence of the wartime horrors can be read in a memoir written just after the war by the Unionist Dennis E. Haynes. In 1866, he put down on paper a thrilling narrative of his wartime exploits.[23] Haynes had been a teacher and lived in Texas at the start of the war. He tried to raise a Union company there. Under threats to his life, he fled to Louisiana. In 1863, he arrived in Rapides Parish and became involved in the deadly clashes between conscription forces and resisters. During the summer of 1863, a Confederate detachment around Hineston, Louisiana, hunted down two Unionists and fired over twenty shots at one man during the course of a long pursuit. "They robbed and plundered the Union men of everything they could lay their hands on," Haynes charged. From herds of stock to personal possessions, everything was carried off by the soldiers. Retribution followed the theft when Union men came out at night to strike back. Haynes described how a refugee family headed to Texas became a target of men who held them up and robbed them of all their possessions. That gang was also hunted down and killed without mercy.[24]

The most notorious story Haynes described took place when Confederate authorities turned over a search for draftees to a conscript hunter. This contractor, described as a person of mixed race, perhaps of Native and African-American heritage, gained a reputation for untold evil. Dubbed "Bloody Bob" Martin, he killed conscripts and beat old men for harboring them. In a long story central to his narrative,

Haynes explained how Martin learned of a plot on his life and set out to hunt down the men who were after him before they could kill him. He not only found them, he tortured them, hanged them from trees and discarded the bodies for hungry turkey vultures.[25]

The Confederate authorities who directed Martin made it illegal to speak out against conscription. Haynes, who had evaded conscription himself and had many a close call doing it, found himself in jail. He escaped from his captors, was shot and wounded, but was able to run away. He moved from one safe house to another, getting treatment for his wound and meals from sympathetic families. Along the way he stayed with a free black man, French Unionist farmers, and even a paroled Confederate who refused to fight anymore. All of them took great risk to themselves for taking him in. Haynes escaped to Port Hudson and Union lines there.

The next spring when General Banks re-organized his army for the upcoming campaign, Unionist Lieutenant Governor James Madison Wells convinced Haynes to recruit scouts for the Federal effort. He went out and located over 100 men, many of whom had been hiding from Confederate authorities because of their opposition to the draft or Confederate war measures. At least one had been hunted by Confederates who used dogs to track him. An associate of Haynes who was granted the opportunity to recruit north of the Red River betrayed the cause and turned into a "Jayhawker" outlaw. Instead of collecting recruits he excelled at robbery. "The Union men on the north of the Red river were not as anxious to join," either because of him or "they did not suffer as heavily the persecutions" as the men south of the river.[26]

Haynes provided twelve horses and two mules for the scouts. The army used them, and he never got the animals back. Following the war, he filed a $2,100 claim for compensation. The government pointed out that given his circumstance of being a refugee recently from Texas, he could not have acquired the beasts of burden legally. "It is not at all probable that he had any money to buy horses or anything else. Yet he claims that within a month he furnished these horses and mules to the government." The claims commission ruled, "The only explanation of this sudden acquisition seems to be that he stole the stock or captured it from the enemy. We reject the claim on this presumption."[27] Haynes would not be getting any money for his contribution.

When Confederates did not volunteer their horses and mules, or sell anything the military needed, authorities confiscated it. For the onerous nature of arbitrary seizure and great burden these activities placed on the Confederate home front, confiscation increased discontent across the region. The head of the Confederate Cotton Bureau defended the actions and provided its rationale. In unabashed terms, William Broadwell, a former cotton factor from New Orleans, explained that the South did not possess public lands to sell, customs revenue to collect, or other dependable sources of income. Confiscation, especially of cotton, he argued, provided a certain revenue stream. "It seems to me," he wrote, "cotton in the midst of a war like this can well be appropriated for military purposes." He complained that the governor of Texas wanted to review the military's cotton policies and veto those that did not meet with his approval. He went on, "If the government has not the power to take the cotton, it certainly has the right." The war was for all the people, and private property would have to come into play in order to best "preserve the rights of the people."[28]

No one would be immune from confiscation and no form of property exempt. The Confederate military asked for slaves to be sent as labor for fortifications. Owners did receive compensation, and many claimed damages when their laborers were injured or died. Planters

Confiscation took a heavy toll on Red River families (*Heritage of Valor*, Louisiana State Archives).

valued their property and were not about to lose a dime of their own money on any dangerous venture. General Richard Taylor remarked, however, that patriotic Southern families would send off their sons to fight more easily than they would turn loose of their slaves. On one occasion in 1863 when planters refused to loan slaves to shovel fuel into the fires of an army steamboat, a Confederate major seized them and took them anyway. "A famous din was made by the planters, and continued until their Negroes were safely returned," General Taylor wrote.[29]

Planters might not be blamed because each knew that their laborers were absolutely essential in their own personal battle to plant, maintain, and harvest crops. Especially in spring time during planting or at fall harvest season, slaves could not be spared for work away from home. Those seasons in 1863 and spring 1864, coincided with major Union campaigns into plantation regions of the state. The troop movements came as an interruption in the agricultural work cycle. The desperation with which labor was needed by the Confederates could be seen in one plea for help.

Governor Henry Watkins Allen issued a proclamation March 22, 1864, appealing for slave labor. "A large number of negroes are required by the military authorities to construct defenses in this State," he pleaded. A Union army and navy had moved into the Red River Valley only a week before. Allen explained that the military authorities were going to seize slaves because "the necessity for immediate labor is most urgent." He explained that if the slave-owners did not cooperate out of fear of losing their investment, the enemy might steal their slaves or drive them into exile anyway. "Your interest and your duty are identical," he argued. Finally he encouraged owners and overseers to accompany their slaves and supervise them personally. The slaves would be more "cheerful and effective" while under the eye of a familiar master or overseer, the Governor believed.[30] The whole tone of the message hinted that it took some major convincing or confiscation to get results. Confederate patriotism had its limits.

Natchitoches planter Phanor Prudhomme kept good records for the slaves who went off for the war effort. He noted the number who went, where they worked, and how long they stayed in 1863 and 1864. When mules, wagons, and drivers were taken for the Confederate army during the Red River campaign, he made notes on those too. He noted how many were taken, how long they were gone, and when they returned, if they came back at all. In the fall of 1864, he rented a slave carpenter for $10 a day and a laborer for $1 a day to build fortifications across from Alexandria. Both worked for over two weeks, and the Confederate engineering department owed him $164 for their service.[31] Additionally, he made claims against the Confederate government for all other property that went for military use. His contributions may have been made from a genuine patriotism yet he kept such strict accounting that one is left with the impression that he considered the exchanges very much business.[32]

Owners valued the work of the labor force and in many cases were not willing to sacrifice them or risk their loss for the Confederacy. These laborers were seen as valuable links in a process that helped bring prosperity and success. For the military, they were the cheap labor needed for fortifications and work that kept armies fighting. Without them the authorities faced the possibility of defeat and having the whole valley overrun by Union occupiers. Very similar to the conscription dilemma that convulsed the region, the military use of slave labor set up conflicting interests. These divisions further hindered unity among Confederates and damaged irreparably their chances for success.

The sacrifices made at home continued to mount every year and grew dramatically every year of the war. The violent turmoil from opposition to conscription never subsided and only raised the level of violence more. Confiscation became a last element that contributed to an erosion of the stable and orderly world that had been put into place prior to the conflict. The pain of sacrifice proved too great to overcome for many families. The war had taken and taken without any promise of restoration of everything that had been lost.

Four

Cotton, Cotton, Cotton
1863–1864

The great success of cotton during the pre-war years made producers believe that their crops would carry them through the war. Anxiety mounted, however, as New Orleans was shut off by Union capture in April 1862 and the whole Mississippi River blockaded when Vicksburg and Port Hudson fell in July of 1863. Only a long and difficult pathway to Texas, and Mexico beyond it, remained open. Few producers could afford or risk shipment in that direction. The prospects of selling bales easily grew more and more remote. With little else to do, and a slave labor force best not left idle, planters and farmers continued in their planting and harvesting. Most stored away all that they produced each year of the war. This curious dichotomy of going about business as usual, producing cotton in great quantities, yet being in the middle of a war could not withstand a great looming truth. War was coming to the Red River, and with it, the distinct possibility of a complete loss of all the effort from one, two, or even three years. Each 400-pound bale represented an investment from years and sometimes generations of struggle. The stored bales were often the best source of wealth anyone possessed beyond slaves, land, and personal possessions.

In the spring of 1861 and 1862, farmsteads buzzed with activity as the people tied to cotton production prepared the land, planted seeds, and went about chores as usual. Thousands of enslaved peoples along the Red River remained in a cyclical and generational rhythm of planting, tending, and in late summer, picking. The cotton bales had to be left either on site, or at nearby centers of commerce at Alexandria, Shreveport, or steamboat landings such as Grand Ecore in

Natchitoches Parish. One took a great risk by sitting on a season or more of a crop. One could lose everything if fire found its way to the coarse fibers bundled so tight. The reality that a Union raiding party might come up the Red prompted Governor Thomas O. Moore to order any cotton close to the waterway be moved at least ten miles away from its banks. Any cotton in danger of being taken by the enemy would be burned rather than letting it fall into enemy hands.[1]

Burning would be a last resort. Cotton was an asset and early in the war the Confederate government established a process whereby produce loan agents would buy stored cotton with bonds. This cotton served as security for loans in Europe that helped finance the purchase of war material. In August 1863, General Kirby Smith created a Cotton Bureau for his Trans-Mississippi Department. New Orleans cotton factor, William A. Broadwell, headed the initiative, and he used soldiers to collect government cotton and get it into the hands of buyers outside the Confederacy. The cotton sold for gold, Confederate money, or even funds drawn on banks in the North. In 1863, a deal for 5,000 bales might gross 1 million dollars in inflated Confederate money, and two other equivalent exchanges registered $250,000 in gold and $100,000 in funds drawn on a New York bank, respectively.[2] Broadwell's arrangements remained secret because the cover story needed to allow the deal to proceed was that this cotton belonged to foreigners, and because it belonged to a neutral party, it could be moved legally through both Confederate and Union lines. It was illegal for private citizens to sell to Northerners or move their goods through enemy lines. One historian has pointed out that since no true explanation could be given to the public for what the Cotton Bureau did, "Patriotic civilians could not understand why exceptions should be made to the prohibition on trade with the enemy." When soldiers were seen transporting these bales, civilians who were in need for necessities themselves assumed those in charge were corrupt. "All of this undermined support for the war on the part of the common people—support that was essential if the war effort was to continue."[3]

Union military planners in Washington, D.C., and at the Department of the Gulf headquarters in New Orleans recognized the tremendous value of the Red River cotton. Its capture or destruction could aid the Union war effort greatly. Unlike Virginia, Georgia or Tennessee, this campaigning area contained an extremely precious asset. Estimates placed price tag of the bales sitting there in the millions of dollars.[4] The leadership decided to make it an objective and made no secret of

Four. Cotton, Cotton, Cotton 69

it. An Indiana soldier billeted in New Orleans wrote his wife a letter about the upcoming campaign: "the army will be pushed forward into Texas, while others only regard it as a Cotton expedition and that the army will return as soon as all the cotton in the Red River country has been sent down the river."[5] As observations go, this one proved right on the money. The plunder of cotton became a major war aim. Historian Ludwell Johnson discussed this issue in the first scholarly study of the campaign, and no historian has disputed the fact since then.[6]

What has not been emphasized enough was how the existence of large cotton stores touched off a pervasive greed for the commodity. The depth of this greed and its degenerating effects could be seen across the ranks. Both Union, and it should be noted, Confederate sides suffered from its corrupting influence. The desire to keep, capture, or destroy cotton raised the stakes for all involved in the military action. Something so tempting and so monetarily seductive would bring misery to those who succumbed to its intercourse. A scramble for it meant that violence, desperation, and war on civilians followed the lust for cotton. The Red River campaign of 1864 became far more destructive because of it.

Basic economics explained why greed became so rampant. The

An idealized view of what Union planners thought they would find in the cotton rich Red River Valley—bales stacked for the taking (*Heritage of Valor*, Louisiana State Archives).

Union blockade of the Gulf and Mississippi River halted regular shipments to distant markets. That action created a scarcity of the commodity at regular points of exchange. An uncertainty about delivery of future goods clouded the forecast as the war dragged on year after year. An inability to easily move the crop due to military actions in the state or highway robbers known as Jayhawkers compounded the problem. A lack of supply and continued demand for cotton in the North and overseas drove the price upward to unprecedented levels. Although specific prices do not exist for 1861 and 1862, good records return in 1863. That year the asking price at New Orleans came in at an outstanding fifty-two cents a pound, that was six or seven times what it had been in the late 1850s. The price in the North could be as much as $1 a pound, or at Boston near the heart of the American textile industry, the commodity soared to $1.90 a pound.[7]

The high price proved to be a fabulous incentive for questionable activity. Even before Vicksburg fell on July 4, 1863, and then especially afterwards, opportunists made their way into the Red River Valley. With greed in their eyes, each dreamed of engineering deals that might move a large number of bales across enemy lines. These men were nothing short of speculators who were able to operate because each enjoyed cozy political or military connections. Oftentimes these relationships reached into both Union and Confederate governments. Unlike typical civilians, these well-heeled gentlemen traversed the borders of the conflict with relative ease. It was not unheard of for them to realize a 300-to-600 percent profit on their activity. Numbers like these kept up a hungry crowd.[8]

Union Admiral David Dixon Porter patrolled the waters of the Mississippi River and ran into more than his fair share of these speculators. He compared them to rats and thought the whole lot were deserving of hanging.[9] One so-called rat, Samuel Casey, a former congressman from Kentucky, stood among the most successful of them all. His ingenuity and pluck gained him a career total of 20,000 bales from all across North Louisiana. When he got wind of the not-so-secret 1864 Union advance into the Red River, he recognized at once that an invasion might disrupt his procurement activities. The pipeline he had laid out so carefully had to be guarded with equal care. He telegraphed none other than President Lincoln, asking for a delay in the planned campaign. That a businessman would contact the President and try to slow a military action for his own personal enrichment illustrated how far one man was willing to go.[10]

Admiral Porter, who had attempted to seize the moral high ground by calling the cotton brokers "rats," proved no better himself. As the U.S. navy entered the Red River in 1864, his sailors set about seizing cotton from plantations and farms along Bayou Rapides, Bayou Robert, Bayou Boeuf, and other tributaries on both sides of the Red and for five or six miles in each direction. A newspaper reported that 800 bales had been sent north and more were expected as the campaign progressed. "In the vicinity of Shreveport thousands of bales are believed to be hidden away; and should our army arrive in time to prevent its destruction a large sum must be realized from this source."[11]

Unlike land forces that had stricter rules to follow, the navy could take possession of enemy cotton and send it to a prize court at Cairo, Illinois.[12] Once there, officials assigned it a value, and then by law all sailors involved in the catch could be given a cash award. From the admiral himself down to the lowly deckhand, all would get a percentage of what they captured on the expedition. All of this was perfectly legal. As the regulations read, half of the value of what was seized would go to a fund for disabled sailors. The crew on the boat then split up the other half. The Admiral, the highest ranking crew member, took home 5 percent of that 50 percent. The remaining 45 percent was divided up by rank for everyone else.[13] The one important stipulation was that the cotton had to be Confederate government property rather than private property. If the cotton did not have "CSA" marks on it, then it was supposed to be off limits. The Union crews contained amateur artists who took up brushes painting CSA on every bale they saw. Gunboat crews joked the "CSA" mark stood not for "Confederate States of America" but rather "Cotton Stealers Association."[14] A photograph taken in 1864 showing gunboats along the river bank next to Alexandria showed clearly cotton bales stacked up on the deck of the *Neosho* monitor.[15] During the campaign, the navy acquired 3,000 bales in Rapides Parish and as many as 8,000 may have been captured from planters along the whole river during the three months duration of the campaign.[16]

When later questioned by Congress about this lucrative activity, Admiral Porter admitted that the whole expedition carried about it the air of one big cotton steal. He never flinched, however, when confronted about his personal gain. He stood firm on the prize law. His conscience cleared for a moment, and he confessed how a thirst for cotton had derailed military operations. "I know that cotton destroyed that whole expedition," he told the inquiry. "If there had been no cotton there we could and probably would have gone on to Shreveport.[17]

Porter's gunboats arrived at Alexandria on March 15, ten days before the army made it there. The sailors collected cotton before the army even had a chance to see what was found. A case of sour grapes developed between the two service branches. The army became jealous, in part, because it had to follow U.S. Department of the Treasury regulations, which did not award prize money to soldiers. The seized cotton went to the government. The cotton's owner had to be a loyal Southerner—by definition one who took a loyalty oath first issued December 8, 1863—for a chance at any compensation. All other bales were deemed contraband of war and lost to the producer. A loyal owner or his agent might expect payment worth only 25 percent of the value. The difference went to the treasury, minus a 1 percent compensation to the registering Treasury agent. At Alexandria the army collected at least "four thousand bales of cotton ... besides large quantities brought in by negroes," a soldier remembered.[18]

An army Colonel, determined the set the record straight, believed that the navy gave the army a black eye on this one:

> One most unjust aspersion was sought to be cast upon General Banks by some of those who most severely criticized the conduct of the campaign. In some quarters it was characterized as a "cotton stealing expedition." This was doubtless suggested by the efforts of the navy to collect cotton, of that there was a large amount in the country, and that was considered "good prize" by that army of the service.[19]

In truth, General Banks received no money personally from the cotton seized, unlike Porter. Ever the politician, Banks played coy by insisting everyone follow regulations, and no new permits for speculators were given by his pen. Nevertheless, he surrounded himself with speculators who brandished impressive presidential passes already in hand. The "bobbin boy" hoped that the cotton he collected for the U.S. government might find its way back to idle New England mills. Being credited for bringing cotton to the starved mills was more valuable to him in his quixotic quest for the presidency.[20]

Cotton was indeed on the brain of Lincoln's army commander. General Nathaniel Banks knew a great deal about white wealth. As a boy, when he started working at textile mills in his home state of Massachusetts, he saw the looms spinning the South's cotton. As a young man, he gained election to Congress as a Democrat in a district that employed many mill workers.[21] When he arrived in Louisiana during the war, he took command in a region that grew large quantities of the raw material. In 1863, as his army made its way along Bayou Teche, the regiments began seizing cotton all along the way. An after-action report he sent to Lincoln reported capture of "from seven to ten thousand bales of cotton."[22] All had been dispatched to New Orleans immediately. This success gave him confidence that a larger operation might gain even more. His very next thought in the report was how an occupation of the entire region might scoop up even more bales. "Should we be successful in our plans, I can loosen, from the Rebels, and open to our markets, from 50,000 to 150,000 Bales of cotton, one half of the net proceeds of that might be paid into the Treasury in the form of a war tax," he boasted. "This is possible—I may say if fortune favors us, probable. It depends however upon the continued occupation of this country."[23] Banks believed that a permanent presence in the untouched parts of the state might cement all that wealth for the Union.

Two examples illustrated well the depth of corruption that followed from Banks' desire for a campaign conceived in cotton. During the middle of the 1864 operations, Captain Deming N. Welch, a

The cotton press compacted the harvested bolls into the sought after bales (Library of Congress).

quartermaster officer, complained about the captain of the steamer *Laurel Hill*. This "scoundrel," Welch charged, had been smuggling cotton during his duties up and down the river. "On the last trip to New Orleans he managed to smuggle through seven or eight bales of cotton," the angry officer wrote to his superiors. "The sooner he is discharged the better." This steamer captain's schemes were halted when he bought eleven bales of cotton for $240.00 at Calhoun's Landing in upper Rapides Parish. Two slaves had hauled the bales down to the river and offered them for sale. The captain received a bargain, given that eleven bales on the open market went for about $2,200 at New Orleans. He stood to profit handsomely. As it turned out, Mr. Meredith Calhoun, the cotton's owner, and one of the most influential planters in the region, discovered the bales missing, and he appeared in front of Captain Welch demanding their return. A search of the captain's vessel turned up ten bales, "& the next morning found one more secreted" away, Welch revealed.[24]

A second example of questionable activity appeared in the form of a murky letter written directly to General Banks by an apparent speculator complaining about an unnamed field officer who must have followed regulations by the book. "He really is the last man for this post," the letter stated. If one reads between the lines it is apparent that this garrison commander stood as an obstacle for getting the "produce out of the country."[25] By "produce," the author could only mean cotton, and in his opinion Banks should do more to facilitate the trade.

A bitter Vermont soldier remembered how the whole Union army, from the top down, oozed of this cotton corruption. His anger continued years later. Giving an address at a veteran's meeting, he was unrelenting in his criticism: "...It is questionable whether the interest of the government and the advancement of our arms was the main object or private speculation and pecuniary motives of men in high places." For evidence, he cited how the army "was supplied with extensive wagon trains, bagging, rope, and other facilities for transportation" of heavy bales. The army's advance provided a ruse or cover for "a vast scheme of Cotton stealing made legitimate by Government sanction."[26] A Confederate veteran who fought in the 28th Louisiana agreed. "The Federals were very keen for cotton. Its possession meant big money for them."[27]

The financial motive existed on the Confederate side, too. An illicit trade between Confederate territory and Union posts thrived by 1863. A Confederate officer and close observer, Felix Poché, described it and condemned the practice, as did David Ray, a common Texas soldier. When word spread of a big sale that brought officers a handsome profit, it "almost produced a mutiny in some regiments," Ray explained.[28] Both men reported hearing rumors that officers were trading coffee and other commodities. These activities were not the officially sanctioned trades that went forward with the approval of the Cotton Bureau. William Henry King, another soldier in the 28th Louisiana stationed at Shreveport, reported that "cotton is being shipped from this place to New Orleans. This is done by the officers, and of course, counted all right." King resented how "if a private or citizens, engage in such business, the act will be regarded as a high crime.... To further quiet matters, a great many men are being furloughed," he claimed.[29] E.P. Petty, a Texas cavalryman, wrote on March 10, 1864, "There is a great deal of dissatisfaction in the army here growing out of the cotton trade. I am afraid it will ruin our army and demoralize the citizens. I am seriously alarmed about it."[30]

The temptation of good Union money or even gold proved irresistible. Orramel Hinckley, a planter situated near Union lines in St. Landry Parrish, wrote to the Cotton Bureau asking permission to trade his crop. The head of the Louisiana bureau replied in a terse missive that laws prohibited it.[31] A cotton bureau agent near the Mississippi River remembered, "One owner of a large lot of cotton stored within a few miles of the river ventured upon offering me a large bribe to engineer his cotton through the lines." He believed that the "stringent regulations ... were violated frequently in a clandestine way," not only by planters but also "by those whose duty it was to prevent it."[32] General Taylor lamented how the Red River's wealth had "made more damn rascals on both sides than everything else."[33]

The same cotton that had established the region's wealth in the antebellum era, now set the Red River on a course for disaster. The rise in its price proved to be an irresistible temptation. Speculators, military leaders, and civilians became caught up in a mad rush to capture or prevent its capture. The Union entry into the valley in March 1864 convinced General Taylor he must get rid of the remaining stored bales. A rear guard of fast moving cavalrymen dashed through the countryside and burned every bale that could be found. A Union staff officer noted in his logbook during the pursuit of the retreating Confederates, "the enemy is burning in all directions."[34]

Another Union soldier on the march offered a Biblical metaphor, "From the day we started on the Red River expedition, we were like the

Israelites of old, accompanied by a cloud (of smoke) by day, and a pillar of fire by night. The rebels had a company of cavalry setting fire to all the cotton along our route."[35] Charles F. Read who rode out in an advance party of Union horse soldiers wrote, "the country seemed to be one fire with burning cotton! The retiring rebels fire all of the cotton that they could find along the route."[36] At times, March winds carried the flames beyond the bales. "From the cotton the flames would spread to the cotton-sheds and out-houses, and frequently reached the dwellings of the planters and cabins of the slaves. This was one of the curious phases of the war—to see the rebels bent on the destruction of their own property."[37]

At Oakland, Phanor Prudhomme's plantation in Natchitoches Parish, family tradition held that Confederates arrived and burned over 1,000 bales in one huge conflagration.[38] Burning parties also hit smaller farmsteads. While it made military sense to burn the bales, the consequences were devastating. Confederate Felix Pierre Poché put it well when he wrote, "My heart was filled with sadness at the sight of those lovely plantations in flames, and to see the work of the honest industry and perseverance of those good old Creoles planters destroyed in the twinkling of an eye."[39]

The vast sums of wealth tied up in cotton bales drove both Confederate and Union forces absolutely mad. Both sides became caught up in corruption and destruction. Cotton strained civil-military relations on both sides. Speculators interrupted and influenced military actions, and local civilians tried to navigate the war policies of both sides. Unlike other areas of the South, generals, soldiers, planters, and speculators knew that hundreds of thousands of dollars were at stake. Men in both blue and gray showed that their true colors were green. The end result would be a disaster for the cotton owners, the Union army that lost the campaign, and anyone caught in the pathway of those taking or burning cotton. While soldiers of both sides gave the last full measure of devotion for their country, an undercurrent of greed as muddy as the Red itself sullied the sacrifice of so many.

Five

The Campaign Begins
January–March 1864

Early on the morning of January 4, 1864, an interesting negotiation began between Louisiana's Union and Confederate armies. The new year of 1864 had arrived only a few days before, and it brought a steady winter rain. The dark clouds hung over all, and the precipitation kept falling in sheets and buckets. "Three days & nights of the coldest weather that I have experienced in many a day," a Texas doctor wrote his wife.[1] He camped near Marksville, not too far from where the military parley took place. Generals Nathaniel Banks and Richard Taylor had some unfinished business. The battles along the Mississippi River the previous summer and Confederate raids across south Louisiana the previous fall left unresolved the issue of prisoners of war. How many did each side hold, and could there be an exchange of these veterans before the next campaign began? To settle matters, Taylor and Banks each sent representatives to talk. Colonel Charles C. Dwight of the 160th New York traveled up the Mississippi River as Banks's man. He arrived at Red River Landing in Avoyelles Parish. There he met Confederate Major William M. Levy, a Jewish Rebel and pre-war U.S. Congressmen. When the two met, discussions moved to a topic that reflected how profoundly the war had changed over the previous year.[2]

General Banks wanted to know if Confederates held any uniformed African-American troops or their white officers. Since the spring of 1863, Union leaders had allowed a large number of black soldiers to fight at the front lines, and all had served bravely at Milliken's Bend, Port Hudson, and on garrison duty at Brasher City (now Morgan City). The Union army knew that many of these troops had been captured. It was reasonable to suppose that Confederates still held them.

Additionally, Union authorities feared that Confederates had executed black soldiers and their white officers. Credible reports had been coming into their lines that raised concerns.

General George L. Andrews, who commanded the Corps d'Afrique at Port Hudson, believed he possessed proof of executions near Jackson, Louisiana. In a reply to a December 2, 1863, inquiry from headquarters, he informed his superior of three witnesses who came forward, and under oath, told what had happened. "He saw a rebel, Lieutenant Shattuck, shoot some wounded colored soldiers then lying on the ground," the General explained. "They also stated that captured colored soldiers were at that time taken into the wood by rebel soldiers, who afterwords state that they had shot them." When Andrews posed the question to the local Confederate commander about the incident, he flatly denied the allegation. Andrews did not believe him and wrote, "I am satisfied that rebel soldiers, with the connivance and assistance of their officers have abused and shot some of our captured colored soldiers." In particular he added, "the Texan troops in Western Louisiana openly state that they will take no colored soldiers prisoners. This statement is made by Texan refugees."[3]

By 1863, Confederates were forced to come to terms with Union war measures that sought to destroy slavery and arm former slaves. In Louisiana, none other than the new Governor Henry Watkins Allen denounced the Union war effort and 1864 creation of a loyal state government that abolished slavery. In one of his fiery public proclamations, he thundered, "The Constitution and Laws of Louisiana that relate to the institution of African slavery are no more recognized but are with the institution of Slavery itself forever to be obliterated!!" Allen stoked fear by throwing out the possibility: "If a negro, one who had been your own servant, should insist upon coming into your parlor and visiting your wife or daughters on terms equally can you prevent it No."[4]

A loyal Louisiana resident explained in a letter written to President Abraham Lincoln that the Red River Valley contained over 121 million dollars in slave property, and he believed that planters would fight to safeguard it at all costs. "Believing that Agriculture cannot be carried on without the labor of Slaves, the slaveholders consider the [Emancipation] Proclamation as effecting the ruin of the state, as well as their own," he explained. When faced with the prospects of ruin, one and only one, solution remained to them: "the persons freed by the Proclamation shall be made slaves again."[5]

To preserve slavery, the Confederates had to re-capture slaves,

Five. The Campaign Begins 79

and those who joined the Union army must go back to their masters. Yet exactly how to deal with the black soldiers? That question became more complicated than it first appeared, and over time it threw a wrench into Confederate politics. Similar to conscription or other issues, civil and military authorities could not agree on a procedure to deal with captured black soldiers. Any proposal had to please military officers, civil authorities, and slave owners—a nearly impossible task. First, Confederates authorities could not acknowledge that the black soldiers had been freed at all, for if they did, it gave tacit approval to the self-liberation that enslaved people practiced in order to get to the Yankee army in the first place. The Confederate government in Richmond then split in its opinion. At first, the army and war department wanted black soldiers and their white officers executed following capture. This policy followed slave codes that stated that slaves acting in insurrection, and anyone inciting them, were subject to capital punishment.[6]

President Jefferson Davis, ever the politician, modified the military's harsh plans and threw the issue back to the individual states. He preferred that the states rather than a military commander make a decision about planter property. Davis directed that each state should take possession of the offenders and handle them according to state law.[7] The de facto policy became that the army returned black soldiers to their owners, plain and simple. No executions by military means would be allowed because it became a civil matter. Additionally, Lincoln and his army generals promised retaliation on Confederate soldiers if executions took place. In no case whatsoever would black soldiers be eligible for exchange. They must shed the uniform and go back into servitude. Kirby Smith ordered his generals to be mindful of the Union threat of retaliation and promptly turn over slaves to civilian authorities.[8]

At the January 1864 meeting, there at the Red River landing, the issue of black soldiers loomed large. In December 1863, Taylor had insisted that he held no African-Americans and instructions from his government precluded him from even considering "that class of persons" anyway.[9] The two officers at Red River landing followed instructions given by their respective commanders and agreed easily to an exchange of other prisoners "heretofore" held by both sides. When the discussion turned to any future prisoners that might be taken, Dwight asked that black soldiers be treated equal to other soldiers. On this point, Levy stood firm and explained how no agreement could be made regarding return of those prisoners. "I informed him that my instructions equally forbade me to make any agreement that should in any manner exclude or discriminate against them," Dwight reported later.[10] In truth, Taylor did not hold blacks or white officers of black units under his command because the whites had been shipped to Camp Ford in Tyler, Texas, outside of his military district of western Louisiana. The blacks had been returned to plantations as slaves; technically speaking, none of those men were in his possession.[11] The two sides remained far apart on the subject. More than anything, this incident illustrated how black soldiers had become symbolic of Union war aims and Confederate frustrations.

Louisiana's slave system, the very foundation for the state's economy and planter patriarchy, showed signs of deterioration as soon as Union forces captured New Orleans. The army camps around the edges of the city became beacons drawing both individuals and families. From 1862 onward, blacks arrived day and night. In Jefferson Parish, west of New Orleans, the army's frontline installation, Camp Parapet, quickly became filled with "contraband." Slaves were called contraband because they were first listed as liberated enemy property by Union General Benjamin Butler. He acted to keep them in Union lines even before Lincoln had a clearly formulated policy or a plan for his commanders on the ground.[12]

In the spring, summer and fall of 1862, along the Mississippi River, Bayou Lafourche and Bayou Teche, the Union army entered areas where the number of slaves was much greater than in New Orleans proper. From the beginning, of the Union movements, slaves began flocking to the stars and stripes. The number of runaways in Union lines rose by the hundreds, and the question of what to do with them loomed large. The destruction of slavery was happening before everyone's eyes. The next spring General Banks, who replaced Butler, marched an army up the entire length of the Teche and into the southern Red River Valley. He carried with him former slaves, now uniformed and armed as soldiers. At Port Hudson, he committed them to combat.[13]

A white Union soldier serving at Brasher City recognized that he was witnessing something profound:

> This war seems base—hard—cruel—unendurable—but there is being brought about one of the greatest Eras in the history of the world—but I just as much believe that God is ruling this all for the best and 3 and one half millions of people are to become Free men & women of the word—who in former years have known nothing of life's joys and its pleasures and have borne the heat of the sultry scorching Sun and been made to bare their back to the Drivers whip

and suffer 40 & 50 lashes for petty crimes—and all this has been done within the very towns and cities where we now are.[14]

A planter south of Alexandria, John H. Ransdell, commented on the transformation too. His opinion could not have been more opposite from the Union solider at Brasher City. He contacted his neighbor, none other than Governor Thomas O. Moore, reporting to him that all the slaves on the neighborhood plantations either ran away or went "crazy" as the Union army marched by the place. Their attitudes and demeanor changed as a spirit of freedom overcame them. He noted in particular how several Union soldiers were spotted conversing with the slaves and telling them outright that they were free. The enslaved men and women freed themselves and then removed other "property" of their master too. Ransdell related how "all the furniture at Elmfield," one of the governor's properties, "was taken out of the house and taken to the negroes' cabins." The slaves stocked their homes with the master's possessions, vividly illustrating how, upon liberation, the slaves turned society upside down.[15]

No evidence exists of how Moore took the news or how he treated his remaining slaves following the rebellion. When the army turned in early May 1863 towards Port Hudson and left many of the slaves on the plantations in Rapides Parish, "things are just now beginning to work right—the negroes hated awfully to go to work again," Ransdell explained to Moore. "Several have been shot and probably more will have to be," he stated. If that did not work, more whippings were needed on all those remaining, he wrote. The slaves had tasted freedom, and it would be hard to keep them down on the farm after this experience.[16]

In 1864, the same thing happened again. As the Union army approached the plantations of the Red River, slaves became jubilantly defiant. "The other Negros were in open revolt, refused to work, and were very insolent," a woman living in Rapides recorded in her diary.[17] A Confederate soldier named William King expressed his own ideas about what was happening to slavery. Assigned guard duty at a jail in Shreveport, he noticed that runaway slaves were brought for confinement before being turned over to their masters. "Five negros brought in … but not taken from among the Federals. While guarding them, many crowded around, and declared the negros out [sic] to be killed," he wrote in his diary. King did not want a lynching on his watch. "It is but natural for them to desire to be free & if they do nothing but run away from their master to obtain freedom, certainly they do not merit death," he stated in his private diary.[18] This opinion, quite surprising for a Southerner at the time, reflected the dilemma facing Confederates with the liberating effects of the Union's 1863 and 1864 military campaigns.

In Sabine Parish, Della Armstrong, who had been a slave as a young girl in the 1860s and then lived into the 20th century, had a story to tell. She reported how slaves heard of "mansipatun" in 1863, yet none of them knew what Emancipation really meant. She claimed a few mischievous fellows told the more gullible in the slave quarters that it "meant they's gonna have yo head chopped off wid a dull axe," she said. The uncertainty of what would happen when emancipation arrived scared so many slaves that she learned of a tragic result of the rumor. "One of my brudders b'lieved it so much he went out in de woods an' hung hisself to a tree."[19] Rather than face certain death, her brother took his own life.

General Banks, maligned in his own time, has also been panned by military historians as a political general who knew little about soldiering. Chief among the criticisms I have heard at meetings of Red River historians was that he placed non-military considerations ahead of sound strategic planning. These complaints will always hit their mark. True, Banks wanted to capture cotton, and that goal eclipsed his military planning. At the scene of action, however, his biggest mistake was that he did not cooperate with the navy. He became a rival with Admiral David Porter for the capture of cotton but also for the glory in what looked like a certain victory. Instead of turning to his own admiral for advice or looking carefully at maps prepared by staff officers such as John Clark, Banks asked for directions from a Captain William Withenbury, a civilian steamboat pilot from Ohio who had only recently signed an oath of allegiance.[20] This captain pointed the army to a narrow inland road as the best route for Shreveport. By giving this direction, Withenbury deliberately guided the army away from the river road where cotton was sitting for the taking. Historian Gary D. Joiner concluded that because of this selfish act, "Withenbury changed the course of the campaign in a single night."[21] Banks should have known better than to trust him.

Historians have thought that Banks was shuffled off to the Department of the Gulf after failure in Virginia for the primary purpose of getting rid of him. This is a seemingly valid point with evidence to support it. While I agree in principle with this assessment, I must offer an alternative or additional reason he came to the Department of the Gulf. Given the President's Reconstruction plans for transforming occupied areas of the South, Banks appeared to be a perfect fit for Louisiana. He had been a political force before the war and that is exactly why Lincoln wanted him there. The former Speaker of the House of Representatives would carry out and supervise political and social goals via military means.

The state could be a showcase for the end of slavery and the start of free labor. Government plantations seized from Confederates along the Mississippi River and elsewhere along fertile bayous emerged as showplaces for presidential policy. Government plantations along the Red would be next, that was if the area could be brought under control. The establishment of Unionists as the new politicos for the state stood as a second big objective. These two steps assured that Lincoln could bring the state back into the Union easily. It made much more sense to have a general who was a political animal to carry out these Reconstruction plans. Following Grant's resounding victory at Vicksburg, a military leader might report back, "Mission accomplished" and then do nothing. Not Banks. He had grander considerations. The opportunity to re-make society into a mold more familiar to New England reformers held a ring to it that was much more seductive in its power.

At the end of February 1864, only a few weeks before the start his spring military campaign, Banks wrote to the Commander-in-Chief to give him an update.[22] This letter did not contain a single ounce of military information. He gave instead strong assurances to the President that he planned to fulfill each of the political objectives he set for the campaign. He was going to hold elections for a state constitutional convention all along his route. He would re-animate local government, placing it in the hands of Union men. Above all he pledged the elimination of slavery. Before the campaign began, he supervised the election of a new governor and other state officials. Banks stepped forward himself to install them properly. First on the agenda would be an elaborate inauguration ceremony held at Lafayette Square in the heart of the American section of New Orleans. All the festivities would honor the newly elected Louisiana governor, Michael Hahn. Platforms festooned with red white and blue bunting filled the space in front of city hall on one side of the square. At great expense and effort, the celebration came complete with children's choirs, bands playing, cannon salutes, and patriotic speeches. The result was a spectacle so common in that day and age that only New Orleans could provide.[23]

Next after this would be those elections for a Constitutional convention to re-write the state constitution. The voting would not only take place at New Orleans, safely under the control of the army, but Banks planned to take ballot boxes with him and hold elections at every stop the army made. The army would be an instrument to carry out a specific political goal of the President. Banks promised Lincoln, "The convention for the revision of the [state] Constitution will confirm the absolute extinction of slavery upon that the election has proceeded and to that every voter has assented, and provide for such extension of suffrage as will meet the demands of the age."[24] All these noble and lofty goals were admirable, no doubt, and yet one comes away from this letter and others Banks wrote thinking that the general wanted political credit for what he was doing rather than a victor's laurels. The army's advance into enemy territory to crush Taylor's army and then capture Shreveport remained well and good yet involved pesky details. Crucial planning would have to be left up to others. The demands of effecting political and social change became too pressing for Banks to be bothered with military strategy.

While Banks played politics, it was his staff who took care of the routine matters. This delegation of duties did not bode well at all. The staff officers, while competent, lacked the talent to make up for their commander's shortcomings. The chief of staff, General Charles Stone, had been a regular army officer before the war. Instead of performing well in 1861, his pre-war experience delivered nothing on a real battlefield. In October, he participated in the ill-fated attempt to cross the Potomac River and gain a foothold in Loudoun County, Virginia. Union soldiers stormed a Confederate stronghold on the river's bluffs, thinking that they could carry it. From the start, the planning and execution miscarried badly. Regiments became trapped, and many men were gunned down beside the river. A great deal of blame for that debacle fell on Charles Stone, some wrongly, yet most rightly. He had been arrested in the weeks following the affair, and although he had not done anything criminal, that arrest sent a chill throughout the whole officer corps of the Union's eastern army. Instead of swift and certain justice, Stone languished without a trial or meaningful command for years until all was swept under the carpet. His second chance arrived with an assignment as chief of staff for Banks in Louisiana.[25]

Instead of assembling a library of detailed maps and other strategic assets, Stone and the staff gathered a minimal cache of material. The Banks papers held by the Library of Congress contains few military maps. One staff officer, John S. Clark, drew maps of his own. They showed Louisiana and Texas that was helpful yet nowhere were the local or parish maps with detailed plots of the roads that would be most helpful for an army on the move.[26] These staff officers found themselves in way over their heads. If military matters were not enough to get them busy, Banks insisted on carrying on large, detailed political objectives. Instead of turning attention to the campaign set to begin only one week later, Banks and his staff planned to launch the new Reconstruction government on March 4, 1864. The Banks papers at the Library of Congress contain a long oath of office written for the Unionist Governor-elect Michael Hahn by Banks himself.[27] Instead of being with the troops as they prepared to leave camp at Franklin, Louisiana, General Banks remained behind to iron out all the details for the inaugural ceremony of a new governor.

"Today has been a great day for Louisiana," Charles F. Read of the 3rd Massachusetts Cavalry wrote after attending the ceremony. "I stayed only a little while," he admitted, yet it was long enough to be quite impressed by "the crowds, the arrangements, and decorations." On the two acres at Lafayette Square in front of City Hall, he noticed "an immense circle of seats ranging upon an inclined plane." A festive "gay assemblage" filled up the rows to capacity, and all around "the decorations with flags etc. was immense. An immense brass band played national airs with cannon accompaniment, and an immense chorus of children sung the same."[28] His repetitive use of the word "immense" said it all. A *New York Times* reporter found the event equally big and beyond words:

> That the pen can do but inadequate justice to the subject, is certain. An approach to a true description of the splendor of the display, or a slightly successful portrayal of the enthusiasm of the mass of the people, would appear to the denizens of the North as exaggerated. The real truth regarding these things, except by an eye-witness, cannot be understood or appreciated.[29]

To catch up to the men who had headed out over rain-soaked muddy roads ahead of him, Banks and staff finished the New Orleans parties and boarded a large headquarters steamer for a river cruise to Alexandria. The fact that their commander choose a stateroom over a saddle could not have been lost on the men as they slogged through mile after mile. The columns arrived a week behind schedule, and Banks alighted from his vessel in a clean uniform. Banks planted himself along the tree-lined streets of Alexandria a week and three days following the navy's arrival there and reviewed the troops.[30]

The regiments who had engaged the Confederates at the start of the campaign in Avoyelles Parish had not been from Banks' army but were

Sherman's men who arrived by boat after a long ride from Vicksburg. They were under the command of the hard drinking, hard fighting soldier's soldier, General Andrew Jackson Smith. His name said it all. He was cut from the same cloth as the president whose name he carried all his life.[31] Smith's mostly western troops of the 16th and 17th corps had been loaned from the Army of the Tennessee with a deadline for return. The lateness of Banks bothered both Admiral Porter of the Navy and General Smith, both of whom did not get along well with Banks for the rest of the campaign. The lack of good communication and cooperation between these three key commanders played a role in the Union defeat.

A word must be said on the composition of the Union army. It was not a well-integrated fighting force. The biggest numbers were brigades pieced together from the 19th Corps and two divisions from the 13th Corps. The soldiers from both corps came primarily from New England or the Mid-Atlantic states. Then brigades from A.J. Smith were from the Midwest and had not fought with their counterparts in a large campaign. The 2,500 men of the African-American unit called

Admiral David Dixon Porter's inland fleet assembles for action on the Red River (*Heritage of Valor*, Louisiana State Archives).

up to the campaign, the Corps d' Afrique, added another element. The Department of the Gulf cavalry, artillery, and support units rounded out those gathered for the mission. This army, a cobbled–together force, had not been conceived as a cohesive entity from day one. A West Pointer might have had trouble making it more integrated or even managing the whole crew. Banks was not a professional military man and devoid of any pre-war military experience. While his staff might have been professional men, they faced a daunting chore in making this beast do what its master wanted it to do.[32]

Instead of spending more time training his staff, making the army units work together effectively, or considering either the best route for his army's march or the order of the column and wagons, Banks committed his time to political matters. This should not be a surprise given he was a politician through and through. His primary interest was to bring about an election at Alexandria on the 2nd of April. The voting was for delegates to the Unionist state Constitutional Convention in New Orleans. Banks had written to President Lincoln back in February, outlining what he thought the true plan for the meeting should be: "The convention for the revision of the Constitution will confirm the absolute extinction of slavery upon that the election has proceeded and to that every voter has assented, and provide for such extension of suffrage as will meet the demands of the age."[33] The Union's Red River Valley expedition became tied into a political agenda that promised economic and social revolution.

The Union men in the Red River Valley who were expected to come forward and vote in the election had opposed secession, or were upset about the Confederate draft, but many had not become abolitionists. Now, they were being asked to come on board with goals that did not mesh well with their own worldview. Upon arrival at Alexandria, Banks wasted no time in finding Charles Boyce, the prewar newspaper editor and Alexandria's vocal Unionist. Banks demanded that he put together a list of prominent citizens who would vote in the election for delegates to the state constitutional convention. A polling place would be established in the city under the protection of United States arms. The only incentive offered was that all those who took an oath of allegiance and signed up to vote received a promise of protection for themselves and their property. Boyce prepared a list of nearly eighty men. The Wells brothers made the list, of course, and other prominent citizens included the mayor of Alexandria and the parish sheriff. It included Bayou Rapides planters Lewis Texada of "Bayouside" and

Robert C. Hynson, owner of the Creole mansion known as "Kent House."[34]

Boyce, Texada, and Hynson all signed oaths of allegiance. Those official documents were dutifully stored in the Department of the Gulf records and survive to this day. Since the grand homes of these men also survived the war intact, and stand to this day, while other buildings such as the Winn and Maddox plantation houses right next door to Texada and Hynson were destroyed by the Union, a willingness to participate in the first steps of reconstruction may account for the seemingly good fortune. The Unionist voters made up a small portion of the planter elite in the parish. This core group was going to step forward and show the way for all others in the region. The Union army promised nothing less than a political and social reorganization of the Red River Valley.[35]

The political atmosphere at the headquarters continued after the election and while on the move. As the army set out towards Shreveport, General Banks kept up a brisk correspondence with officials in Washington, D.C. Topics included discussion about creating a Freedman's savings bank for black troops and Freedman wage-earners on the newly created plantations where former slaves were paid wages for their work.[36] While these efforts remained important and beneficial to Union war aims, and from a humanitarian standpoint remain quite laudable, the time invested in them pulled Banks away from responsibilities that would determine if the whole campaign succeeded or failed. The elections and the freedom for slaves would have no meaning if the army lost the campaign.

The opening weeks in March had lulled General Banks and others into thinking this foray deep into Louisiana would be an easy expedition. All during the month, Union forces had racked up impressive victories. On March 12, General A.J. Smith's 10,000 men landed at Simmsport about twenty-five miles from the major Confederate works at Fort DeRussy. The Third Division 16th Corps acted as a quick-strike force that would take out the only impediment to the navy's pushing up the Red. Fort DeRussy appeared formidable. It included a bastion, rifle pits, and a water battery with heavy artillery right at a bend in the river. A.J. Smith ordered the men to come upon the fort from the rear, land side. "General Taylor was not allowed time to concentrate and cover this important work," Kirby Smith wrote.[37] Taylor did not want to leave his men at the work and ordered a retreat instead. On the morning of March 14, Smith's men assaulted the fort approximately

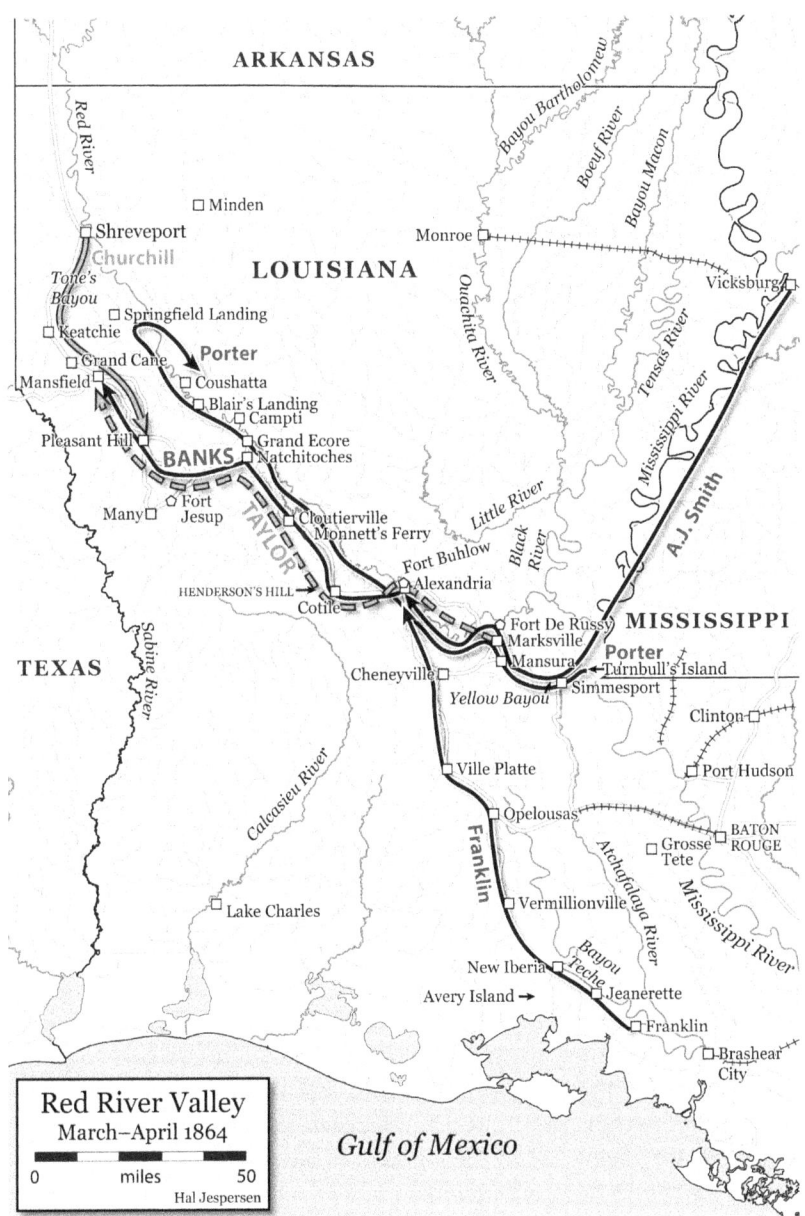

Red River Valley
March–April 1864

350 Confederate soldiers remained in it, and they surrendered quickly. Light losses resulted with seven killed and forty-four wounded for the Union; Confederates counted two to five killed and four to seven wounded. The battle, a mere skirmish really, did little to slow the Union advance. With Fort DeRussy, the Gibraltar on the Red, gone, the river route all the way to Alexandria flew wide open.[38]

On March 15, Admiral Porter's gunboats steamed around the bend and into sight. Union troops unloaded at the levee and entered the quiet town.[39] General Richard Taylor had evacuated and loaded up many supplies before his army retreated on a long march northward, "seventy miles through the pine woods."[40] Colonel William G. Vincent's Louisiana Second Cavalry and Edgar's battery kept an eye on Union activities from a position north of the city. General Taylor depended on this unit because at this point it was his only way for gathering intelligence about Union troop movements. Vincent's cavalry had been overexerted since shadowing the Union forces from New Iberia northward. Taylor knew they had been "jaded by constant service and long marches."[41] On March 20–21, they engaged in brief skirmishes with Union troops. On the night of March 21, Vincent's weary men set up camp at Henderson's Hill, about twenty-five miles north and west of Alexandria. This rise overlooked Bayou Rapides and commanded an open, broad plain for miles to the east.[42]

That night, Vincent's men found their campfires more agreeable than the cold rain and sleet that fell from a darkened sky. Union General Joseph Mower ordered out six infantry regiments and one brigade of cavalry. This highly mobile force totaled 1,000 Union soldiers. Their mission: capture the inattentive Confederates.[43] Union Colonel Lucius Hubbard, who commanded a brigade in the 17th Corps, reported how it was his understanding that "an inhabitant of the country" became a guide for the Union troops.[44] The Department of the Gulf record books stored away at the National Archives contains an order from the quartermaster to pay one John Walker $50 for rendering service as a "guide on the 21st of March at Henderson Hill."[45] The amount—not an inconsequential sum in those days—was paid for navigating Union columns through dark swamps and dense woods. While on the circuitous pathway that night, the units bumped into and captured a Confederate courier whom they questioned and learned the night's countersign.[46] With that intelligence, and the element of surprise, the Yankees completely surround the Confederates.

Lieutenant Colonel William B. Keeler of the 35th Iowa Infantry wrote succinctly, "We arrived in the rear of Henderson's Hill ... capturing the outposts and pickets, and arriving in the main camp about 12 [midnight], surprising the enemy." Keeler's first-hand account mentioned some initial firing. Most Confederates were captured when they came out of their tents and had no time to organize resistance. One of his comrades suffered a "slightly wounded in the mouth by a pistol-shot," Keeler wrote.⁴⁷ Again, the Union forces succeeded in an operation with little loss of life.

In a single swift and daring attack, Union forces had blindsided General Taylor. He lost his cavalry scouts, invaluable artillery, and became momentarily unaware of Union activities. The Confederate chieftain reported, "This disaster leaves me with little or no means of obtaining information in front of a very large force of the enemy's cavalry. I am therefore compelled to fall back."⁴⁸ For all his command savvy, Taylor had made a great blunder by leaving an invaluable asset close enough to be captured. Until General Thomas Green's Texas cavalry arrived and restored good horse soldiers to the ranks, his army remained hamstrung.

Union First Sergeant Charles Read, riding at the head of the 3rd Massachusetts Cavalry, spent the next week after Henderson Hill "skirmishing at the front." As the Yankee infantry lumbered out of Alexandria on the roads to Natchitoches, Read and his men rode out ahead looking for the enemy. The cavalry played a deadly game as they probed the route of advance, and the Confederates would shoot and then fall back. "We have halted at a river and are awaiting the construction of a bridge. Saw some rebel pickets," Read put down in a journal. The skirmishing continued after he crossed over the water. "Passed a dead rebel lying by the roadside. Four negroes were digging his grave," Read explained. Then he mentioned, "At another place we passed a rebel lying by the roadside who had been shot through the head. He was still alive. Looked ghastly pale and was breathing with great difficulty."⁴⁹

One of the most striking characteristics of Read's account or any others has to be the miles and miles covered by the units on horseback and foot. Union and Confederate armies tramped great distances and plowed through varied terrains in all kinds of weather. The Red River was no exception. The daily marching regime of a typical regiment might be sixteen miles, or if pressed, men traversed the distances of twenty to twenty-five miles in a single day.⁵⁰ General Thomas "Stonewall" Jackson was famous for moving his men at such rates during the 1862 Shenandoah Valley campaign. The Red River's Confederate general Richard Taylor had been under Stonewall's command and participated in those feats of marching. Each man carried a knapsack, a nine pound musket, forty rounds of ammunition, canteens, and food for days of campaigning.⁵¹

In the realm of Civil War marching, the Gettysburg campaign during the summer of 1863 is often held up as an example of amazing distances covered by armies.[52] General Robert E. Lee drove his Army of Northern Virginia into southern Pennsylvania from positions near Fredericksburg, Virginia. His divisions took lengthier routes than the Union army that played chase and stayed mostly in Maryland between Lee and Washington, D.C. While a great deal has been made of the arduous Gettysburg campaign marches, practically nothing has been written about the distances covered by both sides during the 1864 Red River campaign. As a general rule, campaigns in the Trans-Mississippi west covered greater distances, and the limited roads made the marches especially uncomfortable. The Red River campaign must be remembered for its unbelievably long marches.

The armies of Richard Taylor and Nathaniel Banks covered greater distances than generals Robert E. Lee and Joseph Hooker/George Gordon Meade during the celebrated 1863 Gettysburg campaign. By using Google maps, I rendered walking directions between selected points of the Gettysburg campaign. General Lee's Army of Northern Virginia travelled approximately 168 miles from a start at or near Fredericksburg, Virginia, and to the Gettysburg battlefield.[53] The selected route travelled through Culpepper and Berryville in Virginia then Hagerstown, Maryland, and finally Chambersburg, Pennsylvania, before arrival at the battlefield itself. Not all of Lee's forces took this pathway but the route is a reasonable approximation for men who fought in the battle. Some units may have gone longer, some shorter. Since Lee made a round trip on this campaign (his defeat bought that ticket), the total miles reached approximately 336 miles.

Doing the same analysis for Red River, with the Union army now as the invader, I found that elements of the 19th and 13th corps made a trudge of 240 miles.[54] Their forces went from Franklin, Louisiana, near the Gulf of Mexico to Alexandria and then Natchitoches before making their way up to a point outside of Mansfield. Then their retreat from Mansfield and Pleasant Hill took them to Simmsport, Louisiana, near the Mississippi River. The length between those points is approximately 154 miles. The grand total marching distance for the Union army came in at 394 miles. Remember, Lee's Gettysburg marches hit only 336 miles.

The diaries and letters from the Union soldiers tell the dreadful tale of their exertions. One unit that steamed down from Vicksburg aboard boats in the first days of the campaign disembarked and "marched nearly 35 miles in 20 hours," a soldier reported.[55] One Indiana unit covered twenty miles on one day eighteen a week later.[56] A soldier

Five. The Campaign Begins 93

in a Maine regiment complained when they were pushed to make thirty-five miles in two days. He detested the narrow roads that strung out the men and wagons for miles and kicked up dust that became a blanket of "an invisible grit that penetrated everything, even to the inside of watches."[57] Another soldier from down east in Maine commented on the 200 miles they covered in the entire campaign. The terrible roads, lack of fresh water, and sheer distances made it "justly regarded as a very credible feat of pedestrianism," he recounted.[58]

For Taylor's Confederate army, its defensive stance meant it marched less. Elements of Walker's division started out near Simmsport and then retreated to Mansfield, approximately 154 miles away. The Confederates won the battle at Mansfield and chased the Union army back to Simmsport for a round trip of over 300 miles. In the Gettysburg campaign, elements of the Union army under General Hooker and then General Meade, also on the defensive, marched only 124 miles to the battle from a starting point in Virginia. They returned to Virginia following a three-day battle. Their mileage never hit anywhere near 300 miles. The Confederates in the Red River campaign went a much greater distance even on the defensive.

One Confederate soldier from Texas summed up his experience well: "Travelled day and night for 5 days & nights…. I am well except my feet—they bruised and sore & road foundered. I think that the fatigue etc. of the trip has made me fall off and that I am not so fat as I was."[59] Another Texan, W. Randolph Howell, kept a journal where he recorded the daily distances that the 5th Texas Cavalry covered to get to the scene of action. This unit arrived from one of the most distant points on the map, Montgomery, Texas. This town, situated in a county of the same name only a few miles north of Houston, was easily two hundred miles from the Red. Once activated, the horsemen moved out slowly and then picked up speed. On March 29 and 30, Howell wrote in his diary that he and the regiment went "17 miles & camp near Many," a town in southwestern Louisiana. He complained, "Again in Louisiana. March[ed] 30 miles & camp near Natchitoches." Only a few days later, the unit had joined up with the rest of the Confederates. In only about two weeks' time, they had covered the entire distance, on average, fourteen miles a day.[60]

When Travis Hensley, a veteran soldier in Waller's Texas Cavalry, received orders that his regiment would be setting out from Hempstead, Texas on a 250 mile journey to join Taylor's army in Louisiana, he took out paper and pen immediately. He realized the impending danger well enough to understand he might not get another chance to share his thoughts. In a fine script that is truly admirable, he composed words that relinquished the heartache of telling his wife farewell. The ever-so-brief missive contained all the Victorian sentimentalism of the day. He reminded her that in only a few hours, his unit would leave, and he might not return. This would be a final chance to tell her and his "darling" children he loved them. When Hensley wrote "good bye" on the page, the steady hand of that seasoned veteran gave way to his other self, that of a loving husband and devoted father. His pen skipped an extra space following this word as if there was a long pause. He then wrote, "O dear one how it pains me to repeat those sad words; but the dearest friends must part. Let us hope to soon meet again when this terrible war is over."[61]

Six

The Most Terrible Charge
The Battle of Mansfield, April 8, 1864

"Now is the winter of our discontent...." With these words, William Shakespeare opened his historical play *Richard III*.[1] In the final scene of the play, Richard is thrown to the ground during battle at Bosworth Field and while casting about for some means of escape, utters helplessly, "my kingdom for a horse." With none to be found, he dies at the hands of an avenger. In an ironic coincidence, the magnificent St. Charles Theater in New Orleans presented Shakespeare's play *Richard III* in early March of 1864, only weeks before the opening of the Red River campaign. Just as winter drew to a close, a young and cultured Union soldier from Indiana attended the play. He had become interested in more melancholy subjects since coming to New Orleans. In a diary, he mentioned a visit to one of the distinctive cemeteries known locally as "cities of the dead." The above-ground tombs made of both marble and gray granite still give the appearance of buildings scattered across acres and acres of ground. These sad, quiet locales remain conducive to melancholy or introspective thinking.[2]

This soldier, Henry C. Sampson of the 67th Indiana, had seen his share of combat and many close calls. He had survived two major campaigns already, and he had been captured twice in close quarter fights, then returned quickly to his lines. In a straightforward and matter-fact style he wrote, "Purchased tickets for the appearance of J. Wilkes Booth tomorrow night at St. Charles. Booth appears as Richard III." Indeed, the lead actor playing Richard was none other than John Wilkes Booth. The *Daily True Delta* newspaper advertised near its masthead for weeks, "entertainment at this theatre, Mr. Booth personating the character of Richard."[3] Booth had traveled to New Orleans and acted in that play one year and one month before he would gun down President Lincoln at Ford's Theater in Washington, D.C. The New Orleans performances would be Booth's last long series. Sampson returned from the play: "Went to see Booth to-night. Was much pleased with his personation of Richard but not with his support." Only three days later, Sampson and his regiment travelled to Franklin, Louisiana. Each soldier was issued a shelter half to carry on the march. When fitted together, the halves made a whole tent for two men. It was a sure sign he and his comrades were starting into a campaign that might be a long period of their own discontent.

Up until the battle of Mansfield on April 8, the campaign did not produce a major battle. The capture of Fort DeRussy had lasted minutes, and casualties there proved light.[4] Admiral Porter's boats captured Alexandria and steamed up to Springfield Landing south of Shreveport without so much as a canon fired against the intrusion. The capture of Confederate units at Henderson Hill on 21 March marked another relatively bloodless engagement where the Union forces surprised and captured sleeping cavalrymen and their artillery battery.[5] In all the actions up to early April, Taylor had continued behaving just as the Union Generals had anticipated he might act. He demonstrated weakness, appeared outnumbered, and his army remained in retreat. The sharpest encounter did not take place until the engagement at Wilson's farm on April 7, that was only a day before Taylor turned the momentum of the campaign around with a large counter-strike that led to the first major battle of the campaign. The desire of both armies for a big fight had been drawn up for almost four weeks, and now they would get one.

Taylor, who had retreated and delayed in order to gather as many men as possible, now found himself backed right against Shreveport. If he followed the orders of his superior, department commander General Kirby Smith, to avoid a battle, he faced the prospect of taking his forces into trenches at the city.[6] There the men who had no experience fighting siege warfare might become sitting ducks. Shreveport would have been another Vicksburg or Port Hudson. The same dismal results could be expected from a move into the city. In Taylor's view, the options did not favor a continued retreat, at least before having a fight. He was running out of space to do that because approximately thirty-seven miles separated Mansfield and Shreveport. One road led into Mansfield from the south, yet three others exited out of it towards

Shreveport. If he moved the army beyond that point, the number of approach routes for the Union tripled, and Taylor would have been spread too thin to stop multiple advances.

Taylor desired a decisive engagement because it fit his typical generalship. Time and again, he retreated, found a weakness of his opponent to exploit, and then attacked, attacked, attacked. He had done just that in the fall of 1863 in the Texas Overland campaign and had stymied a Union advance outside Opelousas.[7] He learned this method from Stonewall Jackson in 1862. Taylor watched as Stonewall defeated an army under none other than Nathaniel Banks himself. Taylor took away from his time in Virginia that he must attack and do so on his own terms. Now in the early spring of 1864, he just had to pick favorable ground for the Union army to stumble into for a beating. In front of the Moss Plantation south of Mansfield, he selected a spot of ground where he might spring his trap.

Just why General Banks and his chief subordinate General William Franklin, with all their experience fighting in Virginia and against Taylor for over a year, fell for the Confederate's predictable plan remains a mystery. Banks allowed his army to advance with a small contingent of men in the vanguard with wagons behind them, followed by more troops and even more wagons. Having wagons stacked up behind the columns of men was not a smart move at all. This boxed in the men on narrow roads with little ability to retreat easily or rush to the aid of those in advance. The Union army ignored Taylor's propensity to attack. The generals simply did not think the Confederates posed a threat. Historian Gary D. Joiner explained that even after riding forward and talking with his Cavalry general, Albert Lee, who warned him about an imminent attack, "Banks still did not believe the Confederates would fight him."[8]

A clue to why this fog shrouded the lead generals can be traced back almost exactly a year before, when Banks rode into Alexandria for the first time. On that occasion in the spring of 1863, Taylor had retreated quickly, and his forces dissipated northward towards Shreveport and west to Texas. In a moment of supreme confidence back then, Banks wrote to President Lincoln that "They can never organize another army in this department—Our movement has been a complete surprise, and the rout fatal to the enemy. It is conceded by all persons whom we meet. Neither Texas nor Arkansas has means of defeating us—The only hope for the rebels is from large accessions from their army East of the Mississippi—I hope they will not escape our forces there."[9] This quote showed that Banks did not believe that the Confederacy could ever assemble the numbers to contest any advances. Fast forward a year to 1864, and this mindset remained the prevailing view. In the opening weeks of the campaign, the evidence showed itself in every move Banks and Franklin made. The senior Union commanders thought Taylor's forces were too small, ill-equipped, and lacking a punch.[10]

What the Union officers did not know was that Taylor had assembled a larger force there than he had possessed at almost any other battle he had fought. Over the weeks of the retreat, sizable numbers of irregular troops made their way into the camps of the Confederates. Additional Texas soldiers had come over, and the assembly of ten batteries of artillery added to the count. Taylor's main army swelled to 12,417.[11] This number included a recently arrived division of Arkansas soldiers who were behind Taylor's main lines and guarded its flanks and rear. A large Missouri Division was marching to the scene, and if they are counted too, the total number on hand in the tactical area of operations reached 14,617. Of these troops, the Confederates committed 10,117 to a battle plan. When the Louisiana and Texas units under generals Alfred Mouton and John Walker commenced a fierce attack on the afternoon of April 8, the misperception that the Confederates could do no harm shattered abruptly. The Civil War was not yet lost in this corner of the South.

The morning of the 8th dawned cool and damp. Mansfield, a "rural and retired" place sitting "on elevated ground," was a "well-built town of some twelve hundred inhabitants."[12] The streets met at right angles and cotton wealth had brought it into existence, and now this ordinary place became a community caught up in war. Over the previous day, Confederate divisions had passed through retreating to points north of the town. The wounded poured in from the daily skirmishing and the big encounter at Wilson's Farm on April 7. The college and churches had been turned into hospitals. Rooms at the courthouse and the jail became filled with prisoners. General Taylor ordered his units to remain close to the outskirts and prepared to move at a moment's notice.

A young lady named Sara Moss had left her farm three miles south of town and had gone into Mansfield to be a nurse at the college. Early on the morning of the battle, she returned home on an errand for butter, eggs, milk, and chickens to supply the hospital. She drove a wagon by herself, or perhaps accompanied a slave, and on her route she passed by the farms of the Phillips, Brown, and McElroy families.[13] She reached the house and gathered all the goods together. Once the food items

Six. The Most Terrible Charge

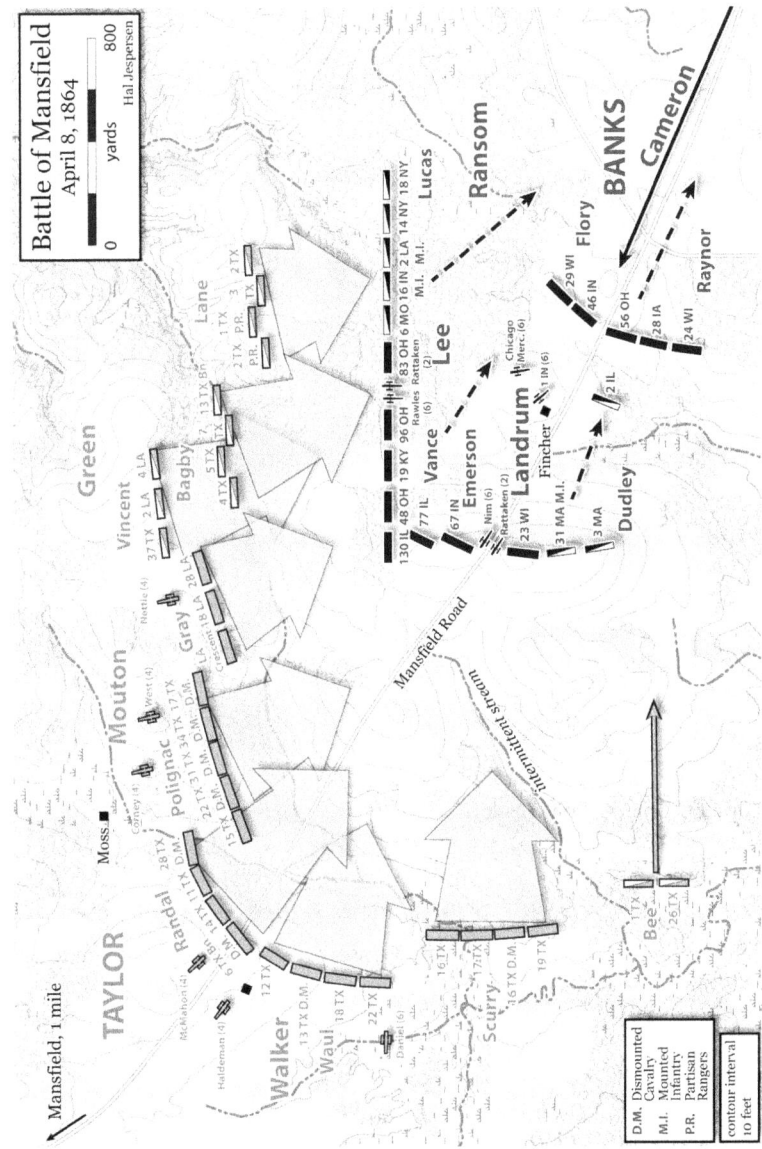

were packed away carefully, she got back on the road for a return trip. As Sara approached the McElroy cotton gin sitting beside the road, she heard a noise she never forgot.[14] The tramp of a large Confederate division came to her ears. The sound grew louder and louder, until all of a sudden large columns of Confederates appeared with battle flags streaming in the morning light. She was shunted off the road to make room for them to pass, and she had to wait a considerable time as brigades of General Walker's Texans passed by making the distinctive tramp and clanking of an army on the move.

All covered in dust and road grime, these soldiers passed by. Only their colors brightened the drab scene. The occasional flash of a musket barrel reminded all of their purpose. This vivid imagery enraptured Sara, and she remembered it the rest of her life. Little did she know at that time the soldiers were headed to where she had been—her family's place. General Walker and the Louisiana division under Alfred Mouton set up battle lines all around the Moss plantation's forest and fields. Taylor had selected that spot for battle.

Earlier while Sara had been away, General Walker's division, the pride of Taylor's army—and nicknamed the greyhounds due to their legendary marching abilities—had paraded through the town to the applause of crowds. Now they were advancing toward the enemy for the first time in the campaign. One of Walker's men vowed, "we would rather die than retreat another step."[15] When Sara returned to town, the women she worked with greeted her with excitement. She had missed the parade, and news was buzzing about when the big battle would start. Later in the evening at the hospital as the wounded began arriving, she met an injured lieutenant, Charles T. Bannerman of the 6th Battalion Texas Cavalry (Gould's).[16] The two fell in love, and the couple married sometime after his recovery.

Moss was intimately familiar with the landscape that became a battlefield, and she gave a great description of how General Taylor aligned his legions. General Walker's Texas brigades were on the west side of the road and to the right of the Louisiana division. She remembered:

> The balance of the troops of Walker's division after marching, counter-marching and maneuvering was formed in the line of battle about 2 p.m. behind a rail fence enclosing the Moss plantation, the left of the division rested on the line of the Pleasant Hill road, Scurry's brigade on the right, Waul's in the center and Randall's on the left. After the line of battle was formed the command was given to stack arms, the fence was pulled down and the soldiers remained inactive about an hour, awaiting the approach of the enemy who were reported about one mile in front.[17]

Among Walker's Confederates awaiting their own fate that day were the Ray brothers, John and David, two sons of the Lone Star State. Their entrance into the Civil War came, like others', at a relatively young age. As teenagers, the brothers joined the 16th Texas Cavalry; by 1864, the unit had lost their horses and fought dismounted as light infantry. John became a sergeant and David a hospital steward. From their letters home, the two appeared to have been the stereotypical "good ole boy" Rebels that the South was and is still famous for producing. They served in Scurry's brigade. At the opening of the battle, these greyhounds found themselves stationed on the right flank of Confederate lines.

When Walker's Division advanced, "the sun was shining from a cloudless sky," a Union soldier remembered.[18] The Texas boys stepped off just after hearing the yells and fighting coming from the left flank where General Alfred Mouton's two brigades of Polignac and Gray drew first blood. John reported, "on the 8 we drove them six miles," he wrote proudly to his mother. During the charge and breaking of the Union lines, "I was hit by a spent ball on the head that caused me to fall," he told her. "I thought the top of mi head was gon but it did not hurt me much," he wanted his mamma to know. He stood right back up and like a good boy carried on and went on to fight the next day as well, "on the 9 we fought again but we did not drive them like on the 8 but we whiped them."[19]

A Union officer who came to the Moss place was not as lucky as John and David Ray. Lysander Webb could be characterized as a frustrated man. His first name, the same as a tragic Greek hero from the ancient writings of Homer, proved to be quite fitting for his life. Born in the lovely Berkshire Hills of western Massachusetts, he was not destined to enjoy an idyllic life. He became orphaned at an early age, and his future might have taken a lesser turn had a wealthy businessman not adopted him and raised him as his own. He attended Yale, but in his third year his patron died, and Webb discovered that the family faced bankruptcy. He never finished his studies. His adoptive mother passed away soon thereafter, and for the second time in his life, he became alone.[20]

Webb took a job in the editorial offices of a Springfield, Massachusetts, newspaper. He found a life-long vocation. Similar to many of his generation, he left the confines of the east for greater opportunities. After a few false starts, he started a newspaper of his own in Peoria, Illinois. The *Transcript* raised the banner of the new Republican Party in a town known as a center of the state's Democratic establishment. The life of an editor in the politics of the 1850s could be tumultuous at best and fatal at worst. Added to the typical dangers from rival newspapers or an offended reader, Webb held abolitionist views. Only twenty years before, that creed had gotten newspaper editor Elijah Lovejoy killed by a lynch mob at Alton, Illinois.[21] Webb knew the dangers and navigated the pitfalls of his day well enough to build in the 1850s a new political party. The state's Republican Party gave the nation

Abraham Lincoln. Webb held a front row seat to Lincoln's rise.²²

Through his political connections, Webb married well, and as the 1850s ended, he passed the state bar exam to make himself a lawyer. Everything pointed to a great political career on the horizon. Once again, fate intervened and delayed any plans he had cultivated for political advancement. The Civil War began, and in the excitement of the first months, he joined the wave of enlistment. His father-in-law, who became the first colonel of the 77th Illinois Infantry, secured the second spot, Lt. Colonel, for his son-in-law.

Lieutenant Colonel Lysander Webb, an Illinois Republican newspaperman who met his end at Mansfield (United States Army Heritage and Education Center, Carlisle, Pennsylvania).

The unit served in the western Union army, and Webb made the most of his time in the regiment by sending letters home to his old newspaper. They of course printed the glowing accounts that highlighted his wartime exploits. One flattering story told of how he protected runaway slaves from their masters in Kentucky. Webb had risked his life when he pulled out two revolvers in the tense standoff. Battlefield glory would be the final ingredient required in his rise to prominence. Congress, the Governor of Illinois—who knew what could happen next? Once again, it was not to be. While he survived a hailstorm of bullets in the two assaults at Vicksburg, his days in the Red River campaign would be numbered.²³

A soldier of his who kept a private diary noted time and again that Webb swore frequently, drove the men hard, and made the soldiers under his command loath the grueling marches.²⁴ The day of the battle, Webb approached his Captain, because, as the soldier reported in the diary, he had a premonition that he would be killed that day. He wondered if he ought to ask if his regiment should be taken off the front lines. Nothing came of it. His unit, the 77th Illinois, found itself at an apex in the front line and at the dead center and focal point of the afternoon's Confederate charge. As the regiment was positioning itself to meet the coming threat, Webb left his command looking for Colonel Landrum.²⁵

A soldier waiting nearby witnessed what happened next:

Six. The Most Terrible Charge 103

About this time also, Lieutenant Colonel Webb of the 77th Illinois—well known to us all as a very cheerful man—came up. But now when he led his regiment into position he wore an unaccountable grave and serious countenance that attracted the attention of all who saw him. He went a few rods to the right, where in a few minutes he fell pierced by a bullet.[26]

Webb had opened his mouth and a musket ball crashed into his face. The ball tore the flesh just below his right eye. The bullet passed completely through the skull and tumbled out his left ear, killing him instantly. The regimental history of the 77th, which reported on the nature of his wound, called him "A generous, impulsive, respected soldier. He seemed to feel a portent of the fate that awaited him."[27]

At the center spearhead of the attack that hit Webb's unit rushed General Henry Gray's Louisiana brigade. The men followed Colonel Leopold Armant, who stood at the head of the 18th Louisiana Consolidated Regiment. Unlike Walker's rough and tumble Texans, Armant, a French Creole from St. James Parish, carried himself with an aristocratic bearing. He had enjoyed a fine education, was well-traveled, and never hesitated to direct his men at great personal risk to his own life. The proud Frenchman had donned a clean uniform for the battle. Early in the charge, as the shooting intensified and a bullet spattered dirt on the breast of his jacket, he became annoyed and claimed that although he might die in battle that day, his uniform would not be soiled beforehand. Similar to Webb, Armant possessed a premonition of his own death.[28]

Before Armant and his men stood a detachment of the 13th Corps under Colonel William J. Landram and commanded by General Thomas E.G. Ransom. Ransom, a young officer with a boyish face, could be tough as nails.[29] He placed his men at the ready in an inverted V formation on top of Honeycutt Hill. As prepared as they might have been, even Ransom did not realize at the moment of attack the numerical advantage the Confederates held on the field, nor did he comprehend the determination of Armant and others in the charge. One of Armant's men in the 18th Louisiana, Arthur Hyatt, noted in a diary that this was his second big assault of the war.[30] Nearly two years to the day earlier, he had been with Confederate forces among the hollows and thickets at Shiloh. "I little dreamt then that I should be in the army two years from that day," he wrote. "Will the war ever end?" His experience at Shiloh would be eclipsed by the carnage he witnessed at Mansfield. As bad as the fight had been at the Hornet's Nest at the 1862 Tennessee battle, what took place in Louisiana turned out to be much worse. Hyatt thought he had been "in one of the most terrible charges of the war."[31]

Exactly what happened to Hyatt and the other attackers can only be imagined. A Union artilleryman remarked that when the Confederates got into range, his battery kept firing canister until they started running short on ammunition. Those rounds turned the cannons into giant shotguns that threw blast after blast of lead that ripped gaping holes in the advancing ranks. The Union gunners "fought like devils laying them out in heaps especially where the regimental flags were." One could walk up the hill entirely on the backs of dead men many with "heads off and bowels out"[32] As the Confederates came in closer, the Union infantry sent a wall of bullets into the attackers.

"The fighting on the hill was now terrific," a Union soldier reported. Despite cutting down row after row of Confederates, "they came on in overpowering numbers."[33] Hyatt recorded that twenty-nine of the forty-two men in the front ranks of his 18th Louisiana unit went down as either wounded or killed. That made for a 72 percent casualty rate. Hyatt himself fell with a deep wound in the thigh.[34] Dozens of others fell in their places as flesh was torn off men in chunks and blood spattered for yards around the dead and dying littering the ground.

Colonel Armant's horse was shot from under him and he fell down

As the Union lines collapsed at Mansfield, Confederates fell upon Union supply wagons, creating chaos (Library of Congress).

abruptly only to rise up and continue on foot. When a color bearer fell in front of him, the colonel grasped the flag himself. That heroic step placed him right in the sights of Union riflemen and Armant's clean, new uniform became riddled with bullet holes. A hazy memory of one soldier placed the colonel down on the ground, his uniform covered in blood. He had raised his body enough to urge his men forward before he died.[35] Nearly all the regimental officers in the 18th Louisiana were killed or wounded. Up and down the whole Confederate lines, nearly the whole officer corps of Taylor's left wing would be lost by the time the men reached the Union lines. The Confederate soldiers remained undaunted by the punishment and continued to press forward until they enveloped the whole Union right wing. "We completely turned the enemy's right," a dismounted cavalryman with the 5th Texas remembered. "The desperate charges of that bloody day will never be forgotten...."[36]

A freedman who had been following one Union regiment as a cook refused to flee when the battle began. Soldiers down the line called out for him to go quickly. He might be killed as the fighting rumbled up the hill. He replied, "If you are willing to stay for me I ought not to be afraid to work for you." One soldier concluded, "The brave fellow had not forgotten about us and had the commanding General been as faithful to his duty as him, this story [of defeat] would never had been told." The former slave remained faithful to his comrades because he knew the battle had great implications for him. "The poor fellow had scented freedom," the soldier wrote, and victory in battle "he has along [sic] known that it meant freedom."[37]

General Thomas E.G. Ransom, the twenty-nine-year old Union general caught up in the fight, saw his lines collapse and took shrapnel in his left knee. As he was carried off the field, General William Franklin arrived and tried to stabilize the situation. He "was wounded, but remained in the saddle until every indication of a renewal of the fight that night had disappeared." Other officers became separated from their men, and formal lines disappeared across the entire front of the Union army. In the shock and confusion of the successful Confederate charge, a complete breakdown of eight army regiments had taken place.[38]

On the hill and down the Mansfield-Pleasant Hill road, Union soldiers fled from the scene. Rifles and pistols and swords were thrown away. Even the artillery pieces of the famed Chicago Mercantile battery that had fought valiantly at Vicksburg were abandoned where they had been parked. Confederates captured them easily. One of the artillerymen complained, "Our once powerful battery as well as our noble little 4th division was sacrificed that day through the ignorance of a political general."[39] The lead element of the army now evaporated and ceased to function. Over a thousand soldiers were missing in action. "We could not do otherwise than retreat across the field to prevent their capturing what few there were of us," one soldier remembered.[40]

General Franklin reached General Robert A. Cameron, who commanded the Third Division of the 13th Corps. Cameron's two brigades consisting of five Midwestern regiments had made their way around wagons and had come up behind the hill about the time of the total collapse. The two generals arranged a second line of defense down the road in hopes of stemming the Confederate tide. Even though General Taylor's brigades had taken horrible losses, the Rebels had not run out of steam. The gray tide encouraged by a total sweep at the top of the hill now surged down the other side. A key problem for the Union became the narrow road where the Union forces tried to rally. On either side grew tall thick pine forests that made movement difficult. All along the narrow road, the wagons had stopped and retreating men blocked the best pathways. "For a mile each side[e] of the road was thick with men and horses giving a hand as they could" one survivor of the 87th Illinois wrote his wife. "The rebels was dashing up into our retreating column cutting & slashing & taking prisoners & capturing artillery & wagons."[41]

Melville Bennett, one of the boys who had lived along Bayou Boeuf in Rapides Parish and worked in the family store before joining the Confederate side, described the scene: "dead Yankees strowed evry where, They was left on the battlefield in some places 7 and 8 deep."[42] A second Union line placed in front of the Sabine Crossroads did not hold either. "The rout of an army is the most awful thing in the world," one New Yorker wrote just after the war. "A painful and terrible spectacle! It is a disorganized mob of screaming, sobbing, hysterical, pale, terror-stricken men."[43] A Confederate doctor who traveled the twelve-mile route of the retreat observed, "The bodies of dead Yankees were numerous for the first 3 or 4 miles and all the way dead horses, broken wagons, ambulances, thousands of muskets and sabres, bayonets, and all manners of implements of war were scattered in every direction."[44]

On the Confederate side that day, victory had been purchased at a high price. General Alfred Mouton, Taylor's Cajun warhorse, who embodied his people's support for the war, fell dead on the battlefield. He had died during one of the last, most successful charges for the

Confederacy. He directed the attack in the midst of chaos when a bullet struck him and he tumbled off his horse. In the confusion, no one remembered the exact spot where he fell, and no one remembered any more specific circumstances of his death. Reports circulated that surrendering Union soldiers cut him down or that he died as the charge began, instead at its height.[45] Whatever the truth, his loss for the Confederates in Louisiana would be comparable to the death of Stonewall Jackson. He had fought in almost every Louisiana campaign since 1862, when the Union army arrived and inspired his men to many brave feats.

Acadian general General Alfred Mouton was cut down at Mansfield during his most successful charge of the war (United States Army Heritage and Education Center, Carlisle, Pennsylvania).

Union soldiers who survived the charge were battered physically and mentally. A Confederate soldier wrote his wife, "Now imagine an army of some 20,000 men all running in thick wooded country and skared our of thar wits." Private Chase Dickinson of the Chicago Mercantile Battery survived the battle unscathed and walked around in disbelief for days afterwards. He had watched as many of his friends and comrades fell dead and wounded all around him. Most galling to him and others was the loss of their artillery pieces. The Chicago Mercantile Battery had all its guns taken, abandoned to the Confederates when escape became impossible. The guns were not just government issue; they had been ordered and paid for by the businessmen in a rising American city and paraded through the streets of the town. They had barked victory at Vicksburg. Now they were lost. It fell upon Chase Dickson to break the news to the patrons and admirers back home. He took up pen and opened his sad letter with the words, "'Now is the winter of our discontent,' and the only vernal hint that breaks the gloom is the thought that we did our duty well, and no one exertion of ours could have changed the result."[46]

Seven

The Union Hold at Pleasant Grove

April 8, 1864

The Union collapse at Mansfield turned into "an utter rout, the road and woods were fairly filled with flying men, riderless horses, mules, ambulances, wagons, etc."[1] In thirty minutes or fewer, the battleground became a swirling mass of confusion. Down the hill went leaderless men, and the remains of a shattered Union division choked the road. In hasty flight, the soldiers threw down their arms and equipment. A Texas cavalryman in hot pursuit stated, "Enemy driven back 7 miles" with the "Road strewn with dead and wounded men & horses knapsacks, canteens, arms and wagon trains." He stopped to count the enemy's "200 wagons, 30 ambulances, & 28 pieces of artillery besides his killed and wounded & 300 prisoners." Thousands of pounds of supplies fell into Confederate hands, confirming General Banks' nickname, "The Commissary of the Confederacy," earned from similar episodes in the Shenandoah Valley in 1862. Confederates broke ranks and swarmed the ground, picking up provisions. Prisoners were being taken by the hundreds. The afternoon had become one of the worst Union defeats of the Civil War.

Union General Robert A. Cameron commanded the Third Division of the 13th Corps, the closest reinforcements. They remained stuck behind a long line of wagons that prevented them from moving ahead easily. His two underpowered brigades consisted of only five infantry regiments and two supporting artillery batteries.[2] He pressed these units to bypass the wagons by going through the tangled woods or along the road's edge. He found an open place to deploy a battle line only a mile from the epicenter of the Confederate attack. The Mansfield-Pleasant Hill road, that he was on, crossed a smaller route that ran from east to west. This spot, named Sabine Crossroads, would appear in Union reports as the name for the whole day's battle.

The Confederates possessed a strong momentum, and they rocketed down the elevation and hit the Union's second position with a thunderclap nearly equal to the afternoon's first stunning blow. A Union Cavalry sergeant wrote in his diary, "Our squad that was keeping together here stopped and tried to rally and form some kind of battle line."[3] That secondary line proved weak, and it gave way under the weight of Confederate General Walker's Texans, who enveloped and pushed aside blue lines of infantry and cavalry assembled before it. The Union cavalryman realized the futility, "after becoming convinced that it was an utter impossibility we gave it up and pushed on toward the rear."[4]

"The enemy had left on the ground, dying and dead, where the battle began about one half their forces," one of Walker's men remembered. "And through the woods and along the road, our cavalry and artillery completely slaughtered them." Over 200 wagons remained idle, more equipment was thrown aside, more prisoners, and more

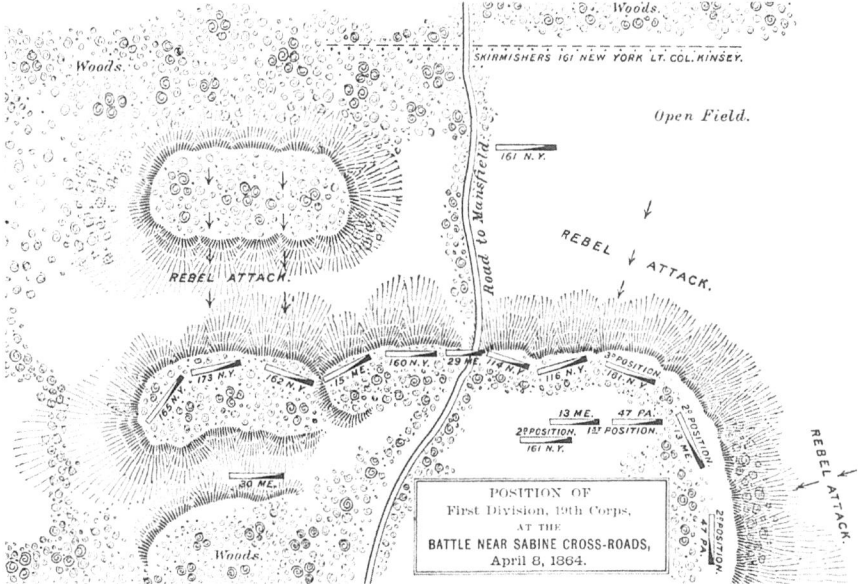

A map of the Pleasant Grove battle. General William Emory placed his regiments on the high ground and repulsed Confederate attacks (*War of the Rebellion Official Records* series 1, vol. 34, part 1: 390).

Union soldiers fled as unit organization melted away. The entire lead of Banks' army had been pulverized. "Horses and men, by hundreds, rolled down together; the road was red with their blood."[5] Without rescue, the whole Union army might become swallowed up by the Confederate juggernaut.

Help was on the way. A force of 5,000 fresh troops of the 19th Corps under General William Emory hurried to the scene. They had been marching up from Pleasant Hill eighteen miles away, and by late in the day when the initial attack began, this contingent had made it within supporting distance. "We started for the battle field and marched very fast about 7 miles," a soldier in the 29th Maine wrote to his future wife. "We found our army badly whipped."[6] Signs of the defeat unfolded as they approached the scene. Men came streaming by, wounded and telling terrible stories of what had happened. The desire to aid their comrades who were in trouble pushed them to extra exertion. "Running about half the time, making we judge four and a half or five miles an hour, that is extraordinary speed for foot soldiers to march at steadily," one regimental history related.[7] As the relief column sped northward and the prospects of meeting the victorious Rebels became more certain by the moment, the need for a good defensive position became paramount.

During his prewar career, General Emory had been a topographical engineer and possessed a sharp eye for terrain. Now age fifty-three, there was no finer officer for the job.[8] He proved to be the right man

General William Emory, a West Point graduate and career officer from Maryland, was a topographical engineer, an explorer of the West, and savior of the Union army at Pleasant Grove and Cane River Crossing (Library of Congress).

Seven. The Union Hold at Pleasant Grove

at the right time. On the march up the road, he located a bayou and small homestead owned by a farmer named Chapman. The home sat astride the Mansfield–Pleasant Hill road. Chapman's small abode sat where there was a slight bend in the road. The farm contained a picturesque orchard, wooden rail fencing around it, and most importantly, the property ran along a ridge that was perpendicular to the road itself. The farm was situated at a geographic high point and thus provided a ready-made defensive position. Emory saw its advantages immediately upon arrival. His position was visibly higher than the one north towards the approaching Confederates. The elevation at the spot where Emory stood climbed to approximately 317 feet above sea level, while down the hill the elevation bottomed out at 275 feet.[9] Emory and other Union officers who fought at the vista named the place Pleasant Grove, perhaps for the orchard or the overall look of the landscape. Matters that late afternoon would be anything but Pleasant.

The Confederates, savoring their great victory, continued flying forward into the late afternoon hours. Although the attack had lost a degree of its might following two major engagements, Taylor's officers had managed to keep order in the lead units. Dozens of men had paused to pillage abandoned wagons, treat wounded comrades, and take prisoners as unit cohesion was lacking across the army. The surviving officers had pressed on, and their men were still reaping great rewards. Every mile they went, more spoils and more success were to be found. Unless they were stopped, this attack would fall upon Union soldiers camped around Pleasant Hill.

Emory acted quickly, and as a first order, he sent out the 161st New York "to engage the attention of the rebels, while the balance of the division were formed in a line," the unit's regimental history reported.[10] Emory's three brigades, led by Dwight, Benedict, and McMillian, deployed in a line of battle north of Chapman's Bayou on either side of the narrow road. The stream, the only water source for miles around, needed to stay in Union hands. The main problem with this disposition was that retreating men of the 13th Corps kept streaming down the road and through the woods towards the colors of these new regiments. Blue uniforms darted in and out of sight in front of the men lined up for battle. It was going to be hard to get a clean shot at the attackers without endangering their own men to the hazards of friendly fire.

A Union lieutenant trying to organize his lines for the coming fight happened to spy Emory at the moment the commander arrived at the front. Immediately, Emory noticed that if his units fired, they might hit as many friendlies as enemy. He became very upset at the chaos he witnessed in front of him. The scene called for order, and it was not there, given the great rush to escape the Confederates. His temper flared, and he fell into an uncharacteristic fit of rage. "He was as savage as an infuriated bear and his conversation was quite sulphurous if not really profane!"[11]

His units had marched up dutifully, put themselves into a strong position, fixed bayonets, and now he watched as all this good work was being threatened by the minute. His hackles raised and his eyes focused like a laser on the Union cavalrymen and teamsters crashing horses into his lines, punching hole after hole into his carefully laid out position. After multiple riders ignored his pointed verbal commands to stop at once, Emory pulled out his service revolver and shot at a rider as he passed by, mumbling something that the report of the pistol obscured. The bullet missed, perhaps by design, yet the general had made his point.[12]

Another soldier running for his life reported how he had lost all his equipment, including his hat, and ran by the fresh brigades pointing and screaming, "Don't go there! It's awful! You can't live a minute!"[13] The scene changed when everyone perked up at the sound of enemy gunfire. Confederates had arrived, offering their calling card of bullets "unpleasantly numerous and spiteful," one witness recalled.[14] For the third time that day, a Union line stood fast as the Confederates came upon them. Emory and his men would have to do better than the first two occasions.

The lieutenant colonel of the 161st New York, on orders from Emory, "deployed the regiment widely as skirmishers across the whole front of the division, in the very teeth of the Confederate line of battle," one history reported. The scene became unnerving because the Confederates charged "rapidly advancing with wild yells and firing heavily as they came."[15] One account stated, "The 161st New York Volunteers, Lieut. Colonel Kinsey commanding, were deployed as skirmishers, and ordered to the foot of the hill, upon the crest of that the line was formed to cover the rear of the retreating forces, to check the pursuit of the enemy and give time for the formation of the troops."[16]

One of the brave men sent out with the 161st skirmishers that evening happened to be a twenty-one-year-old Corporal of Company D named Mahlon W. Barber. He had enlisted two years before at the village of Bath, located in western New York. Barber fought at Port

Seven. The Union Hold at Pleasant Grove

Hudson in 1863 and was serving in his second major campaign of the war. Over among the Confederate ranks, Charles S. Durning, a 2nd Lieutenant in the 16th Texas Cavalry, dismounted and made his way towards the Union skirmish line with the rest of General William R. Scurry's brigade of Walker's Division. These two soldiers, Barber and Durning, could not have known each other before this day. In a short space of time, they would be intertwined in one of the most remarkable diaries of the Civil War.[17]

Barber began keeping a pocket diary in January of 1864—perhaps a new year's resolution. His new commitment was not a burden, as the diary gave space for only a few lines each day. He filled them faithfully. Through January, February, and March he recorded random thoughts. "Fine day" he wrote often on the lines. He mentioned drill, and he gave the name of relatives he wrote or got letters from. Once he told of how he played a ball game similar to baseball, and on several occasions, he reported pulling long hours on guard duty. Nothing he wrote in his diary was all that remarkable. "We have orders to march in the morning," read the March 14 entry. The next day, his unit lumbered out of camp at Franklin, Louisiana, marching for the Red River Valley.

In early April, he reached Natchitoches behind the main columns of troops, and his unit did not leave there until April 6. That day he made a fifteen-mile trek before going into camp. On the next day, his unit pressed on and arrived at Pleasant Hill. Barber's entry for the 7th would be his last: "This morning we march again in the woods." He mentioned seeing Pleasant Hill by the middle of the day and finally: "We marched 22 mile in the pine woods. tonight it raines." The entry for the 8th was blank. The casualty reports showed that among the "rattle and wail of the musketry" Barber fell at Pleasant Grove.[18]

A regimental historian thought the "flesh and blood" of the 161st New York were not enough "to stay the onward rush of the victorious rebels." At the skirmish line, "the One Hundred and Sixty-first lost nearly one hundred men in less than ten minutes, a noble offering from one of the best regiments in the service."[19] At this desperate hour, General Banks himself appeared behind the front line and encouraged Emory's men telling them, "All depends on you!"[20] As the Confederates approached the fresh brigades in front of them, one of the great gun fights of the Trans-Mississippi West played itself out just as the sun set and a blue darkness fell on an otherwise beautiful spring evening. "The Rebels charged upon us and we drove them back again," a soldier in the 29th Maine recalled. He remembered three separate assaults, each repulsed in turn. The "bullets flew like hail stones." While behind the farm's fence, one missile "struck one of the rails in front of us," and sharp slivers flew back into his left hand, but thankfully for him no other bodily damage.[21]

Confederate Frederic Seip, who participated in the charge that evening, recalled how he led two hundred men who "pushed across the creek and on, until we reached the fence of the noted peach orchard, here so many were killed."[22] His unit ran up against a strong position and could not make the Yankee line budge. He ordered his men to lay down and wait for the 18th Texas who moved into position and renewed the attack with two fierce attacks of their own. The 19th Corps poured a deadly fire into them and stopped the Confederate effort cold. A Union soldier wrote, "There came forth a course of reverberating thunder, that rolled from flank to flank in one continuous peal, sending a storm of leaden hail into the rebels' ranks that swept them back in dismay and left the ground covered with their killed and wounded."[23] The Union soldiers had delivered "an immovable wall of fire," General Banks reported. One of Emory's more poetic soldiers recalled, "The musketry sounded very loud in the evening air, and every noise was made more frightful by its echo through the woods."[24]

Oncoming Confederate lines halted, and all momentum evaporated. "Disorganized by the pursuit, through thick woods and by darkness, the Confederate troops were unable to drive the enemy from their strong position," Seip recalled.[25] The Confederates had been stopped by the tenacity of Union arms and a great deployment Emory had constructed on the high ground. As the shooting died down, the wounded of both sides stumbled through the tangle of trees and undergrowth seeking Chapman's Bayou. "The cries of the wounded was dreadful to hear," the Maine soldier wrote. Formless, shapeless voices rent the air with moans and cries for "water, water, water."[26] Those trapped between the lines, unable to move, found no relief. Men who stumbled down the hill and found the twisting and turning bayou that flowed between the lines laid down on its banks, grasping for its refreshing drink. Some of these wounded souls drew a last breath, and many died there as stars came into the evening sky. That unremarkable bayou, unknown to any of them before that evening, now flowed dark red.

Somewhere down the ridge, Corporal Barber lay dead. The diary he kept faithfully did not contain an entry for that day. Yet the entries pick up again on the 9th of April, in different handwriting. The new diarist was Charles Durning of Grayson County, Texas, who somehow

Seven. The Union Hold at Pleasant Grove

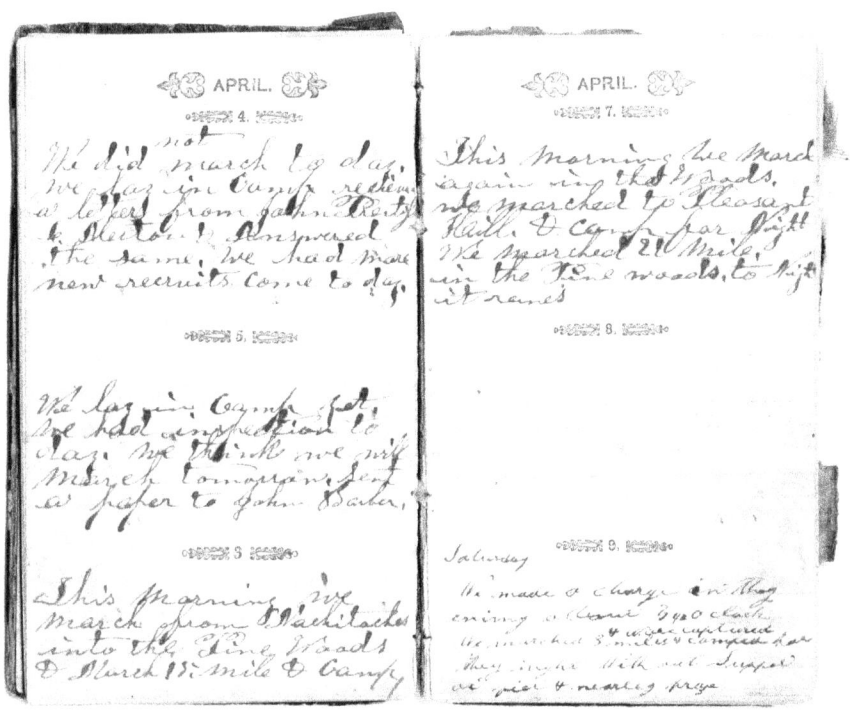

The Barber-Durning Diary. The April 8 entry is blank because Mahlon Barber, a Union soldier, died that evening at Pleasant Grove. The writing picks back up the next day in the handwriting of Confederate soldier C. S. Durning (Dolph Briscoe Center for American History, University of Texas at Austin).

came upon the diary and kept it. His first lines mentioned nothing about Pleasant Grove and provide only a little information about his role at the developing battle the next day at Pleasant Hill. "We made a charge on the enemy about 3 o'clock," he wrote. The Barber-Durning diary is notable for having the experiences of both a Union soldier and Confederate soldier together in the same pages. The tragedy and triumph of that evening at Pleasant Grove is better understood when one examines this unique artifact.[27]

Eight

The Tumult of Pleasant Hill
April 9, 1864

The North Louisiana historian, J. Fair Hardin, had a life-long fascination with the Civil War. Growing up in Desoto Parish and visiting the battle sites near his home, he made a connection between his life and the past. His outings to Pleasant Hill, about fifty years after the fight, enabled him to gather a keen understanding of the terrain: "The village of Pleasant Hill, old site, occupied part of a plateau a mile wide from east to west, along the Mansfield–Fort Jessup Road. Highest ground was College Hill on the west," he explained. His walks across the ground enabled him to locate the Union position: "The Federal lines extended across the open plateau from College Hill (Pierce & Paine) Academy on their left to a wooded height on right east of the road to Mansfield. Winding along in front of this plateau ran a dry gully, bordered by thick growth of young pines, and tangles of fallen timber."[1] He understood how vital the terrain became for soldiers of both sides caught up in the tumult of Pleasant Hill.

Although successful in stopping the Confederates at Pleasant Grove, General Banks ordered his men to fall back on the village at Pleasant Hill. His closest advisors, generals William Franklin and William Dwight, recommended the move to find stronger defensive ground, reinforcements and a good water supply. At 10 p.m., General Emory withdrew his battered division from the ridge and turned them back on the narrow road for a thirteen-mile journey. The chance that a Union army would reach Shreveport or Texas began to fade fast.[2]

A new moon rose that night and it disappeared quickly from view.

Eight. The Tumult of Pleasant Hill

It would be absent for the rest of the night. The sky contained only a few stars and down among the towering pines, the night became an inky dark of impenetrable blackness.[3] The dark night made it difficult for both sides to see where they were going. The cool spring air added to the uncomfortable conditions. "It was a terribly cold night, and with nothing to keep us warm, we shivered," one soldier recorded in his diary.[4] When Union soldiers reached Pleasant Hill through the night and early the next morning, the men found A.J. Smith's divisions halted and in camp. Smith's 16th and 17th Corps had marched from their transports at Grand Ecore. They learned about the Mansfield disaster from harried survivors who streamed in by the hour. Another round of fighting was certain to come when daylight returned to the pines.

"The day was a beautiful one," a regimental historian wrote of April 9. Exactly one year before Lee would surrender in Virginia, two armies in the Trans-Mississippi made preparations for a second day of battle. "It hardly seemed possible that so much beauty in nature was so soon to see the fierce passions of men engaged in bitter strife."[5] The location, although picturesque, presented a number of difficult challenges. A Union officer described the site as "hilly with every species of natural obstacle." His Maine regiment had fought in the eastern theater and was more accustomed to being able to form even ranks on flat ground with clear lines of sight. "We could see nothing of the fight. But we heard the shouts and yells of the victors, and the fresh volleys they poured in," he remembered.[6] Soldiers found themselves bunched together among thick pines, deep ravines, and tangled brush. One hardly ever knew where friend or foe might be and danger could be only a few feet away. Conditions in this part of Louisiana were nothing like Virginia.

General Taylor had spent the night and morning pushing his men down the road in pursuit of the Union forces. He was also waiting for reinforcements sent by General Kirby Smith. A division of Missouri and Arkansas regiments under General Thomas J. Churchill had come down from Arkansas. Taylor spent the morning getting each brigade into place and issuing orders for another strike. His plan, unchanged from the previous day, was to turn both Union flanks.[7] This time he did not have the element of surprise and Union forces had all day to prepare; not until around 5 p.m. did the Rebels emerge into the semi-cleared fields for another round of death and destruction.

Because of the woods and hills, the armies were forced to align themselves in a broken arc of a semi-circle facing each other. Both sides

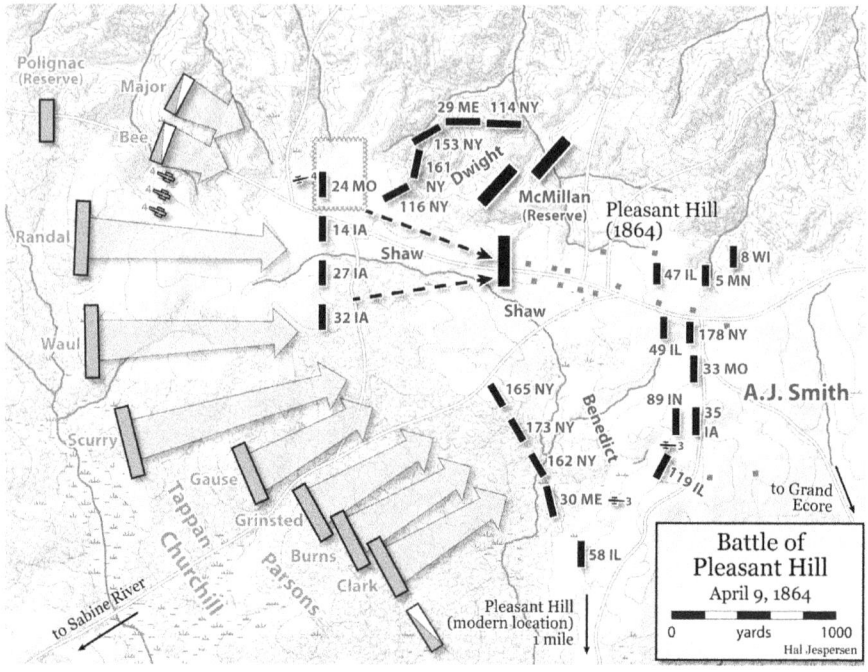

were unable to link their forces together across one continuous battlefield and The Battle of Pleasant Hill degenerated into engagements where brigades and regiments faced each other in close range firefights. From the outset, generals Taylor and Banks had limited ability to direct matters as limited visibility severely hampered command and control. Regimental and brigade commanders on the ground played the most important roles, and many of these officers threw themselves into the thick of things and were either killed or wounded in the resounding cataclysm.

General John Walker and his greyhounds opened the battle with an attack on the Union right and center. "The fight was terrific. Old soldiers say it was never surpassed for desperation," the *Boston Herald* informed its readers.[8] Union artillery that had been silenced the previous day now took up positions in open areas for a strong defense. The gunners opened up with grape and canister. "Notwithstanding the terrible havoc in their ranks, the rebels pressed fiercely on, slowly pushing the men back up the hill, but not breaking their line of battle," one account reported.[9]

The Ray brothers, the Texas boys who had fought at Mansfield, withstood terrible punishment by Union arms. "It was a hard fight," John Ray wrote. "A great many goo[d] soldiers [were] killed," he wrote in a letter to his mother. His preservation was nothing short of a miracle,

Eight. The Tumult of Pleasant Hill

he thought: "I had a blanket around my shoulders shot in nine places and [my] gun shot off by a cannon ball." He gave as hard as he got: "I shot 58 times the last fight. Then I had to surrender." He explained how Union forces rushed into the broken Confederate lines, and he gave up when overwhelmed by the soldiers in blue. John lost sight of "little Dave," his brother, and was taken away without knowing his fate.[10]

Somehow little Dave managed to escape capture or was released immediately because by May he was back in Alexandria with his unit and was writing home. Exactly what happened to him is not clear, other than he survived the near-death experience of battle. He mentioned his participation in a simple matter-of-fact re-telling to his mother,[11] The story of the battle appeared later in his missive, after he inquired about family and crops. No matter what his own circumstances happened to be, family and home ranked higher, and they were far more meaningful to him than the terror-filled moments he spent at Pleasant Hill. Dave and John Ray lived through it. Others were not as fortunate.

General Walker's chief opposition during the battle was a stubborn Midwestern brigade from the 16th Corps, only 1,500 strong, commanded by Colonel William T. Shaw. These men held a position at the center of the Union line. The thick woods and a slight rise to the left of the Mansfield-Pleasant Hill Road afforded the three Iowa and one Missouri regiments a degree of protection.[12] Their position proved a real obstacle to Confederate units. During the opening of the battle, the brigade repulsed a fierce cavalry attack by General Hamilton Bee's courageous troopers. Walker's men then advanced for their own turn in the action. Initial probes and thrusts failed to make any progress. Colonel Shaw thought the attack might have been "more fatal if they had not been protected by the nature of the ground."[13] The first big test of the day's grand assault had come. The Confederates had to take this position and keep going. General John Walker recognized that the Union brigade created an island that provided a natural anchor upon that the whole Union line might pivot and hold fast. He had to act quickly to find a solution that might cause a breakthrough.[14]

Walker located the colonel of his Second Brigade, Horace Randal, and conferred with him. I "asked if he had a regiment that could take the position," Walker reported. Another Texan, Colonel Edward Clark, sat on his horse nearby and perked up as Colonel Randal surveyed the units who might make an attack. His 14th Texas Infantry would take the position and attempt to keep the advance rolling. The battle's outcome hung in the balance, and he was going to tip the scales deep in the woods of Louisiana.[15]

The forty-nine-year old Clark had been born in New Orleans and grew up outside Mobile, Alabama.[16] He was technically a native Louisianan. As a young lawyer, he made his way to East Texas in 1841 and made the growing town of Marshall his home. The skills he brought to the bar carried him into various offices for the Texas Republic. He became a staff officer for General J. Pinckney Henderson during the Mexican War and was cited for bravery at the Battle of Monterrey. His legal career continued in the 1850s, and in 1859 he became Lieutenant Governor of the Lone Star State. His political fortunes faltered in 1860–61 because he had cast his lot early on with the Whig party and the moderates, who fell out of favor during the state's secession crisis.[17]

At the time Texas left the Union, the sitting governor was none other than Sam Houston. The hero of Texas Independence, now old and tired, was no fan of secession. Houston did not want Texas to leave the Union and his vocal resistance got him removed from office. Clark had demurred when first confronted with Louis Wigfall and the fire eaters' demands to leave the Union. But when he saw the direction of political winds in 1861, he bent and embraced secession as a foregone conclusion. With the venerable Houston deposed by a state convention, Clark succeeded him as governor as the state plunged into war. The new governor organized the first state regiments sent off to fight for the Confederacy. Many of these regiments became legendary in both Virginia and Tennessee. The regular election for governor came around in the fall of 1861, and Clark's opponent, Francis Lubbock, beat him by 124 votes.[18]

Clark moved on from political defeat to accept a position as commander of the newly formed 14th Texas.[19] Now he, too, went off to war—from the Governor's Mansion to the colonel's saddle. He spent the next three years as one of Walker's greyhounds. When Randel posed Walker's question to him, a pivotal moment had arrived at Pleasant Hill. Without hesitation, Clark replied curtly, "I have seven hundred men in lines and can take the place if any one can." Walker wheeled his horse around and gave Clark specific instructions. At the end of the brief conference, Clark declared "I move forward at once, sir."[20]

In dramatic fashion, the former governor dismounted and let his horse go. Walking to the center of his regiment, he commanded, "Right shoulder, shift arms, forward, double quick, march." Just a few feet in advance of his men, he moved steadily forward, his sword drawn. As

Eight. The Tumult of Pleasant Hill

the Texans came within thirty yards, the Federals opened fire and Clark fell wounded from a ball that struck just under his knee. The injury sparked anger among the Texans, who raised the rebel yell and rushed into the Iowa regiments. The old muskets of the 14th fired buck and ball at close range, delivering a devastating blow. The Texans shattered the Union position. Colonel Shaw withdrew all but one regiment, which remained trapped as the Confederate tide swirled around it. Shaw reported losing 500 men during the course of the battle.[21] Clark was carried to the rear and recovered enough to serve on crutches for the rest of the war. He won promotion to general and wore his red badge of courage into the 1870s.[22]

Governor Edward Clark was wounded leading a successful charge at Pleasant Hill (State Preservation Board, Austin, Texas).

On the Confederate right, Thomas Churchill's legions pushed through the tangled pines and burst into sight of Union lines. The ambitious flank moment struck Union lines like a thunderclap. One Union soldier remembered, "It was our time to turn pale."[23] Four brigades carrying the flags of Missouri and Arkansas, over 4,000 strong, flew like a spear point aimed at the Union left flank. The Confederates carried new Enfield rifles, among the best arms available, and each rank fired as they stumbled forward through the overgrown clearings. A contingent of the 30th Maine regiment and a brigade of New Yorkers stood on a small rise with only a wooded gully lying between them and the Confederates. Skirmishers from several units encountered them first, including a company from the African-American 84th USCT regiment. These men had been placed far to the left of the main postings because they were not expected to see action. Suddenly they found themselves right in the teeth of the developing battle.[24]

General Taylor had waited anxiously to see how his grand flank attack would fare. From the beginning, this tactic was a gamble of enormous risk. Churchill's columns had not participated at Mansfield, yet they were hardly fresh troops; they had marched forty-five miles in thirty-six hours just to arrive at the scene of action.[25] The forced march had taken a heavy toll. For several key hours that morning, they had to stand down and rest. Would they be rested enough to play a decisive role in the battle? Only time would tell, and Taylor had lost much of it getting everything ready.

A year earlier, Taylor's mentor, General Stonewall Jackson had marched his corps twelve miles and crumbled the Union's 11th corps near the crossroads tavern of Chancellorsville, Virginia. At that battle, the flank march had worked beautifully. Confederates at Pleasant Hill would be covering only two miles to reach the Yankee flank, with far fewer men, but they ventured into an area they knew practically nothing about. Landmarks to guide by were even fewer and farther between. Limited intelligence had been gathered about the exact location of the Union flank. The gullies, ditches, and undergrowth made the area difficult to scout.[26] Taylor anticipated difficulty with this maneuver and sent a former sheriff of the parish as a guide.[27]

This man, T.J. Williams, did not understand Taylor's plan well enough. He led Churchill and his men down the first forest pathway to the east they met. This wrong turn placed the divisions only on the flank of the most advanced Union troops. It did not put the attack in the rear of all Union forces, as Taylor had envisioned. Churchill's men should have turned on the Fort Jessup Road farther south. The mistake proved costly. Pleasant Hill would not be the Chancellorsville of the Trans-Mississippi.

As it was, the weight of Taylor's hammer came down hard on the left flank of a brigade of the 19th Corps led by Colonel Lewis Benedict.[28] This New Yorker had arrayed his men a half mile outside of the village of Pleasant Hill. His right sat on the Logansport road and extended along a slight rise in a vacant, fallow field. A slope and ditch provided a slight defense to the left, and woods extended beyond it.[29] The unexpected appearance of Confederates from that direction brought him into one of the fiercest struggles of the whole campaign. His men had not fought at Mansfield, yet they were at Pleasant Grove that evening. Their determination carried over to this day's fight, and it meant a fierce close-quarters contest.

Colonel Benedict sat mounted on his horse near the color bearer

Eight. The Tumult of Pleasant Hill

when the Confederates started pouring in a thick, deadly fire. The columns advanced quickly and kept up the shooting as they closed on Union lines. Soldiers described the Confederates letting out a rebel yell, charging their bayonets, and crashing into the first Union line at the gully. Benedict was no stranger to close quarter combat. He had a horse shot from under him at the Battle of Williamsburg on May 5, 1862. As bullets whistled by him, he urged his men forward. As the Confederates counterattacked and overwhelmed Benedict and the men around him, he surrendered in front of the enemy earthworks. As a prisoner of war he was held at the infamous Libby Prison in Richmond, and then the stockade in Salisbury, North Carolina.[30] While prisons were typically destructive to the health of inmates, Benedict kept up his constitution and spirits.

Colonel Lewis Benedict, Albany attorney and courageous brigade commander, was killed at Pleasant Hill (Library of Congress).

Benedict had been born and raised in Albany, New York. He received a fabulous early education, graduating from prestigious Williams College in 1837.[31] He studied law and began a successful legal career in the two decades before the outbreak of the war. He supported the Whig party, and although he did not run for high office, he was a power behind the scenes. "There was no high council of the party held during a generation in that the voice of Lewis Benedict was not heard and his power felt," his son boasted.[32] An ardent Unionist, he once responded to the charge that the Civil War was fratricide by saying, "I do promote the cause of liberty by slaying even my brother, if, with traitorous and patricidal hand, he dares to tear down the flag of our common country." He celebrated Independence Day even in prison, and his perseverance kept all of his fellow inmates from succumbing to despair and depression from the grim confinement. He had been anti-slavery before the war and praised the 1863 Emancipation Proclamation. "The slaves, he says, are all our friends," his son related. "He would use the freedmen in all the ways they could serve."[33]

In early 1863, following release from prison and exchange, he accepted a promotion to Colonel of the newly recruited 162nd New York. This fresh unit embarked at Fortress Monroe and joined General Nathaniel Banks and the 19th Corps in the Department of the Gulf. Benedict caught up to Banks at Alexandria in May 1863 just before the army turned towards Port Hudson. An excited horse reared up as he came down off a boat, and it nearly killed him. He recovered from the injury in a short time and led attacks against the fortifications at Port Hudson. He remained steady and calm as shot and shell tore through men around him. There was not a more solid and committed Union officer than Colonel Benedict.[34]

As Churchill's men crashed into his line, the chaos of hand-to-hand combat swirled around Benedict. His unit fell back from the onslaught of the gray and butternut masses. A Maine officer remembered, "He was in full view of the whole attacking line of the enemy. The Brigade fell back over that slope and I did not see him afterwards."[35] No account mentions the hail of lead that brought the Colonel down. One minute he was on his horse, the next minute he laid comatose on the ground, riddled by multiple gunshot wounds. The able New Yorker had been pierced by at least five shots that stained his uniform with gaping wounds in the arm, foot, legs, and head. The brigade colors rested on the ground beside him. At his funeral back in Albany, where dignitaries packed the 2nd Presbyterian Church, including the Governor of New York, the pastor concluded his eulogy: "Before this coffin, then, my hearers, in the very valley of this our sorrow, let us devote ourselves, with no outward ritual, but in the deep recesses of our hearts, to this our cause as it was his, the cause of 'Freedom and the Union,' with the solemn resolve of a perfect consecration."[36]

Benedict's brigade collapsed and retreated back towards the village of Pleasant Hill.[37] The Confederates followed and ran right into the teeth of Union regiments waiting for their turn to fight. Unknown to Churchill or Taylor, General A.J. Smith's forces had massed just off Churchill's right flank. These men had been in camp around Pleasant Hill, and General Taylor believed they were back at Grand Ecore guarding the gunboats.[38] This intelligence failure would be a huge mistake.

Unlike the 19th Corps, these men were rough and tough Midwestern soldiers. Colonel Lucius Hubbard, who commanded a brigade of them, remarked how the eastern troops were, "handsomely equipt with new uniforms, arms, and the officers wore all they could." In appearance they were "the proudest army in bearing and appearance that had graced the valley of the Mississippi during the war." His unrefined farm boys, wearing the same uniforms they had donned for the Vicksburg campaign, were "shabby" by comparison. General Smith's poorly dressed yet seasoned veterans advanced as a blue bulwark against the oncoming fury.[39]

The *Boston Herald* remarked how the Confederates ran right into what became a death trap, "all heedless of the long lines of cannon and crouching forms of as brave men as ever trod mother earth." Witnesses were amazed when Smith's men opened up on the attackers. "Words cannot describe the awful effects of this discharge of 7,000 rifles and several batteries of artillery," the newspaper reporter wrote. The guns, "loaded to the muzzle with grape and canister, were fired simultaneously, and the whole centre of the rebel line was crushed down, as a field of ripe wheat through that a tornado had passed."[40] Several hundred men may have fallen from among Churchill's men. The Confederate charge halted in its tracks.

"They gave the rebels one volley and then went for them with the bayonet," Colonel Hubbard, a future governor of Minnesota, recalled.[41] It looked as if a million men had struck the Confederate lines. Smith's regiments fought with a resoluteness that the Union army had lacked at Mansfield. "This unexpected movement threw the victors into utter confusion," one Union source reported.[42] The depleted Confederate lines were stunned and then hit with hand-to-hand combat. A dramatic scene played out as the two sides clashed back and forth over the same ground. General A. J. Smith, known also as "Whisky" Smith for his drinking habits, sat astride a black charger, gesturing and yelling commands in a vain attempt to control the action. Colonel Hubbard remembered that the melee appeared to him as the "hardest fighting and bloodiest work" of the entire war.[43] Smith's men were determined to win or die trying in the wilds of Pleasant Hill.

The Confederates were not ready for this fierce counterattack, and in shock they reeled backwards. Dr. William McPheeters, a surgeon working on wounded behind Churchill's lines, had been in high spirits at the start of the attack. "I was startled by the announcement that our lines were broken and our army falling back at all points," he wrote. He learned the army was "outnumbered and outflanked." Troops began streaming rearward past the field station where he worked on wounded and prisoners. "The Missourians broke first and soon the whole line gave way. I shall not attempt to describe the scene. A complete panic and stampede defies description." At nightfall he packed up his bloody instruments and left his station. After the last of the wounded were put away in ambulances, he mounted and dashed off with Minié balls whistling all around him.[44]

"A large portion broke and fled," the *Boston Herald* explained, "fully 2,000 throwing aside their arms."[45] A Vermont unit's regimental history described how "the Missourians left the ground covered with their killed and wounded."[46] A Confederate battery that had been too close to the action became a casualty of the day, including some re-captured ordnance: "[T]wo guns of Nims' battery, the Parrott guns, taken from us last fall at Carrion Crow, and one or two others, belonging to the rebels, besides 700 prisoners."[47] When the safety of the army, and perhaps the whole campaign, hanging in the balance, Smith's veterans had saved the day, at least on their part of the battlefield.

One of the most unusual participants in the battle, private Lyons Wakeman, survived the fighting and slept the field that night. "I feel thankful to God that he spared my life and I pray to him that he will lead me safe through the field of battle and that I may return safe home," she wrote. Her real name was Sarah Rosetta Wakeman. She had dressed as a man before the war to obtain work. When the 153rd New York began recruiting in 1862, she fell in like the rest of them. Wakeman survived the campaign, but became ill and died in New Orleans a month after its conclusion. Her secret identity remained hidden until the late 20th century.[48]

Both armies had taken a terrible beating. Official counts listed 1,200 Confederates killed and wounded and 426 taken prisoner. The Union losses that day stood at 289 killed, 773 wounded, and 1,062 missing in action.[49] Left where they fell, the wounded wailed. "You can't imagine the sound of the moaning of the wounded men who had to lie on the field all night," a young German immigrant in blue reported.[50] The "air was filled with groans, and shrieks, and delirious yells. Maddening curses and blasphemies, were all enough to test the power of human endurance to the utmost. Such touching appeals for pity; such earnest prayers; such tender references for home and friends, from dying lips."[51] At daylight the wounded were taken to nearby houses, outbuildings, and other places for shelter. "Both friend and foe were put there, all the men who were seriously wounded were together."[52]

Eight. The Tumult of Pleasant Hill

"That same night our army withdrew, because we didn't have anything more to eat, and we had to march back to our supply ships," the young German wrote.[53] When the order came to retreat, leaving the apparent gains made that day and many wounded behind, General A.J. Smith was enraged. Had he not won the battle and saved the army and the campaign from embarrassing defeat? Evidence of the sacrifices made that day littered the ground. When Smith discovered that Franklin and Banks had decided without consulting him to withdraw, marking the Mansfield encounter as an enduring defeat, Colonel Lucius Hubbard witnessed an apoplectic Smith spitting sulfurous wrath from his mouth. Each four-letter word he gnashed out "illuminated ... that frosty April morning."[54]

As the sun rose on April 10, dead bodies and horse carcasses littered the ground for twenty-one miles, beginning at Mansfield and ending at the village of Pleasant Hill. A Union soldier who survived both Mansfield and Pleasant Hill wrote his family and remarked, "You can't even imagine how horrible it was. The battlefield was strewn with dead and wounded."[55] Confederate Félix Poché, who walked the Pleasant Hill battleground, called it a "dismal and sorry spectacle." Dead bodies "mutilated, some without heads, the faces of other[s] completely mangled, others again had their legs crushed and turned inside out, leaving entrails exposed to view and one could see flies crawling all over them." He found a Yankee soldier who had been hit in the face; the bullet had crushed his jaw and drove teeth into his skull. As the pathetic man

General Andrew Jackson Smith, the hard-fighting soldier whose counterattack saved the Union army at Pleasant Hill (Library of Congress).

lay writhing in agony unable to speak, Poché noticed how his head had swelled up to the size of a pumpkin. "He was a truly terrible sight."[56]

"Loss on both sides very heavy," Dr. William McPheeters wrote. He had barely escaped being wounded himself and now spent days "amputating limbs, adjusting fractures, elevating depressed skulls, and etc., etc." As the Union forces retreated back down the road to Grand Ecore, the Confederates became burdened with the responsibility for the "killed and wounded." They [were left] "in our hands," the doctor remarked in frustration. "How long Oh God! Wilt thou permit such destruction of life?"[57]

One wounded Iowa soldier remembered the loneliness of being left at Pleasant Hill. His knee and hip had been "crushed by the bullets that fell among us like hail upon the house top." His comrades lay dead nearby, and nearly half his regiment was gone. Then, "I was stripped of my outer clothing." A scavenger walking around searching for anything of value turned out his pants pockets. As he pulled the Iowan's

Smith's men stop the Confederate attack at Pleasant Hill (*Heritage of Valor*, Louisiana State Archives).

Eight. The Tumult of Pleasant Hill 129

hand out and found it covered in blood, the Southerner recoiled and dropped the $85.00 that came with it. Another comrade among the walking wounded looked for help because "a Minnie ball had entered his mouth, cut off his tongue, and passed through his neck. The poor boy could not speak or eat, and at the end of about nine days died of starvation." Another wounded man asked the soldier to take a rusty knife and cut out a ball lodged under a shoulder blade. The soldier did not have the strength to do it and refused the horrid task.[58]

Residents who lived in Sabine Parish arrived by the dozens to help at the two battlefields. Two young boys who had wandered over to the Pleasant Hill battlefield found the soldiers of both sides "mixed up like salt and pepper, horses spinning like windmills, some without eyes, some looking like shells had gone clear through them. Men were crying for water."[59] The wounded would be carried to dwellings near the battlefields and into the buildings in Pleasant Hill and the town of Mansfield. A parish history published in 1912 explained that "the dead were buried in pits and several days were spent in clearing the field of the carnage. The bullet scarred trees there still bear evidence of that stubborn conflict."[60]

In a surviving document from the surgeon of a Texas regiment, the grim results of the fighting can be seen on a long list of the killed and wounded.[61] The detailed surgeon's report on the 14th Texas regiment, commanded by the former governor of Texas Edward Clark, stands as a ghastly catalog of what happened to men at Mansfield and Pleasant Hill. Forty-three men are listed on the casualty list. They came from different companies in the regiment, all ranks were represented among those hit, and in the line on the form for the wounded soldier's occupation most reported being farmers. Age range is widest. The youngest was nineteen and the oldest wounded soldier had reached fifty-three years of age. A fraction of the men, twelve to be exact, were wounded on the 8th, the day of the great charge at Mansfield. The 14th regiment served on the Confederate right at the opening of the battle, and as it turned out it was a considerable distance away from the center of action at Honeycutt Hill. The regiment shifted to the center of the fight the next day. At Pleasant Hill thirty-one men fell wounded. Overall, Walker's division of which the 14th made up an important part suffered 36.2 percent casualties out of the 4,000 men in the ranks.[62] Most of the men of the 14th on the casualty list suffered gunshot wounds to "thigh, neck, hand, chest or leg." For others their wounds speak of horrible moments when lead ripped into soft flesh: "Wounded in Bowells,

Contusion in Groin," or "beneath the Clavicle, fracture of the tibia," or "in the face maxillary bone." Just glancing down this regiment's report gives one an intimate and horrifying view of Civil War combat.

A Union chaplain who visited a field hospital gave his own ghoulish descriptions of what he saw: "One man shot through the bowels, who had evidently not many hours to live ... another lay on the bare floor quietly, and almost motionless, while his brains, were running out of a large hole in his skull, and yet he was uttering mangled sighs and groans." Other wounded included patients who did not conform to the Victorian sense of quiet, noble dying. "Still another powerful man," he recorded, "with a large hole in his head, and covered with blood, kept tossing and plunging about in an unconscious state, striking his head against a bare bedstead." It would take a strong nurse to hold him down and keep the patient from harming himself. The experience made the man of God ponder the condition of man and reflect on "the awful criminality of those who make war without good notice."[63]

In one of the worst episodes to befall the wounded, a hospital at the Baptist Church at Mansfield caught fire:

> At dark on the eve of the tenth, one of the nurses lighted a candle and holding it in one hand attended the patient with the other, but the delirious patient struck down the candle and the light, catching the loose cotton used as bedding, set it on fire, and in a moment the flames filled the building. To save the wounded from death by burning, the men who were in Mansfield rushed in and carrying the patients through the fire or casting them out of the windows saved about 200 soldiers from a horrible death. As the rescuers were about to abandon the work, a young Creole Confederate soldier suffering from slight wounds and a young Union soldier arrived upon the scene and answered the wild calls for help from within. The fatigued rescuers joined them and another dozen of the men were saved from the flames. The Baptist Church burned to the ground.[64]

As the shock of the conflict altered lives in and around Mansfield and Pleasant Hill, reaction to the battles fell predictably along the fault lines that had long defined the two belligerents in the Civil War. Northern newspapers bemoaned the defeat at Mansfield and played up the engagement at Pleasant Hill.[65] Confederates celebrated both encounters as great victories. One Confederate soldier, Reuben Pierson, a relative of David who had been the reluctant Confederate from Winn Parish in 1861, was away serving in the Army of Northern Virginia. He was only weeks away from the beginning of the spring 1864 campaigns that would take him to the Wilderness. Almost as soon as he learned of the

Yankee advance into the Red River, he obtained a Northern newspaper and it reported the defeat at Mansfield. He rejoiced. The "wretches," he thought had not "polluted" the soil of his home. Union arms had failed in their wicked attempt to "enslave us," he asserted boldly.[66]

General Camille Polignac, who had commanded a division at Mansfield and Pleasant Hill, offered his men thanks and praise. In a speech given on April 12th that was later printed in a newspaper, he called the "gallant charge" on April 8 at Mansfield "worthy of an army of veterans." What the Confederates had lacked in numbers, he believed they had made up for in a sprit marked by "determination and consciousness of a just cause." The attack at Pleasant Hill that had been so stubbornly resisted by A.J. Smith's men he brushed over that and credited his boys with driving the enemy "from, every position in that they attempted to oppose you." The bulk of his words turned, however, to the great sacrifices made on the battlefield.[67]

He noted how General Alfred Mouton "fell while facing the foe and urging our troops to victory." Union Soldiers spilled his blood, "gushing out at once from five ghastly [sic] wounds." The mighty Cajun general, once so proud, became lifeless "too soon to enjoy the fruits of victory." Then he was put to rest "beneath the soil for that he fought, and among the relics of the brave he led so well." The imagery resonated with Catholic symbolism. From the five holy wounds of Jesus Christ, to the victory on the cross, to the use of the word "relic," all of these turns of phrase would have been understood by Cajuns and Creoles as sacred references. In this speech, Polignac elevated Mouton to the status of a Confederate saint. A large number of other officers had fallen as well. "The heroic colonels "Taylor, Armant, and Beard, and Lieut. Cols. Walker, and Noble, and Major Canfield were killed." The final words of the noble Frenchman drove home the religious theme. "These will now enjoy the blessing of a quiet home, with the consoling thought of having done their duty towards God, their country, and themselves." These dead Confederates "will wear in Heaven the crown that is due to their devotion to our most sacred and holy cause."[68]

In a similar fashion, General Taylor evoked scripture and compared the battles his men fought to the Old Testament contest between David and Goliath. He went over the overwhelming numbers and long odds stacked up against his Confederate army at the beginning of the campaign. He then explained what his men had done. Along three hundred miles of river and across two hundred miles of land, he claimed, his army met the enemy and beat them. "You have matched your bare breasts against his iron clads, and proved victorious in the contest!" His orders roused his army to future fights including an allusion to re-capture of New Orleans that had been a goal of Taylor's since coming back to fight in Louisiana. "Soldiers! These are great and noble deeds," he wrote of the battles at Mansfield and Pleasant Hill. "They will live in chronicle and song as long as the Southern race exists to honor the earth."[69]

In contrast to the patriotic bravado, a Texas family felt nothing but heartache. Robert Neblett had enlisted in the 12th Texas regiment and fought in Waul's brigade of Walker's division. His brother William had been standing in a crowd waiting for the arrival of a locomotive at the Houston, Texas, train station. He remembered the 8th of April as a beautiful spring day. A soldier in among those waiting made the casual remark that he thought a great battle would be fought that very day. William remembered that at the very moment when the stranger made reference to a battle he had a promotion that his brother would die in the fighting.

When word arrived on the 11th of a victory at Mansfield he became even more concerned for his brother. He wrote, "I feel more anxious to hear from Robert. He must have been in the fight." William worried most for his Mother who became "sick with anxiety" as she waited for news about her son's fate. On the 18th, a newspaper published a list of killed and wounded. Robert's name appeared among the long black columns of names. He had perished not at Mansfield but the next day at Pleasant Hill. He had been struck right near the heart. The family sent a slave to retrieve his remains. William's wife wrote to console him, "Oh Will! Will this horrible war! Will it never cease until every hearth stone in the C.S. is made desolate, and every heart filled with unutterable woe."[70]

NINE

The Old South and Cane River Crossing
April 23, 1864

The battles at Mansfield, Pleasant Grove, and Pleasant Hill had left both armies bruised and battered from two days of terrible fighting. Regiments had been shattered, and the wounded of both sides reached into the thousands. The Confederates watched as the Union brigades turned around and moved back down the narrow roads to their supply base at Grand Ecore on the Red River. Following twelve days there, the army packed up for a retreat back down the Red River Valley.[1] During this withdrawal, a major battle took place at Cane River Crossing. Also known locally as Monett's Ferry, the engagement illustrated how the war was tearing at the social relations of the Old South. The slave society of the Red River that had begun to crumble in the early phases of the campaign now came apart at the seams. The once stable and structured society gave way to a more chaotic world.

The chief agent of the change came as the momentum of the campaign shifted to the Confederate side. When the army of General Banks and Porter's navy turned and withdrew down the valley, Taylor's army became the pursuers, and the Union side became the ones on the run. Across the countryside, this transformation had a profound impact on the enslaved people. The trend of slaves running away from their masters started during the advance of the Federals accelerated and took on greater urgency with the Union army in retreat. African-American freedom a part of this campaign from the beginning was thrown into complete jeopardy. The Union army, once believed to be there for good, was not going to stay. To obtain freedom, slaves would have to leave with it.

The total number of runaways who escaped and gained their freedom is hard to estimate. The *St. Louis Republican* newspaper claimed that the U.S. navy took away six or seven thousand freedmen on their transports when they left Alexandria. Thomas C. Manning, an ardent Secessionist, advisor to both of Louisiana's Confederate governors, and State Supreme Court Justice, considered the topic when making an official report in 1865 that described the damage sustained in the campaign. "I have made a careful estimate of the number of slaves taken from this Parish by the enemy in the two expeditions of May 1863 and March 1864," Manning wrote. "After comparing my own with that made by others, [I] have no hesitation in stating the number at eight thousand."[2] A modern historian who tackled the subject could not pin down an exact number and wrote thousands escaped from their masters.[3]

The impression from contemporary Union sources confirmed a high number. A Union soldier remembered how all the slaves he ran across understood that soldiers in blue uniforms meant freedom. "The expressions of joy with that these poor ignorant beings received us were wonderful and must have rendered any reliance their owners had placed on their fidelity of little value." Another soldier confirmed that slaves moved about the countryside by the hundreds. "It was a sight to be remembered," he recalled. "Fantastics of the Fourth of July could not be compared with these dark sons of toil, seeking liberty with their household goods that they carried upon their heads or placed upon mules, as was most convenient."[4] A Union officer who took in dozens at his unit reported how he asked them where they thought they were going and one replied, "We will goin wid you all, Masser." That officer believed the most fitting place for the men was the black regiments where "they will be sent to do battle for 'Uncle Sam.'"[5]

That officer noted that the biggest problem became the lack of support they could offer the freedmen. The Army and Navy, while prepared for a military campaign, did not possess the quartermaster supplies for a growing refugee population. Little thought had gone into what would happen when the Union invaded a rich plantation region. The slaves who ran away turned to the Union army for protection, food, and transportation. None of these were in abundance. For the Confederates, their army lacked the resources as well to guard or recapture the large numbers of people who escaped and did not want to return with them. The organizational and logistical void meant that freedmen largely fended for themselves.

None of them left for the promise of food, shelter, or wages on

Nine. The Old South and Cane River Crossing   135

government plantations. The enslaved people of the Red River desired freedom alone. Historian Susan Dollar found an account of a Union sailor on a gunboat who spotted slaves on the banks of the Red who were jumping, waving, and shouting, "Hurrah for Lincoln!" They wanted to be picked up and taken away to their liberator. A lieutenant in a Wisconsin regiment marveled at the flood of people he saw: "the Darkies by hundreds took occasion to come with us." The officer, John Demerit, thought that the sight of the young and old weighed down with their bundles "pitiful especially when their prospect is before us." He knew all were taking a huge risk to flee to his army. He had heard "from several sources that several Negroes had been killed because they attempted to go to the Yankees."[6]

At least 200 hundred runaways managed to board the Union transport, *Champion No. 3*, in Natchitoches Parish. The side wheeler paddled slowly down the river, and near Calhoun's Landing in what was then Rapides Parish (now in Grant Parish) Confederate artillery caught the boat along an open stretch of water. The boat, laden down and with little or no armament of its own, made for a tragedy waiting to happen. A St. Mary Parish battery opened up a brisk fire and

Champion No. 3 seen prior to Confederate fire hitting the steam boiler, killing nearly all the freedmen aboard (*Heritage of Valor*, Louisiana State Archives).

peppered the boat. The early shots inflicted several casualties. One salvo struck the steamboat's boiler, and it exploded in a tremendous blast. It was "a fearful sight, being crowded with negroes, dead and dying, scalded by explosion of the boiler": one artilleryman remembered.[7] Approximately 175 refugees died, and many more were maimed as the boat broke apart into pieces. The scale of this grisly incident illustrated the risk each slave took when he fled.

Not only did slaves leave in great numbers from plantations but many traded their slave clothes for a blue uniform. On the Prudhomme plantation named "Bermuda," with lands stretching alongside the Cane River in Natchitoches Parish, a young laborer escaped slavery and followed the retreating army into Alexandria. There he enlisted in the Union army. He took the name William Smith and was enlisted in a black engineering company.[8] An important element often overlooked in this campaign was the significant contingent of African-American infantry and engineers that marched with the Union Army. These regiments numbered 2,500 strong.[9] The Corps d'Afrique, as they were called, had been organized in 1862, and thus far had participated in several campaigns around the Mississippi River Valley. During 1864, national military policy brought a re-naming and re-numbering of the black units. Those in Louisiana, as in the rest of the country, became the United States Colored Troops (USCT) and took regular regimental numbers. No longer the Corps d'Afrique, the black regiments in the Department of the Gulf became the 73rd, 75th, 84th, and 92nd USCT infantry regiments. William Smith joined the 99th engineering regiment, and the 97th engineers were also with the expedition.[10]

Typically, black soldiers were placed in non-combat roles and in menial tasks. Not much had been expected from them by anyone. They had been slaves without identity or freethinking abilities so the racist reasoning of the era went. Their stellar performance during an ill-fated charge at Port Hudson in 1863 gained the respect of many doubters. Still, they were kept in non-combat roles during Red River. The corps guarded nine hundred wagons in the long trains on the marches. Others served as engineers for building pontoon bridges at bayou crossings or laying down logs to make muddy roads more passable. All of these tasks were vital for the army, yet none of them so spectacular to earn the same glory of front-line soldiers.

The most significant role they played would be as living recruitment posters for more African-Americans to join the corps. By marching into the region, they became a visible point for runaway slaves to

Nine. The Old South and Cane River Crossing   137

see and emulate. Numbers show that they did this job well. Following the easy capture of Fort DeRussy in Avoyelles Parish, a report stated that 257 slaves around the fort enlisted in the Union army during the months of March and April 1864. Other Union garrison points such as Alexandria, where William Smith joined, and Grand Ecore served as recruiting stations. Several hundred came into those places making a total of around 600 African-Americans who joined the army.[11] That number was a significant size regiment gained in less than two months' time. The social revolution that saw slavery erode had been accelerated by not just the presence of the Union army but by the presence of black role models in uniform. Their presence proved an important psychological element, inspiring slaves to leave their masters, angering Confederates wherever they went, and expanding the boundaries of service for the U.S. Army.

African-American service came with its share of struggles. The officers of the USCT were white, and discipline could be severe. On the march to Mansfield, one black soldier discharged his weapon without permission. Rifle fire could alert the enemy to one's location. The punishment that came down was quite severe:

> Special order no 21 HQ Corps Afrique Western Louisiana April 6, 1864 Private Daniel Dickinson F co. having discharged his musket without authority while on the march contrary to the articles of war is hereby ordered to forfeit his pay during his time of service and shall upon arriving in permanent camp have his head shaved and be drummed out the military service of the US." By command of Henry Fuller.[12]

Another episode illustrates one of the many other challenges they faced. After arrival at Alexandria in March 1864, Colonel William Dickey, the brigade commander of the Corps, demanded that the colors of the First Infantry regiment be replaced at once. The old flags appeared ragged and discolored from wear and tear. The Colonel had issued a new set right at the start of the campaign, yet the unit continued to display their cherished flags. The men had carried those banners at Port Hudson and did not want to give them up. The noncommissioned officers, musicians, and privates of the First Infantry (part of the famed Louisiana Native Guards) petitioned General Banks, demanding an exception so they might be allowed to keep them. The petition charged that their defiance had angered Dickey. "Dickey Said it was a dam petticoat and A disgrace to the brigade he also Curesed our Regt and Said we wer the dam Smart Nigers." The protest further explained other wrongs made against them. When he saw it, Colonel

Dickey wrote an endorsement below the complaint in that he cited the "old faded and ragged" condition and how the colors did not meet army regulations. He insisted, "no such language as is mentioned in the communication has ever been used by me."[13] A headquarters notation indicated that the appeal made it to Banks' staff but was returned without action that meant that the request failed and new colors had to be brought forward.

During the middle of the campaign, General Nathaniel Banks took time and implemented the re-organization of these units into numbered regiments of the USCT. The Corps d'Afrique would no longer exist in name and a transition of those black units from experimental endeavors to fully functioning U.S. army units would be completed while on the move. General Banks embraced the changes and made sure the designations were done immediately. At the same time, he communicated with the Secretary of the Treasury, lobbying for a savings bank for black soldiers and freedmen who now collected wages for cotton cultivation at experimental sites throughout the state. Banks worked as hard on this aspect of what was early Reconstruction policy as he did plotting strategy and operations of the campaign itself.[14]

A good illustration of the aid that African-Americans could make came during the first days of the retreat. Just south of Cloutierville at a nondescript crossing of the Cane River in southern Natchitoches Parish, a helpful slave would save the Union army. At the crossing called Monett's Ferry, the slow-moving Cane River became "lined with extensive 'cane-brakes,' that in some places cover many thousand acres, and furnish grazing for large herds of cattle."[15] On the north side approaching the crossing, the land fell flat with large tracts of cotton fields. On the south side, high hills rose to 135 feet in elevation and thus looked over the deep, slow water flow below. The road that crossed the river happened to be the most direct path from Grand Ecore to Alexandria. That in and of itself made it important to Union forces. Without really understanding the topography of the area, General Banks placed over 25,000 Union soldiers on that road, marching south down the forty-five-mile long and seven-mile wide island created by the Cane River on the west and Red River to the east. The spring had turned warm by the time the army reached this point and the "suffocating southern heat and scorching sun, as well as dust so think you couldn't see a comrade 4 paces away, sapped our energy completely," a Union soldier reported.[16]

On April 23, 1864, a Confederate force of 1,600 cavalry, only four

Nine. The Old South and Cane River Crossing 139

African American soldiers listen to a speech on duties of freedman in Louisiana (*Heritage of Valor*, Louisiana State Archives).

brigades, and several batteries commanded by General Hamilton Bee stood in the way at the crossing. Bee arrived there first and placed his men on the hills on the south side facing the crossing. He blocked the path of the retreat. "It was a very strong position," veteran James A. Jarratt wrote, "and should have been held by General Bee."[17] General Taylor's one remaining division pressed the Union from the rear, and a smaller force stood ready on the east bank of the Red prohibiting movement that direction. Taylor believed he had trapped General Nathaniel Banks. A quick glance at a map would show that with the aid of the Cane River and Red River, the Confederates cut off movement north, south, east and west. Two important factors worked against Taylor's encirclement. The total number of troops Taylor possessed was fewer than 5,000 due to General Kirby Smith taking away Churchill's and Walker's divisions for operations against a Union army moving on Shreveport from Little Rock.[18] Banks still commanded over 20,000 effectives. His army outnumbered what was left in Louisiana by five to one. By sheer weight of numbers, he could have broken free by applying his superiority in any direction. Secondly, the Union force still had fight left in it. The rear guard commanded by A.J. Smith gave ground grudgingly, and the 19th Corps contained units that had fought valiantly at Pleasant Grove and Pleasant Hill. Although beaten, and in retreat, Banks led an army that still possessed a will to fight.[19]

When the 19th Army Corps, the lead element of the army, arrived at Bee's position, General William Franklin, who had been wounded at Mansfield, turned over corps command to General William Emory. No better selection could have been made. Emory had rescued the army at Pleasant Grove on the evening of the battle of Mansfield, and now he faced another dire situation. Unless he found a way to break through, the army would suffered more unnecessary losses. Once again the battlefield's terrain played a great role in what took place next. Because Emory had been a topographical engineer, he knew his forces could not carry the strong position by storm without large loss of life. He had to find a way to cross the river somewhere besides the road crossing and possibly flank the enemy. Scouts went out first downstream where they did not locate a shallow spot anywhere that might allow an infantry crossing. About this time, the 96th Ohio Volunteers, who manned the front lines in front of Monett's Ferry, noticed a dark figure leap out of the earthworks at the top of the bluff opposite and dash from tree to tree down the slope.[20]

When the man passed the advanced outposts of the Rebel skirmish line they did not anticipate someone from behind them coming from that direction through the lines. They hesitated but when the man plunged into the river, the pickets opened fire "splashing all around him, a shower of balls."[21] He survived that danger miraculously and when he reached the opposite bank, the Buckeye soldiers almost opened fire. He stopped them from leveling their rifles by yelling, "Don't shoot, Yank, I'se your friend." It was a slave who had run from his master over in the Confederate lines. The wet and exhausted slave said his name was Tom, and he wanted to be taken to the General because he wanted to convey some helpful information. When brought before General Emory, he claimed to know the location of a hidden ford two to three miles upstream. Tom had used it many times when out hunting. He was given a chance to prove himself. The slave led the doubting soldiers to the spot and then walked carefully across in waist deep water making it safely to the opposite bank. Others followed in

Tom's footsteps exactly, except for a few men who missed a step and plunged under water, much to the amusement of their comrades. The ford proved passable and Tom had given Emory the option he needed for a flanking attack.[22] Another regimental history claimed without any specific details a "negro woman pointed out the best place for crossing."[23] Either way, a slave contributed the vital intelligence making an escape plan possible.

General Emory dispatched General William Birge with a division that included Colonel Francis Fessenden, son of Lincoln's Secretary of the Treasury who now commanded the late Colonel Lewis Benedict's brigade, and the remains of the 13th Corps under General Cameron. Without opposition, the strike force crossed at the ford and made its way towards the Confederate left flank. When the regiments arrived in front of the Confederates and commenced firing, Emory laid down a covering barrage from his artillery batteries. The Union fire split the attention of Bee's gunners, who aimed shots at the batteries in an attempt to silence them and as a result did not concentrate all their fire on the Union attack. When the battle started, Bee discovered an enemy both in front of his position and now on his left.[24]

General Birge pushed his men forward, leading one of the most aggressive assaults mounted by his side during the entire campaign. The Union regiments crossed through dense bottomland woods, a cotton field, and with fixed bayonets hit Colonel George Baylor's 2nd Arizona cavalry. The 2nd Texas Partisan Rangers joined Baylor after he fell back to a second position behind a rail fence. Colonel Fessenden fell on the field with a leg wound just as the Union forces prepared for a charge against their opposition. Baylor dispatched a frantic message to Bee asking for reinforcements, and instead of support, Bee ordered him and the rest of the Confederates to abandon their positions. Bee thought he had lost the day and he ordered a general retreat. A final factor in his decision process had come when Emory had sent a Cavalry force in the direction of Bee's right flank, and although a feint without any hope of crossing the river anywhere, the move convinced Bee he was being closed in on from all sides. The Union army had executed a plan flawlessly and Birge's soldiers had attacked with aggressiveness. For heroism at the scene, William S. Beebe, a recent West Point graduate, won the Medal of Honor.[25]

When Emory found that Bee had withdrawn, he sent African-American engineers from a USCT unit to lay down pontoon bridges. The army crossing proceeded through the night and into the next morning. Black refugees made their way across the bridges with the army. The freedmen would not be left behind here as was to happen when General William T. Sherman's 15th Corps crossed at Ebenezer Creek in Georgia and left refugees behind.[26] The bottleneck at Monett's Ferry had been broken, and the blue lines continued on down the road to Alexandria. The Confederates had not been able to hold the Union army and force it to give up. With the aid of a slave and a good battle plan, the blue coats were successful.

The disappointed Confederates turned on the commander, whom they believed had failed them. Augustus Ball, an army physician from Bowie County, Texas, thought the battle's outcome might have been different if Bee had not been in command. He complained, "He is the poorest excuse for a Gen[eral] that I ever saw."[27] Another Texas soldier remarked, "But even though Bee had a good stronghold he let the Yankees through and they chased our troops 6–7 miles in front of them." The soldier had also heard of the growing storm between Taylor and Bee. "Because of his cowardice gen Bee is supposed to be under arrest."[28]

Bee's decision to withdraw made Taylor furious. Why could he not hold his position to the last extremity as ordered? Bee became the scapegoat for Taylor's frustrations and anger. Bee was not an incompetent. By birth, Hamilton Prioleau Bee claimed a long French

General Hamilton Bee, shown here in 1863, commanded Confederates at Cane River. He disappointed General Richard Taylor by withdrawing and leaving the road open to Alexandria (DeGolyer Library, Southern Methodist University, Lawrence T. Jones III Texas Photography Collection).

Nine. The Old South and Cane River Crossing

Huguenot lineage. He began life in Charleston, South Carolina, and grew up steps away from Tradd Street, only the most distinguished avenue in the most pretentious city of the South. Additionally, he came from the first state to secede; the convention was held in his birthplace. Everyone knew he was the older brother of the fallen hero Barnard E. Bee, who died at Manassas after giving General Thomas J. Jackson his nickname, crying "There stands Jackson like a stone wall!"[29]

In 1839, at age seventeen, Bee moved with his parents who made their way to the Republic of Texas.[30] Vast new cotton lands were being opened up there each month. Hamilton Bee cut his political teeth by taking several minor government posts. He then distinguished himself by fighting in the Mexican War as a Texas cavalryman. In the 1850s, he became a planter near the site of the 1836 Goliad Massacre. It is reasonable to assume that he knew the story of what happened there; how a brave band of Texans stood defiant, became surrounded by Mexican troops, and then were cut down without quarter.[31]

Bee entered state politics in the 1850s and became a speaker of the State House of Representatives. In 1862, he became a Confederate Brigadier general. Instead of field command back east similar to his brother, however, he left for an important desk job. He coordinated supplies being brought into the Confederacy from Mexico. This assignment proved to be an invaluable part of the war effort because the Union blockade had prevented military stores from reaching Southern forces. At Brownsville he stayed for the first years of the war making sure foreign shipments came into Texas and then shipped to armies across the Confederacy. His first field command came in 1864 for the Red River expedition.[32]

He rode over from Texas with Tom Green's cavalry contingent and arrived at Taylor's army not long before the Battle at Mansfield. When the April 8 attack began, his men headed towards the Union left flank but because of dense woods few of them ever made it into the thick of action. At Pleasant Hill, however, he made a brave charge into the face of Union forces that laid down a withering crossfire. A Union soldier explained, "Our men waited until they were near and then poured a volley into them. Another line," he related, "poured in a cross fire and it hardly left a man or horse alive."[33] Of 300 cavalry that moved forward, one estimate stated that not fifty of these men returned to Confederate lines. Bee lost two horses shot from under him and suffered a slight wound. He explained, "The cavalry command was literally swept away by a cross-fire at close range from an enemy concealed behind a string of fence perpendicular to the enemy's line of battle. This fire was as unexpected as disastrous." He went on to report, "Fortunately there were ravines of young pines on our right that furnished somewhat of shelter until the shock could be recovered from, but the empty saddles, the men shot and falling in all directions, the confusion, produced a scene imperishable on my memory."[34]

Following the withdrawal from Monett's Ferry, General Taylor relieved Bee of command and accused him of "ruining his plan" to trap the entire Union army and showing "no generalship."[35] Louisiana's soldier prince had become fixated on destroying the entire Union force. Flush from his Mansfield victory and the Union retreat following Pleasant Hill, he possessed delusions of grandeur. Taking the whole Union army would have been difficult to carry out even with many more infantry, strong entrenchments at Cane River, a better commander, or other circumstances that did not exist. Ever since the battle, Taylor's supporters have pondered the "what if" scenarios and insisted that the circumstances provided a real opportunity to capture General Banks and all his men.[36]

This contention could not be more mistaken. It completely minimizes the Union's leadership. General Emory devised an excellent plan and with a brilliant execution carried the day. Also underestimated has been the great fighting ability of the Union officers and men one of whom won the Medal of Honor. The sheer determination of the Yankee force held Taylor's Confederates at bay in the rear while a bold attack in front pushed Bee's men off their position. Lastly, a slave delivered key information that compromised the Confederate position. All these factors were just as important as Bee's mistakes and General Kirby Smith's withdrawal of two divisions for service elsewhere. Smith's determination that Arkansas demanded greater attention than a retreating force in Louisiana should not be seen as a blunder. Looking at the troop withdrawal for what it was, a policy decision, places the Battle at Monett's Ferry in its proper perspective. The Confederates did not stand a chance of capturing the entire Union army even if they had retained the veterans of Walker and Churchill.

Following the Union breakthrough at Cane River Crossing, Taylor snapped and lashed out at both Bee and Smith. He flew into a rage at Smith because he withdrew the divisions. In a written tirade, the peptic commander castigated his superior: "I have supported you when your policy was fatally wrong, for I believed it my duty to give my commander a warm and earnest co-operation." One too many things had

Nine. The Old South and Cane River Crossing 145

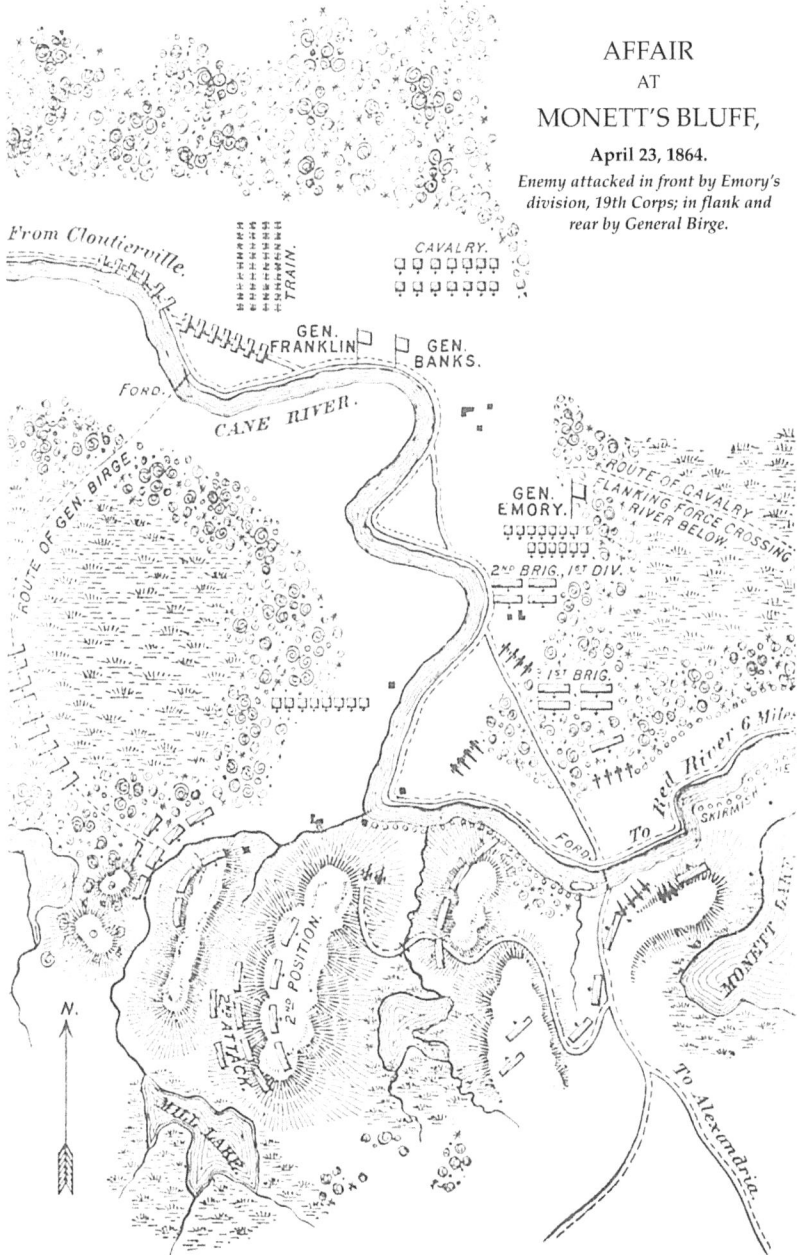

A map of the Cane River Crossing or Monett's Ferry battle (*War of the Rebellion Official Records*, series 1, vol. 34, part 1, 233).

Union army crossing the Cane River (*Heritage of Valor*, Louisiana State Archives).

happened and Taylor now declared, "I cannot do my whole duty under your command."[37] Smith read the insubordinate remarks and did not give them the dignity of a response. He merely returned the communication with a note calling the missive "unjust" and adding that Taylor must not be feeling well.[38]

General Taylor solicited support for his firing of Bee following the battle. He found a willing ally in division commander General John Walker. Although not present at the Monett's Ferry battle, the greyhound's commander agreed that Bee performed poorly. The failure of the cavalry at Pleasant Hill earlier in the month colored Walker's negative assessment. His beloved Texans died in greater numbers and he himself suffered a slight wound on the field because the cavalry had failed in their change there. The infantry had to pick up the slack. To him, the collapse at Cane River Crossing was but one more mistake Bee had made. Walker believed "the position itself was so advantageous that with a more skillful handling of his troops, and more vigorous resistance[,] the Federal army would have found it extremely difficult to dislodge their enemy and to force a passage."[39]

In his own defense, Hamilton Bee responded with the very important point that his orders were totally unreasonable. "That I was not successful was because success was impossible," he explained. "An army of 25,000, marching at their leisure on the main road at Alexandria, could not be long impeded by a force of 2,000 horse in position on a river fordable and easy of access and approach. There was no time to prepare for the advance of Banks' army ... the whole of it was suddenly thrown on me." He went on to lambast his critics, "Those who, distant from the scene, imagined that the enemy, demolished and disorganized, were fleeing before our triumphant forces might have expected other results; but those who saw that splendid army spread over the valley of the Cane River as far as the eye could reach were not surprised that the road had to be yielded to them."[40]

General Smith supported Bee, writing after the war, "General Taylor's force was, however, too weak to warrant the hope that he could seriously impede the march of Banks's column."[41] Bee's trusted subordinate, General John Wharton, contacted his benighted superior at the time and wrote, "I have heard that you are censured in Texas in reference to the Monett's Ferry affair by stragglers from the cavalry, who would have been as loud in condemnation had you remained until defeated by Banks' army, as would certainly have occurred."[42] He asserted that gentlemen would support him and understand what really happened there. His words harked back to that antebellum pillar of Southern society, honor. Wharton believed Bee had acted with honor and his detractors wrong to lambast his decisions. Notably, Bee could have challenged Taylor to a duel, yet he did not issue a message asking for one. Trading barbs with pens rather than swords turned out to be the favored approach. It certainly was not keeping with the "honor and violence" that triggered physical confrontation in the antebellum South.[43]

Bee requested instead Smith hold a court of inquiry to clear his name. Before one could be convened, he accepted Smith's suggestion that instead of a formal review he assume a new command. Then Taylor received the thanks of the Confederate Congress and a promotion to department command east of the Mississippi River. With the two men separated, Smith no longer had to deal with the ugly controversy in an official way.[44] The matter would remain a source of bitter contention among Trans-Mississippi Confederate leaders for years.

Colonel George Baylor, whose men took the brunt of the Union attack on the left of the Union line at Monett's Ferry, continued to hold a grudge against Bee. He remained angry because Bee had not sent reinforcements when he needed them and instead ordered a retreat. Baylor never let go of the affair. He tangled with General Wharton, who continued to defend Bee, and found plenty of other issues to fight about in sharp exchanges lasting for nearly a year. Both officers were too proud to forgive and too stubborn to forget. On April 6, 1865, the two Texans happened to meet up at Confederate headquarters in Galveston. When Wharton called Baylor a liar and slapped his face, so the story goes, Baylor pulled out a pistol and shot him dead. In a matter of speaking, Wharton became the last casualty of the battle at Cane River Crossing.[45]

Ten

Gone with the Wind
The Burning of Alexandria and the End of the Campaign, May 13–18, 1864

Following the breakthrough at Cane River Crossing, the retreating Union army limped back into Alexandria. Union forces dug in at this time, and for a week in early May, all waited anxiously as Admiral Porter's eleven big gunboats stood above the river's falls stuck in low water.[1] The Confederate engineers had succeeded in making passage up the river difficult and now, with only three feet four inches of draft left, passage became impossible. Confederate pickets hovered outside the city and skirmishing continued briskly. Day by day, both sides remained on edge as each attempted to figure out the next move of their enemy. No more dangerous point in this game came along the river's premiere tributary, the Bayou Rapides that extended to the north and west and formed the northern boundary of Alexandria's modest urban development. All routes into the city from the northern part of the parish followed the stream's pastoral meanderings.

The bayou, an old bed of the Red River, could be dark and deep at points and then wide and swampy at others. Its winding course through the flat countryside could be followed at a distance from the sight of the numerous cypress and oak trees often draped with moss sitting silently beside it. Bayou Rapides contained some of the parish's largest plantations. The mansions, mostly Greek Revival or Creole in architecture, appeared tall and proud, set as they were beside the road or Bayou's bank for miles leading into the town. Each of these cotton complexes boasted regal names that evoked the great manors of

Europe: The Kent House, Tyrrone, Lakeland, and Geneva, just to name a few. These spacious places, boasting elaborate gardens and communities of outbuildings, should have reminded one young Confederate cavalry officer of his own substantial seat back in Brazoria County, Texas.[2]

Major George McNeel proved a notable exception to the popular notion that the Civil War was a rich man's war yet a poor man's fight. McNeel came from one of the richest families in the South. The cotton and sugar cane of his father's Ellerslie plantation placed that household in the top tier of all Texas planters. In the years leading up to the war, George headed north for a college education at New Jersey's Rutgers University. He graduated in the class of 1860, which included a Vanderbilt and a number of social elites. McNeel's yearbook, among the first to be produced for the preservation of school memories, has survived. It contains many poignant farewell messages from his classmates. A comradery still existed among these students even as the sectional crisis divided America.[3]

At the outbreak of the war, McNeel joined the 8th Texas Cavalry, known as "Terry's Texas Rangers." In 1862, he became a staff officer for General Hamilton Bee. He fought at Mansfield, Pleasant Grove, and Pleasant Hill. He had two horses shot from under him and many of his fellow troopers fell dead all around him in the ill-fated charge at Pleasant Hill. The dedicated staffer went out under a flag of truce following the end of hostilities that day so he and others might recover the large amount of wounded

Born to a wealthy Texas family and educated in the North, George McNeel died outside of Alexandria. His grave has been lost to time (Photographic History Collection, National Museum of American History, Smithsonian Institution).

left on the field. McNeel could rightly claim to be a survivor of one of the deadliest charges of the war.[4] For his accomplishments, he seemed poised for lost cause glory and post-war political leadership. Similar to General Alfred Mouton, the Cajun son, it was not to be for this Lone Star prodigy.[5]

In one of the great tragedies of the war, McNeel died on May 7, 1864, while scouting in front of Union lines. Just outside of Alexandria, along the middle bayou section of Bayou Rapides, he went out alone to probe the Union lines.[6] General M. K. Lawler, a Union officer, gave a terse account: "Major McNeil ... was killed on this day by Cameron's pickets reconnoitering our lines."[7] In another account, the 46th Indiana regiment's soldiers stated that after 5 p.m., shots were fired at a young Confederate officer spotted on the other side of the Bayou Rapides Bridge. The soldiers who fired on him advanced to the spot, found him shot dead, and searched his body. They took from him $700 in Confederate money and "very important papers," the account states.[8] Little more than this bit of information is known. His final resting is even a mystery. He is not in the family cemetery back in Texas or at any of the regular burial grounds in Rapides Parish. A descendent is still searching for his grave.[9]

At the end of the campaign, General Bee compiled a list of his staff officers killed and wounded. The last line in the report rendered a fitting epithet for the planter's son: "My regrets for George McNeil will be appreciated by all who knew him."[10] His stepmother back at home jotted an entry next to his name in the family Bible: "Aged 26 years, and 7 months, and 10 days. His life has been given in noble sacrifice in his country's service."[11] McNeel's death symbolized the tragic results of the war for many of the young and bright participants on both sides.

An equally terrible result would be the destruction wrought on the countryside in the path of the maneuvering armies. In this campaign, private property became specific targets. One Texas soldier of German descent who insisted that the Union had not burned houses around Pleasant Hill at the time of the battle there remained unequivocal about what happened following the retreat down the Cane River Valley: "The houses, Gin's, Negro-Houses, and Korn-kribs lay in smoking ruins, we didn't see any people living there, and not an ear of corn will be planted this year."[12] A Union soldier, marching by what he called the "Lecomte" plantation in southern Natchitoches Parish, noticed the magnitude of the damage: "All the cotton houses had been burnt," he remembered, "the fire that was five days old was still blazing."[13] Another Texan who marched through the neighborhood recorded at the time how the retreating Yankee soldiers were "[b]urning all houses and destroying property."[14]

For French citizen Pierre Poete, a relative newcomer to the Cane River, the destruction during those days brought disappointing financial loss. Pierre had been born in France, arrived in America in 1853 and by all accounts was living the American dream. At age thirty-two, he and his brother opened a successful bakery. They enjoyed a good reputation, and the first years of the war passed uneventfully. Then Poete saw an opportunity, and he took a great financial risk. In late 1863, he purchased twenty-seven bales of cotton from Theodore Rachal, who ran a place on Cane River near the twenty-four-mile ferry above the French town of Cloutierville. Rachel had stored away cotton bales in a gin house, representing crop harvests for 1861, 1862, and 1863. Following the sale of the twenty-seven bales, Poete stamped his mark on his share and accepted a receipt for the large amount of cash he turned over to Rachel. The transaction value at the time was at least $6,000. Neither man knew that the next spring the Red River would be the target of the Army of the Gulf.[15]

In early April 1864, the Union army approached the plantations along the Cane River and swept the retreating Confederate cavalry away from the neighborhood. According to Poete's brother, who filed a claim for damages in 1882, the plantation's cotton remained untouched by the Confederates, who left in a hurry. Someone had moved the bales safely into the woods and they escaped General Taylor's burning parties, who torched cotton for fifty miles up the Cane River, all the way to Campti.[16] When the danger subsided, an overseer had slaves collect it, and they stored it under the gin house's open shed.

The overseer was mistaken to think that the danger had passed. Following the defeat at Mansfield, Union forces returned the way they had come, but now in full retreat. This time a far larger number of Union soldiers poured into the area and remained close by for a day and a half. An elderly brother-in-law checked with the overseer when the federals arrived for the second time, expressing the misconception that he thought the Yankees would not burn a Frenchman's cotton. "And he told me they would not respect anybody's property, not even a woman's."[17]

"Yankees were everywhere," a former slave recollected when interviewed by an agent investigating the claim. The freedman presented a simple yet vivid description of soldiers moving down both banks of the Cane River and slaves joining them from all directions. White soldiers and black refugees filled camps in the neighborhood. Union soldiers sought out the slave and urged him to join them, he explained, and he also noted that he remembered seeing regiments of blacks wearing blue uniforms. Despite having a good memory, he could not say for certain who burned the cotton in question. All he remembered was seeing Union soldiers and the next thing he knew the cotton was burning.[18]

A brother, Philippe Poete—Pierre had died in 1869—made the claim for over $60,000 in damages, adding additional information about two fine horses, worth $1,000 each in Confederate money, that he purchased in 1863. These horses stayed in a warehouse at Natchitoches where Union officers stayed after their arrival in that town. The officers rode off on them. Poete apparently chased after the thieves without ever finding them. The brother thought he deserved compensation for the cotton and horses because, as French nationals, both he and his brother had avoided taking sides during the war. Although they belonged to a home guard unit, this company remained in the parish and never marched or carried ammunition. The strong assertions of Poete and their one witness did not go unchallenged.[19]

A second equally plausible narrative came in from a neighbor, Emmanuel Dupree, a free Creole of color. Living along Cane River since colonial times, the free people of color had carved out a place for themselves as planters and farmers.[20] A number had owned slaves themselves. Dupree stepped up, and he possessed a sharp memory. He spoke of seeing retreating Confederates arrive in the area in early April, before the Union, and a group visited the gin house, the location of the cotton in question. The overseer had not hauled the bales into the woods as directed, nor as he testified under oath. The Creole claimed the gray-clad soldiers removed the bales to the riverbank and burned them. His testimony contained important descriptive details about the plantation setting and Rebel soldiers that lent credence to his words. On its face, the testimony contained more credibility than the others'.

He even approached the squad doing the burning and asked the men to spare four of the fifty bales for the orphan children of the owner. When pressed, he maintained that he saw none of the other witnesses walking around the gin house that was located on the opposite side of the river from the main dwelling. His words were supported by a second witness, this time a Confederate soldier, Green Morgan, who served in the 2nd Louisiana Cavalry. He testified that his unit burned cotton all along the Cane River, up to the Catholic Church above the so-called twenty-four-mile ferry. He specifically remembered the French brothers and meeting a Creole who asked him to save four bales for orphans. With these two strong counter-witnesses, the Poete claim lost steam. It would be denied. The cotton was gone, and the indiscriminate hand of war had consumed it. In the confusion of advance and retreat, private property came under the torch of one side or the other. It did not matter. Each army destroyed what they came across and only the lucky went unscathed.

It did not matter if one was a white Southern Confederate, French Unionist, Creole of color, French national, Catholic priest or a convent of nuns; the harm came down indiscriminately. Soldiers might burn down buildings or just as easily steal valuable items such as horses, mules, and food. These items might be seized officially or unofficially and often were taken away at gunpoint and could not be replaced easily. In late April and early May 1864, Louisiana's Civil War had taken a particularly destructive turn. The physical destruction and theft brought with it an atmosphere of anger and resentment. Civilians began to take matters into their own hands. Whenever they found a target to act out their revenge, they struck with deadly effect.

The regimental history of the 77th Illinois explained how soldiers in that regiment came to blame civilians for sniper fire and every ambush of foraging soldiers. "The flanks and rear of our army were constantly annoyed by these cowardly sneaks—men who had not the courage to enlist and fight like soldiers." Instead, they pretended to be civilians when the army passed their home, "then, seeking the cover of the brush, acted their mean, contemptable part in the capture or killing of our men." The resentment built up and "the boys showed their contempt for all such claims by acts of wholesale destruction as they passed along." As in the wars of other eras, the anger of the troops was vented in vandalism and pillage. The conditions created a vicious cycle, often repeated, of ambush and then retaliation that created the darkest days of the campaign.[21]

One Texas cavalry trooper expressed shock at the turn of events:

> The whole stretch that we covered yesterday, down through the Cane River Valley, for about 30 miles there were fields planted with corn but all the fences lay around. The houses, the gins, the negro places and the grain silos were still smoking ruins, one sees no inhabitants, and nothing will be grown here this year.[22]

Ten. Gone with the Wind

Another Texan who had chased Union soldiers into Alexandria reflected on his experience in a long thoughtful letter: "My heart has been made sick by the miserable success of destruction," he informed his parents. At twenty-four years of age, he had witnessed a lifetime of burnt buildings. "A great many families that have had every thing taken from them and burned out of house and home by the vile miscreants of the North," he wrote, adding that a few folks kept only the clothes on their backs. Apparently, Unionists who had taken the oath of allegiance found no greater protection for their loyalty. "They had no respect for the person. Those that had taken the oath just about the same as those that did not."[23]

The leading Unionist of Cloutierville, a president of the 1861 Union Club, Dr. Samuel O. Scruggs, counted only three outbuildings standing at his homestead as the Union army passed by on their way to Alexandria.[24] Following the war, he made a claim to the federal government for a whopping $18,534 in personal damages.[25] When a French citizen in the same neighborhood flew the tricolor and scrawled a note on his gate, "Neutrality Here," he found that this tactic did not afford any better results. A Union officer spotted the flag and remarked, "had I been where I could have reached it I would have cut it down with my sabre."[26] Phanor Prudhomme, the cotton planter at Oakland along the Cane River, was detained when the Union arrived at his home. Two of his sons and a son-in-law were fighting for the Confederacy, and he was forced to walk twelve miles to Natchitoches. His plantation home escaped destruction, yet plenty of supplies disappeared and his gin house was burned to the ground. According to family legend, a soldier who walked through the home stabbed the portrait of his first wife and left it with a large ugly hole. At fifty-seven, and in poor health, the personal losses and strenuous march to town confined him to bed. He never recovered fully and died the next year without being able to see Oakland again.[27]

His heirs and related family members made seven separate claims for damages after the war, totaling more than $130,000, a fantastic sum in that day. That damage estimate stood out as the largest monetary claim of any family in the Red River Valley. The estate of John Compton in Rapides Parish made the largest individual claim, however, coming in at over $21,621. Almost all of these claims would be denied because one had to prove beyond a shadow of a doubt that the claimant had "adhered to the Union cause" and did not become a Confederate or aid the Southern side. Most notably, James Madison Wells, the Unionist

Lieutenant Governor, turned in his estimate for damages at $19,675. The United States government approved $4,080 of it, compensating him for supplies appropriated by the U.S. quartermaster and hospital staff.[28]

The late historian, James G. Hollandsworth, Jr., who researched this subject extensively, found that General A.J. Smith's detachment of the 16th and 17th corps carried out the majority of the destruction and stealing. These western veterans had extensive practice in the destructive arts. General William T. Sherman had employed Smith's men for his Meridian, Mississippi, campaign in February 1864. From east of Jackson almost to the state line, these troops tore up railroad tracks and torched homesteads all along their route of march. Their pathway became a sorry scene of desolation. The campaign stands today as a rehearsal for the Red River, Georgia, and the Carolinas. The purpose of the destruction proved to be two fold. One, to destroy the will of the people to carry on resistance, and the second was to remove their capacity to fight on. The Red River Valley contained many more plantation complexes to plunder and homes to burn than found in the piney woods of Mississippi. The amount of destruction visited upon the Red would be that much greater.[29]

The idea of an expanded war wrought on property and doing damage to civilians changed the nature of the Civil War itself. Many months before the celebrated burning of Atlanta or Columbia, South Carolina, the Red River Valley experienced the harshness of total war. Why did the Union soldiers turn so viciously on the population and property? The answer it seems can be found in the condition of the soldiers themselves. Following long marches to Mansfield and Pleasant Hill and the harassment of a retreat that included for many another engagement at Monett's Ferry, the Union soldiers were certainly pushed to a breaking point.

Joseph Minis, a Union soldier, not yet twenty and serving with the 11th Wisconsin, explained how terrible the conditions were on the retreat. His unit happened to be aboard a transport, a circumstance one would think was generally safe. It was not. "I cant remember half of it but I can remember that we have been fighting most ever day," he explained. The danger came in fits and starts and placed everyone on edge as they waited anxiously for the next round of attacks. Minis mentioned that, "we went as far as [G]rand [E]core then [B]anks got whipped so we stayed thare four or five days." As the Union army continued southward, he joined the columns on land and recalled how he found himself no better off: "Our corps had to stay in the rear and cover [Banks'] retreat so the rebs would attacked us in the morning and we had to fight them all day then [Banks] would be so far ahead that we would have to march all night to catch up with him he kept us a going so far about three weeks while we got so tired we could not do hardly anything."[30]

A member of Company C of the 161st New York remembered, "We had to march night and day during the retreat, starting at one or two in the morning, and frequently not halting until late the next night. We traveled forty-five miles, at one stretch in twenty-four hours!"[31] Lieutenant Colonel Lucius Hubbard, a future governor of Minnesota, confirmed that his men were "worn out by our continuous day and night duty in marching, skirmishing, and fighting."[32] A soldier noted that the army appeared to him "greatly depressed."[33] Their frustrations with the fighting, retreat, and ambushes bubbled to the surface.

"Our cavalry burnt every building on the route," a soldier in the 161st New York reported. "They must have destroyed over a million dollars worth of cotton alone, besides corn and other stuff. Before we left Grand Ecore our men set fire to the town and burnt to the ground nearly every house in it."[34] Across the river at Campti, a skirmish took place with Confederates, and as the Union abandoned that place, the men set the buildings ablaze. The fate that befell these tiny steamboat landings proved to be harbingers of bigger things to come. A Union soldier lamented that during a long night march of over twenty miles, "the way was occasionally lit up by burning houses and barns; a disgraceful and needless barbarism, that excited our disgust but could not be wholey [sic] suppressed."[35] A Confederate explained, "They fight us on every foot of ground burning every corn crib, fence around corn fields & many dwellings—completely devastating the prettiest country in La., or the world I presume."[36]

Upon arrival at Alexandria, the tired and frustrated soldiers remained cooped up in camps for more than a week. Confederates in Pineville, just across the river, laid down sniper fire into the city. The Union response came swiftly. The trapped gunboats lashed out with a barrage of shot and shell. Most of a day and throughout the night, the bombardment continued at regular intervals. Everyone, friend and foe, stayed awake from the deep sound of man-made thunder. The Unionist newspaper editor Charles Boyce owned a home on the banks of the Red in Pineville. A long cherished, and often repeated, family tradition claimed that during the bombardment a shot passed straight through the mansion's opened first-floor front door, sailed through the central hallway, missing everyone and everything inside, and wrecked the outhouse in the backyard before coming to rest.[37]

The Union gunboats trapped above the falls needed a solution to their precarious position. Wisconsin ingenuity came to the rescue. Lt. Col. Joseph Bailey stepped forward with an idea for how to save the trapped gunboats. Before the war, Bailey had worked in the lumber industry at the Wisconsin dells, a site where natural obstructions hampered the flow of timber on the river. Bailey utilized winged dams that raised water levels so that valuable logs could continue flowing to saw mills downriver. His knowledge of this civilian enterprise, combined with a natural engineer's mind, made him the man of the hour. He went to work designing a dam that might put some drag on the trickle of water in the Red and, inch by inch, raise its level. He needed six to eight feet of draft and thus far the river stood at only three feet. His superiors supported the plan and provided legions of men as laborers because, absent another idea, this plan might be their only hope.[38]

Bailey slowed both the underwater and surface flow enough to raise the water quickly and get the draft needed at the middle point of the river. The Official Records Atlas contains several diagrams and maps that outline the genius of what Bailey was able to do.[39] His hydraulic masterpiece, named Bailey's Dam in his honor, required three thousand laborers working nearly around the clock. A first task was to dismantle buildings for finished lumber. The David Store on the Pineville side of the river, and many more on the Alexandria side, were pulled down in a mad scramble for planks.[40] Dozens of trees had to be cut down and rocks collected to anchor the pointed logs in place, firmly attaching them to the riverbed. James H.C. Barlow of Alexandria claimed sixty-five bales of his cotton, valued at $9,000, had been seized and employed in the construction of the dam. Tons of iron rails dumped on the levee three years before, left there during a dispute between a shipper and a Texas Railroad Company, were put to good use as well. "Night and day the work was carried on without cessation, the men working willingly and cheerfully, although many were compelled to stand up to their waists in water during the damp and chilly nights, and under a burning sun by day, and notwithstanding very many had no faith in the success of the great undertaking."[41]

The work was done so well that more than a century later, the logs could still be seen at low water, set uniformly in the muddy river bottom. Dozens of people have commented to me how they walked on

Ten. Gone with the Wind

Remains of Bailey's Dam were still visible at low water well into the second half of the 20th Century (Historic American Buildings Survey, Library of Congress).

Bailey's Dam in the years before the Red River Waterway Commission deepened the channel. All of the laborious effort was done under Bailey's direction and to his specification.

African-American soldiers provided the bulk of this labor, done over the first two weeks of May. Measurements would be taken daily, and when it was clear the dam was working, Bailey could claim his place as one of America's great military engineers. A crowd of spectators gathered on the levee waiting to see the gunboats pass. In preparation, General McMillian gave instructions to lighten the gunboats: "Fling overboard every d— pound of cotton, and fling the d— proprietors over after it!"[42] When the day arrived, the gunboats slid passed the falls with relative ease. Admiral Porter could not say enough about Bailey:

> He has saved to the Union a valuable fleet, worth nearly $2,000,000; more, he has deprived the enemy of a triumph that would have emboldened them to carry on this war a year or two longer, for the intended departure of the army

was a fixed fact, and there was nothing left for me to do in case that event occurred but destroy every part of the vessels, so that the rebels could make nothing of them. The highest honors the Government can bestow upon Colonel Bailey can never repay him for the service he has rendered the country.[43]

The regular gunfire from Union pickets outside the city reminded Union officers that although the fleet was free, the army remained in a precarious situation. If Taylor possessed more men, Banks might have been in a worse situation. The Southern manpower deficit that had haunted nearly every aspect of the Confederate war effort in the Trans-Mississippi placed Confederate operations here at a distinct disadvantage. The Union army packed up and made preparations to leave the city.

On May 13th, 1864, around 8 a.m., about an hour after the front of the columns of the Union soldiers left town, a new tragedy unfolded in Alexandria. A fire began near the Ice House Hotel, at a point where Bayou Rapides still empties into the Red River. The smoke and flames spread quickly. Union soldiers set the fire at that particular spot because of the wind direction that morning. The object was to inflict as much damage as possible. A Confederate reported, "The Yankees left Alexandria about May [13], after burning two-thirds of the town. Whether it was their intention to burn the whole place, or only some of the public building, warehouses, &c., does not clearly appear. The wind was very high and the fire could not be managed. A considerable quantity of stores was destroyed."[44]

Recent examination of the documents and a post-war map of the town by the late historian James G. Hollandsworth, Jr., has pointed to an "orchestrated arson."[45] The soldiers laid turpentine-soaked rags and

Admiral Porter's gunboats escape through Joseph Bailey's ingenious dam (*Heritage of Valor*, Louisiana State Archives).

other combustibles on fences and threw them inside of buildings. The fire had been set at a hotel on the northwestern edge of town to take advantage of the prevailing winds that morning. An eye-witness at the time ascribed the fire to "men belonging to General Andrew J. Smith's command." Another made it clear that "the burning and plundering was the work of the 16th and 17th Army Corps, composed exclusively of Northwestern men." The Unionist Dennis Haynes rode into town later that evening to see his family before riding south with the army. "The town was on fire, and nearly all burned—all the front portion of it, lying on the river." The tragedy had to be "the work of several persons."[46]

Although no order had been issued to fire the town, and Union General Nathaniel Banks covered himself by writing protection orders for the town, he never took steps to enforce his wishes or punish those responsible. A few Union officers tried to help civilians. Charles Reed of the 3rd Massachusetts Cavalry ordered a squad to grab blankets, soak them with water, and climb up on the roof of a home in danger of the advancing flames. A woman and her daughter, the only ones living there at the time, needed assistance. Other men went from room to room and carried all their possessions outside and into a vacant lot adjacent to the dwelling. The items included a very heavy piano requiring several strong backs. These kind souls exhibited the characteristics of "Christian people and native gentlemen" a witness testified.[47]

Other soldiers were not as Christian. A few of them approached the town's Catholic Church clutching their torches. The priest in charge, Father J. B. Bellier, was not about to let his beloved house of worship become the next victim. He placed himself at the front door, so the legend goes, holding a sword or a brace of pistols, and dared the soldiers to enter. Little did they know, the native Frenchman had been in his country's cavalry before taking vows and leaving for America. The arsonists would have to come through him, if they wanted to set a fire. Another account says that he impersonated General Banks himself and ordered the soldiers away. In either case, the priest saved the building. Most churches were not so blessed, and the fire consumed several others on its unrelenting march through the main streets of Alexandria.[48]

The flames carried the destruction across the entire length of the community. Most tragic for the legal community and historians ever since, the courthouse and all its vital records burned to the ground. The parish's original property transactions, plats, criminal proceedings, and probate records became lost to history.[49] All total, twenty-one blocks, or nearly one-half of the town, consisting of businesses and residences would be flattened into a smoldering ruin. Only a few clusters of buildings located in the extreme north and very south end of the city escaped total loss.[50]

An Iowa Soldier of the 27th Iowa who took part in the arson justified his actions:

> Of course, there was no apology for the incendiary—nor is there much sympathy in the army for the citizens. They have brought, by their rebellion, an army into their midst, and they must expect not only to submit to the proper and authorized results of military occupation, but also to suffer from unmilitary, unauthorized and wanton acts of those bad men who are to be found in every army. As to making war upon women and children, the only question in my mind as to whether it is most proper to shoot the rebel father and husband, or to burn down the shelter of his family, is one of policy. If, by the latter course, he could be induced for a brief season to forego the exercise of his amiable intention to kill me, and devote his little furlough to the reinstatement of his household goods, I am almost certain that I should incline to the incendiary policy.[51]

The ashes left at Alexandria reflected a darkness that fell over all the commanders and combatants. A whole city had been torched by those who were frustrated, angry, and indifferent. From greed to fear to revenge, the range of emotions among the soldiers in the Union army moved inevitably towards this fire.

Upon learning the news of the town's burning, a jaded Confederate soldier who believed he had seen it all still expressed astonishment: "I do not believe none but a black heart would be guilty of such deeds!" He thought the burning of a city containing four to five thousand inhabitants, mostly women and children along with refugees from fighting in the countryside, to be a most heinous crime. "Burning the property of citizens is savagism," he avowed.[52] The governor, Henry W. Allen, expressed similar outrage at the destruction. He called it, "one of the most brutal and diabolical acts of this wicked war."[53] He promised an investigation that would bring out every detail of what had happened.

True to the governor's words, Thomas C. Manning, Secessionist and advisor to two Louisiana governors, collected depositions and published them in 1865 as *The Conduct of Federal Troops in Louisiana*. This publication appeared in print using the very limited ink and paper the state possessed during the last months of the war.[54] The document presented heart-wrenching stories of the destruction that affected several of the Red's parishes. Because of its combative tone, the publication could be classified as propaganda, yet upon close examination, the pages contained special value as micro-history. The details in the testimony collected delivered insights not to be found anywhere else. At the very least, the anger that flows from every one of its pages confirmed beyond the shadow of a doubt the deep pain of civilians caught in war's fury.

As Union and Confederate armies tramped south of Alexandria, the destruction continued, and the two armies played a deadly game of cat and mouse. A Texan of German descent remarked that "the Feds take away the best Negroes and mules, and now the remaining grain is set on fire, our troops break open the sugarhouses and destroy more than they eat. This area is being completely devastated."[55] The armies arrived in Avoyelles Parish where two final battles took place. The encounters at Mansura and Yellow Bayou illustrated how the Civil War in the Trans-Mississippi had shifted from Napoleonic maneuver to the "attack and die" charges of World War I battlefields.[56]

In the flat bayou country of the parish, the roads proved to be little more than "a wilderness, most of the way through the pine woods, up and down short hills, sandy, rutty, rooty, stumpy, gullied—in short combining all the conditions of meaness that could possibly pertain to a road."[57] On May 16, Banks' retreating brigades encountered General Taylor's Confederates outside of Mansura, a tiny village located on the flat expanse of the Avoyelles Prairie. Taylor's lighter and smaller regiments had managed to squeeze between the Union forces and the roads leading to the steamboat landing at Simmsport. The Federals would have to push aside the Confederates. A visitor four years before described the Avoyelles Prairie as "elevated at 65 feet above the Red River and grass lands with dotted patches of trees and homesteads. 10–12 miles long and 5 to 7 wide."[58]

Before sunrise, Taylor had formed a line reaching across the landscape for about 1,000 yards. Generals Arthur P. Bagby and James P. Major, in command of Texas dismounted cavalry, formed up on the right with nineteen cannon, while Major General Polignac's infantry, with another thirteen guns, stood on the left. Taylor boasted to Colonel S.S. Anderson of the Trans-Mississippi Department, "The broad open prairie, smooth as a billiard table, afforded an admirable field for artillery practice and most of our guns were 3-inch rifle and 10-pounder Parrots captured from the enemy."[59]

The battle opened when Confederate artillery threw their deadly missiles across the battlefield at Union lines. For the next four hours, the Union responded with their own guns and a long range artillery duel caused the loud echo of thunder to shake the prairie. A 4th Texas cavalryman reported that, between the two sides, the shock waves made him estimate that at least 100 pieces participated in one of the largest artillery fights in the Trans-Mississippi. "The boys describe it as the most terrific bombardment they had ever been in and if you can imagine skirmishing with fifty guns on a side firing all as fast as they could load and fire you can form an idea."[60]

Much to the relief of those who dodged the incoming rounds, the engagement proved to be a relatively bloodless affair. Confederate Major Thomas A. Faries described how "[t]he enemy fired 3-inch, 12-pounder, and 20-pounder rifles, also 30-pounder Parrot shot and shell, with rapidity and with more accuracy than I have before observed, the most of his shot and shell falling in and near the batteries, but few of his shell exploding, however, that accounts for so few casualties."[61]

At 10 a.m., Union reinforcements arrived from the 16th Corps, raising the Union troop count of 10,000 on scene to more than 18,000 men. Realizing the overwhelming odds against his 5,000 battered veterans, Taylor withdrew as the Union divisions began massing for an attack.[62] The Confederates conducted an orderly withdrawal southwest toward the settlement of Evergreen. Union General William Emory complimented the 19th Corps: "At Mansura, on the 16th of May, you met the enemy on an open plane, and, supported on your right by the Sixteenth Army Corps and Colonel Lucas' cavalry, drove him from the field."[63] The Confederates expressed equal satisfaction at their performance. Major Faries wrote, "The officers and men of all the batteries behaved with the most becoming coolness and gallantry and retired when directed in perfect order."[64] The tone of the officers' words harked back to the honor and formality of past warfare.

Confederates had managed to slow, yet not stop, the Union retreat. Similar to the battle at Cane River Crossing, the Confederates did not possess enough men to successfully halt Union movements. An ambush attack on the 92nd USCT regiment failed due to the determination of that unit. Instead of being trapped, helpless, and passive, the black soldiers stepped up and defended the wagon train they were guarding. Although armed with Springfield smooth-bore muskets "of very inferior and defective quality," they confronted their attackers without hesitation. Similar to the fights at Milliken's Bend or Port Hudson in 1863, the 92nd acquitted themselves well. "I must say that their conduct," Lt. Colonel John C. Chadwick, a white officer of the unit wrote, "was as good as that of any troops. There were instances of cool courage and determined bravery." The men lost two killed, four wounded, and six missing.[65]

As the rear guard actions continued, the head of the Union column arrived at Simmsport. The commanders ordered the men to dig in and put up a defensive perimeter as they awaited transport across the swollen Atchafalaya River. The Mississippi had reached spring flood stage, as was normal for May, and the tributaries near the confluence of the Red, Atchafalaya, and Mississippi began to rise. Pontoon bridges that would work on any other river were useless against the wider, stronger current. To ferry thousands of men and supplies across under these conditions might take weeks.[66]

Again, the generals turned to Lt. Col. Joseph Bailey, whose dam saved the navy at Alexandria. Now, he sprang into action for a second time. He came up with the ingenious solution of lashing steamboats together side by side and having them push against the current with their engines. Then he connected their decks with planks that covered the gaps between them. From boat to boat, the infantry scurried across and also hauled its artillery and supplies until everyone arrived safely on the other side. Given the dangerous current and distance, a big solution was called for and Bailey again proved his knack for problem solving and the resiliency of the Union army in tough situations.[67]

Hovering outside the Union's hastily dug entrenchments, and only a few miles away at the Norwood plantation on Yellow Bayou, the Confederates watched and waited. General Taylor possessed one infantry division, some cavalry and artillery, still only enough to harass Banks. General A.J. Smith spotted Taylor's men and wanted to buy time for Bailey's latest project. He could not let a Confederate force remain untouched so close to Union lines. Three brigades made a reconnaissance in force in their direction. When lead elements of the 4,500 man force crossed the tepid waters of Yellow Bayou, they stumbled upon Confederate pickets two miles beyond.

Instead of waiting for the Union forces to strike first, the Confederate infantry of Polignac's Louisiana and Texas brigade advanced and opened an attack. Their commanders planned a drive that might push the blue coats into Yellow Bayou. With courage and determination, the Union soldiers endured tremendous punishment. The 95th Illinois infantry reported being caught in "one of the severest fires of artillery it ever experienced in a field fight."[68] As the two sides blazed away, casualties began to mount and bodies littered the field. After several failed attempts to dislodge their foe, General John A. Wharton, Confederate cavalry commander, ordered his subordinate, William Parsons, forward for another attempt. By this point, it was painfully obvious he faced a stubborn foe. At first, Parsons did not comply. He knew another attack would be suicide. When ordered a second time he remarked, "If I must, I must."[69] Into the fray the dismounted troopers plunged, many never to return to their own lines again. During their failed attempt, the unit lost twelve killed, sixty-seven wounded, and two missing. May 18 became the single worst day for the unit during the entire Civil War. Parson's hesitancy when given a direct order illustrated that he saw no point in sacrificing good men in a charge that would accomplish little.[70]

A Texas soldier remembered crossing over a mile of ground in the face of twelve to fourteen pieces of artillery in an attempt to get close enough to the batteries to drive the gunners from their posts with musket fire. Dark blue ranks of infantry, three deep, advanced upon them and forced a retreat. "Our loss heavy to day—nearly 600 killed, wounded, & captured," he reported. Once the battled ended, the Texan noticed that unlike other fights, his fellow fighters appeared different. "Men & horses completely broken down. Don't look like themselves." A Union officer found that the ferocity of the battle surprised him. "I never heard such volley of musketry and the cannonading was very heavy."[71]

The desperate fighting continued until a brush fire ignited by gunpowder blasts threatened to burn the wounded lying on the field. The slaughter halted so each side might collect their disabled men. When the truce came, parts of the battlefield gave the appearance of a charged, lunar landscape. In other places, the mangled bodies of the dead and wounded littered the ground clustered in groups where they fell together. General Joseph Mower, the Union general at Yellow Bayou, who could have advanced and hit Taylor's men again, stood fast and did not press his successful defense. He withdrew back to the rest of the army. The sharp fight at Yellow Bayou saw over 350 Union soldiers killed and wounded. The Confederate losses from the ill-fated charge, as the Texas soldier recorded, exceeded 600 killed, wounded, and captured.[72]

The large number of wounded overwhelmed the local capacity to house and care for all those requiring immediate care. At make-shift hospitals in buildings on plantations and farmsteads, women became nurses for the injured and dying. A house in Evergreen, over twenty miles away, became a hospital ward and the site of one of the most haunting reminders of the war's tragedy. The nurses lined up beds against a white-washed wall. Bandaged, bloody, and broken soldiers rested side by side there. An unknown Confederate lying in one bed took a pencil, reached over to the wall and scrawled in dozens of lines, in every space he could reach, "I will not die. I will not die. I will not die." The writing remained visible well into the 20th century.[73]

The carnage at Yellow Bayou anticipated the forthcoming battles of 1864. In Virginia and Georgia, terrible assaults at the Wilderness, Cold Harbor, and Kennesaw Mountain accomplished little, and wasted the lives of good men. Major Silas T. Grisamore, who served with the 18th Louisiana, could only express disgust following the two hours of fighting. He wrote, "The whole affair was unnecessary and utterly barren in its results."[74]

The Battle of Yellow Bayou demonstrated that General Taylor could not trap, stop or inflict great damage on the Union force; he could only annoy and harass them. A much larger army would be required to do real damage. Had he retained the divisions withdrawn by General Kirby Smith for service in Arkansas, he still could not have matched the numbers and determination of the Yankee army. Northern soldiers, black and white, proved a tenacious bunch. Engaged on an open battlefield, the Union army could put up a successful defense and inflict significant casualties. The destruction of property and loss of lives on battlefields continued unabated so long as Taylor and Banks remained locked in struggle in Central Louisiana. Yet the Confederates had driven an army and navy out of the heartland of Louisiana.

Conclusion

Forty years following the end of the military actions along the Red, and a few years into the 20th century, Lieutenant Colonel Lucius Hubbard, a brigade commander for the Union, looked back and called the campaign a "conspicuous failure."[1] The military losses amounted to 4,600 men killed, wounded, and captured for his side. The Confederates lost nearly the same. If the large number of soldiers captured at Fort DeRussy and Henderson Hill at the campaign's start are counted in the total figure, Confederate losses rose over 5,300 killed, wounded, and captured.[2] Even before the last shots had been fired, leaders in Washington knew the whole operation had been a fiasco. An emissary from Washington, D.C., left for the scene in late April, carrying important dispatches. Major General David Hunter traveled a great distance with news that General Ulysses S. Grant had been given command over all of President Lincoln's armies. Once on the Red, Hunter thought the Union's defeat arose from "cotton and politics."[3]

General Banks had emphasized political goals and failed at his military ones. The results were nearly predictable: another major disaster for the Union cause. General William T. Sherman, who had lived in Pineville before the war, used more colorful language: "One damn blunder from beginning to end," he remarked.[4] It was 1864 and too far along in the war for failures such as this one. Red River looked more like an 1862 debacle than the spring 1864 defeat that it was. "I hope such mistakes will not cover our army again with misfortune but I hope our Genls, our armies and our people will look to God & trust in him to give us victory," a Union soldier wrote.[5]

Leaders in Washington wanted to make sure Banks had made his final mistake. General Grant informed him that General Edward R.S. Canby had been given charge of a newly-created department, the

Military Division of West Mississippi. That re-organization elevated Canby over the Department of the Gulf, and General Banks found himself out of a command. He spent the next year trying to work political connections for reinstatement, all to no avail. At war's end, Banks returned to Massachusetts where he won election to Congress, and there he remained, one election after another, until his death in 1894.[6]

In the immediate aftermath of the campaign, the U.S. Congress launched an investigation. For months, the Joint Committee on the Conduct of the War took testimony.[7] Generals Banks, Franklin, Smith, and Emory, Admiral Porter, and lesser ranking officers, paraded in front of the committee. Already Radical Republicans and their moderate opponents sparred on the particulars of what caused the grand failure and who was to blame. General Banks and the Lincoln administration received the most attention. The final report, that ran hundreds of pages, became an important historical document. Throughout its pages, a reader finds explanations and justifications of those Union men involved in the campaign. Rather than a careful expose of what went wrong and how to fix things, the report did a better job at preservation of the reflections of its commanders.

In the parishes along the Red's banks, far from the halls of Congress, the impact of the campaign could be felt in every household. The Red River's enslaved people faced the most uncertainty. Those who had escaped and run to the Union army or navy were free unless they did not make it to Morganza where the army camped in the months following the expedition. These people in between slavery and freedom found themselves running and hiding from patrols. For months after the campaign, runaways would be hunted down and returned to their masters. An Alexandria newspaper reported that a slave who had gone with the Union army returned over a year later, malnourished and clothed the same way as when he left. "This is Yankee freedom and philanthropy with a vengeance," the editor smacked.[8]

William Smith, who had run away from a Prudhomme plantation along the Cane River, became one of those people who lost his bid for freedom. He had escaped and joined the 99th USCT engineering regiment at Alexandria. He assisted in the construction of Bailey's Dam and endured days and days of hard labor. His effort exhausted him, and he fell ill. Too sick to move, Smith had to be left behind as the army evacuated Alexandria. When he tried to catch up, a vigilant patrol captured him. The patrol carried him back to the plantation on Cane River. In summer 1865, when war's end brought real freedom, he left the master's neighborhood and enlisted with the U.S. army as a "Buffalo Soldier," as blacks were called in the service. He never returned to Louisiana, preferring instead the military to sharecropping on the master's old place.[9]

For white civilians, recovery would take years and sometimes decades. Planters and farmers threw all they had into cotton or sugar cane production. Cotton, that had caused greed and destruction for the valley, came to be relied upon for redemption. Wealth that had been built up for generations disappeared. Plantations and farmsteads in Natchitoches and Rapides Parishes, especially, had been made into smoldering sentinels of war. "The people in the interior are in many places in the most destitute and starving condition. There will be untold suffering, both among the white and black population, unless some relief is afforded," a St. Louis newspaper reported.[10] In June of 1864, one resident complained that Confederate money provided no hope as it "was worthless.[11] Governor Henry Watkins Allen contacted a state senator about conditions across the region and concluded, "God help the suffering people of Rapides." He promised to do everything in his power to get needed supplies down the river from Shreveport to stave off starvation.[12]

In the years following the war, the United States Congress established a claims commission for war damages of loyal citizens. Unionists who could prove a loss might receive compensation. The established rules included strict requirements. One had to prove that he never served in the Confederate army nor aided the Southern cause in any way. Losses caused by Confederate armies or loss of slaves were not valid either. The losses inflicted by Union forces had to be established using legal rules of evidence. Sworn testimony was required, and the government pursued its own independent investigation. The government sent special agents out and gathered their own depositions in hopes of denying fraudulent or faulty claims. Southern claimants in Avoyelles, Caddo, Desoto, Natchitoches, Rapides, and Winn parishes filed 116 requests for compensation. The lion's share, not surprisingly, originated from Rapides and Natchitoches parishes. Only a handful of were lodged from Avoyelles, Caddo, Desoto, and Winn parishes. From an examination of the 116 filings, the majority were for food, quartermaster supplies, horses, livestock, cotton, sugar, molasses, dwelling houses, and personal items such as furniture and books.[13]

A few claims from Rapides Parish are illustrative. May M. Barlow asked for $9,999.00, the value of sixty-five bales of cotton that "were used in the building of 'Bailey's Dam.'" The government denied the claim on a technicality. "This was use of a property not coming within the terms of the act of Congress, the cotton not being 'stores and supplies' in the sense of the act, but property taken in the course of and for the purpose of military operations." Louisa Schrader, a widow of Pineville, asked for $2,100 to cover a house, stable, outbuilding, fencing, ten cows, and a few beef cattle. She and her husband had boarded a naval transport for New Orleans a few days before the army left Alexandria. He worked as a carpenter in the city. She would also be turned away without any compensation. "Aside from the claimant's assertion of her loyalty to the Union cause there is literally no evidence whatever to establish that important fact."[14]

Landry Baillio, an old French Creole cotton planter living twelve miles south of Alexandria found he was caught by the same problem. He filled out the paperwork for $9,329 and asserted, "I took no part, and never expressed myself; I never cast my vote for secession; I remained neutral." A government agent collected evidence and discovered his two sons fought for the Confederacy, and he "was never threatened, molested, or injured on account of his Union sentiments." The most damning material appeared in two depositions, one from James Madison Wells, and the other from A. H. Mason, a Confederate quartermaster who had bought supplies from planters in Rapides Parish. "From their statement it is very certain Mr. Baillio was not in sympathy with the Union cause." Baillio lost; his plea was denied.[15]

Charles W. Boyce, the pre-war Unionist editor, and his father Judge Henry Boyce asked for a combined total of nearly $40,000. Damage to dwelling houses, a store house, horses, mules, fencing, quartermaster supplies, and a number of other items rounded out their list of things damaged or lost. The government found that, in the case of Charles, "there is proof to show that he opposed secession and was then regarded as a Union man, but the proof of his subsequent disloyalty is conclusive. He became a lieutenant in the confederate army." A modern database turned up a service record where Charles's name was put on the rolls of a Confederate unit. The staunch Union man had buckled during the war and gone over to the Confederacy. A special agent learned his father "voluntarily furnished supplies to that army and was in full sympathy with the confederate cause." The commission ruled: "The claim is disallowed."[16]

The case of Whitty M. Sasser became one of the most complicated ever considered, and with its conflicting testimony, it filled nearly two big pages in the claims commission report. At the time, most entries contained a paragraph or only slightly more. Sasser, a well-connected planter in Rapides Parish, contested his claim in 1873, had it denied, and unlike most others, managed to have it referred back to the commission for a second review in 1874. He demanded the astronomical sum of $100,498.14. The large amount might explain why he contested the case for so long and how he brought in so many witnesses.

His inventory of losses included, among other things, 20,678 bushels of corn, 4.5 tons of fodder, 162 horses and mules, 26 cords of wood, two farm wagons, and 10.5 miles of rail and board fencing. The claim hinged on Mr. Sasser's loyalty. The government sent Enos Richmond, special agent, to take depositions. He learned that Sasser had been a Whig until President Buchanan's election in 1856, and then he became a Democrat. In 1864 when General Banks arrived in Alexandria, Sasser took the Oath of Allegiance and presided over a Union meeting that elected delegates to the Reconstruction Constitutional Convention. Following the Union retreat, Confederates arrested him and placed him in a Shreveport jail for disloyalty to the Confederacy. William Levy, a Congressman who had been on Taylor's staff, confirmed these facts and claimed that during the war Sasser refused to sell supplies to Confederate armies.[17]

Richmond spoke with a number of men in Rapides Parish. His investigation proved that Sasser had been a Unionist in spring of 1864. Before that, however, he had been a full-fledged Confederate. A number of witnesses testified to his Southern sympathy. William W. Whittington told Agent Richmond that he "lived within a mile and a half of Sasser and have known him since 1838; had frequent conversations with him with regard to the war." In the course of conversations, "he was regarded friendly to the confederate cause; talked very often as a friend of the cause. Some times when he had been drinking, he was pretty wordy on this subject." Documentary evidence showed that Sasser had sold cotton to the Confederate cotton bureau, and for $100 a month, for nearly two years, he had kept cattle for the Confederate quartermaster. Josiah Bailey, who had been a slave of Mr. Sasser's during the war, gave the most damaging testimony: "My master, Mr. Sasser, was and always claimed to be a rebel during the war up to the time General Banks came to Alexandria; then he changed to that of a Union man." With his loyalty in question, Sasser lost his claim.[18] Only a small fraction of those who filed claims ever received any money from the United States government.

Conclusion

Citizens of Britain and France who made Central Louisiana their home and who suffered losses from the Union army received their own international claims commissions.[19] The British one met from 1871 to 1873. Only eight British subjects filed for damages incurred during the Red River campaign. All but one lived in Rapides Parish. Sixty-two percent of the claims were accepted for payment. The largest reported losses were from theft or destruction of horses, wagons, and cotton. A few claimants found their gold and personal items missing once Union troops had left the area. The Queen's subject with the largest claim, Samuel Simpson, asked for $80,178.74. He had watched helplessly as cotton bales he had secured for transport out of the region became confiscated by Federals. Simpson appeared to have a great case until he presented safe-passes from both the Confederate and Union authorities. His cotton speculation in Texas, Louisiana, and Mexico with Confederate agents doomed his claim. The United States refused to allow anyone who traded with the enemy to receive compensation. A few other claims were rejected due to the British subjects aiding the Confederates through trade or serving in their armed forces.

For French citizens, their commission was not established until 1880, and it met until 1884.[20] During this time, the three-member commission looked at forty-five claims from the Red River campaign. The bulk of them came from Natchitoches and Avoyelles parishes. Similar to the British, the damages had been from the loss of horses, wagons, and cotton. Personal items, mostly poultry and livestock, rounded out the list. Significantly, twenty percent of the Frenchmen claimed loss of dwellings that was higher than the British, who mostly lost other assets. A cook, tavern owner, and businessman Louis Paul Cayer of Mansura forfeited his claim when he turned in an inventory of possessions prior to his loss of supplies. The inventory included one slave. French law from 1848 forbid its citizens anywhere in the world from purchasing or possessing slaves. The penalty for the infraction meant loss of citizenship. Without citizenship, the claim could not be honored. The commission disallowed 74 percent of the cases presented before it. Unlike the British who paid the majority of their claimants, the French commission and the United States claims commission struck down far more claims than they paid.

When Confederates retained control over the Red River, Unionists found themselves in a most precarious position. Over 1,500 Confederates had taken the United States' oath in March and early April when all believed the Star Spangled Banner had come to stay.[21] Many of these people had been Unionists going back to the 1860 election or the Secession crisis. Others had taken the oath to protect their property or for political advantage. Both John Elgee and Lewis Texada had been prewar politicians who took the oath and were courted by the new regime. Unionist Lieutenant Governor James Madison Wells had asserted at the time that "the protecting shield of the Federal Government had been permanently thrown around them...." These words, written in a letter, ironically, on the 8th of April, proved only illusionary. It was a mirage that evaporated in the heat of the battle of Mansfield fought that very day. The victorious Confederates took a dim view of those who pledged loyalty. A Texas refugee wrote to former governor Thomas Overton Moore, "I rejoice to hear that Mrs. Moore did not take the oath and much regret to hear that so many of the citizens of Rapides have taken it." He believed, "We cannot know when to put confidence in those that have taken the Yanky oath."[22]

Those who had cooperated as soldiers in the Union army faced charges of treason. What could happen to those who served was reported in a New Orleans newspaper. In early May 1864, a band of Unionist French Creoles in Avoyelles Parish armed themselves and went looking for recruits. The Captain, F. W. Masters, and a Lt. Cease rested with ten other men at a vacant house one night. During the wee hours of the morning, all twelve of them were surprised and overtaken by a Confederate patrol. One man escaped into the night and two others were only young boys who lived nearby. After a neighbor interceded on their behalf, they were released from custody. The rest, all nine, the article stated, were stripped naked, lined up, and shot dead at 9 a.m. the next morning. This terrible act of retribution outraged Unionists who called for "vengeance," the newspaper declared.[23]

Despite defeat in the military campaign, Unionists kept their faith and admired General Banks for his commitment to them. In December of 1864, a group of them from Central Louisiana wrote to President Lincoln praising the general: "By his noble, just and upright policy more than three fourths of the voting and producing portions of Louisiana are now as loyal as the State of Illinois—."[24] They applauded his commitment to ending slavery and setting up government plantations. "He has solved the problem of what we shall do with the freedmen and has pointed out how they can be profitably used in the development of the agricultural resources of the country & at the same time lifting them from the danger of falling into a state of destitution & want & at the same time has set in operation a system that in time must elevate them in the scale of civilization."[25] Lastly they applauded his recruitment of Unionists:

> He has by his wise & equitable course enlisted under the Union banners ten thousand whites and more than fifteen thousand of the colored population—by him the Union man has been strengthened—the doubtful have been confirmed & won to the Union and hundreds of the erring have been won back to their true allegiance.[26]

In their mind, Banks deserved accolades for what he had tried to do, those political objectives for the campaign, and not for his failure in military matters.

The Unionists then reported on their desperate circumstances. "I have seen hundreds, who have been in the Red River country, since the withdrawal of Gen Banks and the vials of Confederate wrath have been poured upon those who were seduced into open & manifest efforts, of co-operation, believing they would be protected." The numbers, they believed, were large. "Hundreds & hundreds of the friends of the President & the Union, have been reduced to beggary. They cannot get away—all they can hope for is from the lands they live on. The enemy have no supplies to give—and these people must starve if their friends in [New Orleans] will not be allowed to send them food."[27]

The Unionist scout Dennis Haynes confirmed what the others had put in writing. He related how Confederate General Richard Taylor expelled families of Union men from their homes. Women and children left for Union lines south and east of the Red River. The Confederate army confiscated their property and, in some cases, burned down existing homes. "They did the work of destruction with celerity and cheerfulness," Haynes related. Conscript hunters such as "Bloody Bob," and regular army units, patrolled Rapides and Sabine parishes looking for any remaining scouts hiding out in the woods. "Not a Union man that stayed at home, and was caught, but was 'shot with bullets as thick as they could stick in him.'" His people, the loyal Unionists, became pitiful, starving refugees.[28]

President Lincoln learned of their plight from an army general. He contacted the authorities at New Orleans and asked that the army help. The people, the President wrote "are in great destitution—almost absolute starvation—their condition is greatly aggravated by Gen. Banks' expedition up Red-River, last Spring, in reliance upon that they mostly took the oath of allegiance—Of course what Gen. Bailey asks is permission to carry provisions to them" he explained. "Do for them the best you can, consistently with the interests of the public service."[29]

The battles along the Red River would be Louisiana's last Civil War campaign. For General Richard Taylor, he would be voted the thanks of the Confederate Congress. Instead of celebration and toasts, he and General Kirby Smith traded barbs as arguments and accusations flew. Smith was unwilling to give any ground, he remained generous and composed in his responses, and finally he accepted Taylor's resignation.[30] The Confederate Congress in the meantime promoted Taylor to Lieutenant General and gave him a department command. The Alabama, Mississippi, and East Louisiana post moved him to an unimportant spot out of Louisiana and east of the Mississippi River. About the time he assumed command, Mobile, Alabama, fell to the Union navy. After war's end, he became a Democratic Party insider and died in 1879, the same year he published his influential memoirs.[31]

In the post-war years, Taylor's rival, General Kirby Smith, became president of a telegraph company and then served as an administrator or professor at academic institutions in Tennessee until his death in 1893.[32] One of the most lasting of Smith's legacies would be his unwavering commitment to a fortified defense of the Red River. The victory at Mansfield, and his wrangling with Taylor, did nothing to change his mind. With Taylor gone, no one was in his way to oppose his strategy. In the summer of 1864, his engineers devised additional plans to stop future Union advances up the Red River.

Better forts would do the job. Fort DeRussy had been on low ground and easily surrounded by a Union landing party. Two new fortifications farther up the river rose on the high ground opposite Alexandria. Engineers Christopher Meyer Randolph and Alphonse Buhlow oversaw the construction of dirt, stone, and timber walls, and gun emplacements for eight pieces of artillery at each fort. Most notable were the large bombproofs built to withstand heavy naval guns. Soldiers from parole camps around Pineville and conscripted slaves went to work through the fall and early winter. Forts Randolph and Buhlow, whose remains are still visible today, became central to Smith's deterrence strategy. Although small, undermanned, and both praised and lampooned by Union and Confederates who saw them, their presence fulfilled a need to defend the Red. While the Mansfield battle has loomed large and Taylor's reputation became enshrined in the Lost Cause, Smith's engineering defense and able administration should be held in as high a regard.[33]

Because the Union army and navy did not return to the Red River in fall of 1864 or spring of 1865, a lull ensued in the region for thirteen long months. Union planners elected to pursue the capture of Mobile, Alabama, and that campaign went forward in August 1864.[34] The Trans-Mississippi department short on men and materials languished without any major activity until word of surrenders in the East prompted their own capitulation. On June 2, 1865, General Kirby Smith surrendered the last major department command of the Confederacy.[35] The 1864 victory in the Red River campaign, while notable in military terms and a source of pride, amounted to not much more than that. It did not help the South win the war, and if it extended the conflict, it was only for a short time. Its most far-reaching effect was to cement a strong Confederate ethos in North Louisiana. The Southern families who endured the campaign and suffered its consequences remained "unvanquished" as William Faulkner might have written. Their side had won and they never forgot it.

The Confederates vowed to win the peace. Freedom that came for African-Americans in 1865 became short-lived in the murky social, economic, and political questions of how to rebuild a society based upon labor-intensive cotton-sugar cane cultivation. The Confederate victory in Red River made Louisiana's Reconstruction more difficult, violent, and perhaps doomed from the start. The ten-year history following the Civil War witnessed incredible violence along the Red. Two bloody massacres of freedmen took place near where Union and Confederate armies had clashed. At Colfax named for the Republican vice-president, of the United States in the newly formed Grant Parish, named after the Union general and president, white Democrats ended Republican rule with violence. A second clash took place at Coushatta in newly formed Red River Parish in 1874.[36] Politics, Unionism, black equality, all became combustible fuel for intense conflict. What had been a stable agricultural economy, a growing and prospering place, descended into murky uncertainty. Wounds from the war and the trials of Reconstruction surfaced in the region from time to time over the decades since and continue over 150 years later.

Chapter Notes

Preface

1. Gary D. Joiner, *Through the Howling Wilderness: The Red River Campaign and Union Failure in the West* (Knoxville: University of Tennessee Press, 2006), introduction.
2. Gary D. Joiner, *Lincoln's Brown Water Navy* (New York: Rowman & Littlefield, 2007), 155.
3. *Ibid.*, 156–157.
4. Ezra J. Warner, *Generals in Gray* (Baton Rouge: Louisiana State University Press, 1959), 117.
5. George P. Lord to Admiral David Porter, May 8, 1864 in United States, Naval War Records Office, *Official Records of the Union and Confederate Navies in the War of the Rebellion*, series 1, vol. 26: 112.
6. James G. Hollandsworth, Jr., "Preparing the Place for Hell: The Burning of Alexandria in 1864," *Louisiana Cultural Vistas* (Spring 2008): 22–29.
7. Joiner, *Through the Howling Wilderness*, 300.
8. Ludwell H. Johnson, *Red River Campaign: Politics and Cotton in the Civil War* (Baltimore: Johns Hopkins University Press, 1958).
9. John Winters, *The Civil War in Louisiana* (Baton Rouge: Louisiana State University Press, 1963).
10. Shelby Foote, *The Civil War: A Narrative Red River to Appomattox* vol. 3 (New York: Random House, 1974).
11. Gary D. Joiner made the first remark. Donald S. Frazier, "Geography Is Destiny: The Mouth of the Red River and the Fate of Confederate Louisiana," Civil War Sesquicentennial Commemoration, Marksville, LA May 31, 2013. Dr. Frazier claimed a Virginia scholar made the statement to him.
12. T. Michael Parrish, *Richard Taylor; Soldier Prince of Dixie* (Chapel Hill: University of North Carolina Press, 1992); James G. Hollandsworth, Jr., *Pretense of Glory: The Life of General Nathaniel P. Banks* (Baton Rouge: Louisiana State University Press, 1998).
13. Gary D. Joiner, *One Damn Blunder from Beginning to End: The Red River Campaign of 1864* (Lanham: Rowman & Littlefield, 2003).
14. Michael J. Forsyth, *The Red River Campaign of 1864 and the Loss by the Confederacy in the Civil War* (Jefferson, NC: McFarland Publishing, 2002).
15. Gary D. Joiner, *Little to Eat and Thin Mud to Drink* (Knoxville: University of Tennessee Press, 2007); *Through the Howling Wilderness: The 1864 Red River Campaign and Union Failure in the West* (Knoxville: University of Tennessee Press, 2006). For Joiner's preservation efforts, see http://friendsofmansfieldbattlefield.org/default.aspx and Deborah Fitts, "Satellite Photo Aids Mansfield Battlefield Supporters" *Civil War News*, May 2004, accessed May 12, 2012, http://www.civilwarnews.com/archive/articles/satphoto.htm.
16. Jeffery S. Prushankin, *A Crisis of Confederate Command: Edmund Kirby Smith, Richard Taylor, and the Army of the Trans-Mississippi* (Baton Rouge: Louisiana State University Press, 2005). Also see Dana M. Mangham, "Oh, for a Touch of the Vanished Hand": Discovering a Southern Family and the Civil War (Murfreesboro: Southern Heritage Press, 2000). Also see William R Brooksher, *War Along the Bayous: The 1864 Red River Campaign* (Washington: Brassey's 1998), Stephen G. Visco, *The Red River Campaign: An Analysis* (Carlisle Barracks: U.S. Army Military History Center 2001); Samuel W. Mitcham, Jr., *Richard Taylor and the Red River Campaign of 1864* (Gretna: Pelican Publishing, 2012).
17. Charles Royster, *The Destructive War* (New York: Alfred A. Knopf, 1991).
18. Daniel Sutherland, *Seasons of War: The Ordeal of the Confederate Community, 1861–1865* (New York: The Free Press, 1995); Daniel Sutherland, *The Emergence of Total War* (Buffalo Gap: State House Press, 1998); Sutherland, *Guerrillas, Unionists, and Violence on the*

Confederate Home Front (Fayetteville: University of Arkansas Press, 1999); Sutherland, *A Savage Conflict: The Decisive Role of Guerrillas in the American Civil War* (Chapel Hill: University of North Carolina Press, 2009).

Introduction

1. John H. Bering, and Thomas Montgomery, *History of the Forty-Eighth Ohio Vet. Vol. Inf.* (Hillsboro, OH: Highland News Office, 1880), accessed June 11, 2008, http://www.48ovvi.org/chap15.html.
2. Bennett Wall, ed. *Louisiana: A History* 5th ed. (Wheeling, IL: Harlan Davidson, 2008), 101–197.
3. *Ibid.*
4. John M. Sacher, *A Perfect War of Politics* (Baton Rouge: Louisiana State University Press, 2003), 259–301; Chester G. Hearn, *The Capture of New Orleans, 1862* (Baton Rouge; Louisiana State University Press, 1995).
5. John Winters, *The Civil War in Louisiana* (Baton Rouge: Louisiana State University Press, 1963), 152–153.
6. *Ibid.*, 113–124.
7. Ezra J. Warner, *Generals in Gray* (Baton Rouge: Louisiana State University Press, 1959), 300.
8. T. Michael Parrish, *Richard Taylor Soldier Prince of Dixie* (Chapel Hill: University of North Carolina Press, 1992), 344.
9. Arthur W. Bergeron, Jr. "General Richard Taylor as a Military Commander," In Arthur W. Bergeron Jr., ed. *The Louisiana Purchase Bicentennial Series in Louisiana History*, vol. 5, Part B. (Lafayette: Center for Louisiana Studies, 2004).
10. Richard Taylor, *Destruction and Reconstruction.* (Edinburgh: William Blackwood & Sons, 1879).
11. Moore to Jefferson Davis, December 26, 1863 quoted in Parrish, 315.
12. Ezra J. Warner, *Generals in Blue* (Baton Rouge: Louisiana State University Press, 1964), 18.
13. Winters, 226–229.
14. Donald S. Frazier, *Thunder Across the Swamp: The Fight for the Lower Mississippi, February-May, 1863* (Buffalo Gap, TX: State House Press), 275.
15. Winters, 235–238.
16. *Ibid.*, 242–281.
17. David C. Edmonds, *Yankee Autumn in Acadiana: A Narrative of the Great Texas Overland Expedition Through Southwestern Louisiana, October-December 1863* (Lafayette: Center for Louisiana Studies, 1979). Richard Lowe, *The Texas Overland Expedition of 1863* (Fort Worth: Ryan Place Publishers, 1996).
18. Gary D. Joiner, *Through the Howling Wilderness: The Red River Campaign and Union Failure in the West* (Knoxville: University of Tennessee Press, 2006), 15.
19. Winters, 325.
20. Gary D. Joiner, *One Damn Blunder from Beginning to End* (Lanham, MD: Rowman & Littlefield, 2003), 37.
21. Orders of battle and a list of naval vessels that participated can be found in appendices 1 and 2 of Gary D. Joiner, ed. *Little to Eat and Thin Mud to Drink* (Knoxville: University of Tennessee Press, 2007), 265–284.
22. Joiner, *One Damn Blunder*, 38–43.
23. United States. *Official Record War of the Rebellion*, series 1, vol. 22, part 2, 781–82. Hereafter cited as OR.
24. Warner, *Generals in Gray*, 279.
25. Paul Escott, *After Secession: Jefferson Davis and the Failure of Confederate Nationalism* (Baton Rouge: Louisiana State University Press, 1978), 282.
26. Edmund Kirby Smith, "The Defense of the Red River," *Battles and Leaders of the Civil War* vol. 4 (New York: The Century Co., 1884), 374.
27. Sarah A. Dorsey, *Recollections of Henry Watkins Allen* (New York: Doubleday 1866), 249–250. A historical marker stands at Smith's headquarters location near the Shreveport, LA Sci-Port science museum.
28. Joseph Howard Parks, *Edmund Kirby Smith, C.S.A.* (Baton Rouge: Louisiana State University Press, 1954).
29. Smith, "Defense," 369.
30. The discussion in this paragraph and the following one comes from reading Jeffery A. Prushankin, *A Crisis of Confederate Command: Edmund Kirby Smith, Richard Taylor, and the Army of the Trans-Mississippi* (Baton Rouge: Louisiana State University Press, 2005).
31. Joiner, *Through the Howling*, 41.
32. Steve Mayeaux, *Earthen Walls, Iron Men: Fort DeRussy, Louisiana, and the Defense of Red River.* (Knoxville: University of Tennessee Press, 2007).
33. *Ibid.*, Chapter 2.
34. *Ibid.*, Chapter 6.
35. Joiner, *One Damn Blunder*, 16–17; 24–27.
36. Lucius F. Hubbard "Civil War Papers," *Collections of the Minnesota Historical Society* vol. 12 (St. Paul n.p., 1908), 588.
37. General Kirby Smith to Lieutenant Marshall, March 18, 1864 in OR series 1, vol. 26, part 1, 164.
38. John Andrew Prime, "Shreveport's Civil War Defenses," accessed March 3, 2013, http://www.home.earthlink.net/~japrime/lagenweb/defenses.htm.
39. *Ibid.* Also see Joiner, *One Damn Blunder*, 26–29.
40. Joiner, *Mr. Lincoln's Brown Water Navy* (Latham, MD: Rowman & Littlefield, 2007),

93. Joiner *Through the Howling*, 22–23 and 41. National Underwater and Marine Agency, Inc., "2006 Magnetometer and Side-Scan Sonar Remote Sensing Survey For: Three Confederate Civil War Submarines, Cross Bayou, La.," accessed June 17, 2013, http://clivecusslershipwrecks.com/WordPress/NUMA/expeditions/confederate-submarines.
 41. Joiner, *One Damn Blunder*, 18 and 41.
 42. Taylor to General Camile Polignac quoted in Dorsey, 261.

Chapter One

 1. Darwin Spearing, *Roadside Geology of Louisiana* (Missoula: Mountain Press Publishing Co., 1995), 143; Carl Newton Tyson, *The Red River in Southwest History* (Norman: University of Oklahoma Press, 1981), 96.
 2. Quotations Harris H. Beecher, *Record of the 114th Regiment NYSV* (Norwich: J.F Hubbard, 1866), 299–300. Hubert Davis Humphreys, "The 'Great Raft' of the Red River," in B.H. Gilley, ed. *North Louisiana: Essays on the Region and Its History*, vol. 1 (Ruston, LA: Louisiana Tech University, 1984).
 3. Spearing, 136–137, 141, 197.
 4. Benjamin Moore Norman, *Norman's New Orleans and Environs* (New Orleans: B.M Norman, 1845), 35.
 5. Thomas Overton Moore to Col. King n.d. 1836 in Claude Hunter Moore, *Thomas Overton Moore a Confederate Governor* (Clinton, NC: Commercial Print Co., 1960), 7; Also see History of Caddo Parish, accessed November 14, 2011, http://www.caddohistory.com.
 6. Phillip C. Cook, "The North Louisiana Upland Frontier: The First Three Decades," in Gilley, ed. *North Louisiana*.
 7. *Ibid.*
 8. Norman, 34.
 9. *Red River Republican*, June 29, 1844.
 10. James E. Boyle, *Cotton and the New Orleans Cotton Exchange* (Garden City: The Country Life Press, 1934). See tables in Appendix I.
 11. J.D.B. DeBow, *The Seventh Census of the United States: 1850* (Washington, D.C.: Robert Armstrong Public Printer, 1853), 484. For what the largest planters were producing see "Some Large Landholders of Avoyelles, Bossier, Caddo, Natchitoches, and Rapides, Parish, 1850" *Louisiana History* Vols 24, 25, 28 and 29 (1983, 1984, 1987, and 1987): 48, 154, 402, 380, and 388. .
 12. Walter Pritchard, ed. "A Tourist's Description of Louisiana in 1860," *Louisiana Historical Quarterly* 21 (October 1938): 1168, 1171, and 1161.
 13. Joseph C.G. Kennedy, *Agriculture of the United States in 1860* (Washington, D.C.: Government Printing Office, 1864), 67.
 14. St. John Richardson Liddell, *Liddell's Record* (Baton Rouge: Louisiana State University Press, 1985), 171.
 15. Taylor, *Destruction and Reconstruction* (Edinburgh: William Blackwood & Sons, 1879), 115.
 16. Charles Mulholland Memorandum Book, August 9, 1850, Mulholland-Polk Family Papers. Central Louisiana Collections, James C. Bolton Library, Louisiana State University at Alexandria, Alexandria, LA.
 17. Moore to Col. King, July 26, 1833 in Claude Hunter Moore, *Thomas Overton Moore*, 7.
 18. Moore to Col. King n.d. 1836 in *Ibid..*
 19. *Ibid.*
 20. Lewis Gray, *History of Agriculture in the Southern United States to 1860* vol. 1 (Gloucester: P. Smith 1958), 531.
 21. Solomon Northup, *Twelve Years a Slave*, Sue Eakin and Joseph Logsdon, eds. (Baton Rouge: Louisiana State University Press, 1968), 126.
 22. *Ibid.*
 23. Maris L. Deloach Papers. MSS 370, Historic New Orleans Collection.
 24. Brigadier General E.L. Tracy to Major General John L. Lewis, November 17, 1860 in Rebel Archives Adjunt General Correspondence, Louisiana State Archives, Baton Rouge, LA.
 25. Sandra Prud'homme Haynie, *Legends of Oakland Plantation* (Shreveport: LaPress Co. Printing, 2001), 37–47. Visit to Oakland Plantation by the author April 14, 2008.
 26. "Some Large Landholders of Desoto Parish, 1850" *Louisiana History* 26 (Summer 1985): 300.
 27. Goodloe Stuck, *End of the Land: A South Carolina Family on the Louisiana Frontier* (Ruston: McGinty Publications, 1992).
 28. The Original Red River Sankofa Project, accessed November 23, 2011, http://www.redriversankofa.org.
 29. Beecher, 307.
 30. Bennett Store Records. Sue Eakin Collection, Central Louisiana Collections, James C. Bolton Library, Louisiana State University at Alexandria, Alexandria, LA.
 31. Bayou Boeuf History, accessed April 7, 2014, http://Bayouboeuflouisiana.Blogspot.Com/2013/07/Stop-2-Lamourie-Locks-In-Bayou-Lamourie.Html. White's Landing was renamed Lecompte after a famous racehorse in the 1850s.
 32. William C. Davis, *Three Roads to the Alamo* (New York: HarperCollins Books, 1998), 149–164 for land speculation and 209–218 for the duel.
 33. Donald S. Frazier and Andrew Hillhouse, eds. and trans. Anne Ball Ryals, *Love and War: The Civil War Letters and Medicinal Book of Augustus V. Ball* (Buffalo Gap: State House Press, 2010), 54–55.
 34. Prichard, ed. 1172–1173.

35. Joseph C.G. Kennedy, *Population of the United States in 1860; Compiled from the Original Returns of the U.S. Census* (Washington: Government Printing Office, 1864), 194.
36. S.B. Buckley, "Agricultural Resources in Texas" *Debow's Review* vol. 4 (October 1867): 327.
37. J. Fair Hardin, *Northwestern Louisiana: A History of the Watershed of the Red River, 1714–1937* vol. 1 (Shreveport: Historical Record Association, 1939), 349.
38. Edith McCall, *Conquering the Rivers: Henry Miller Shreve and the Navigation of America's Inland Waterways* (Baton Rouge: Louisiana State University Press, 1984); Carl Newton Tyson, *The Red River in Southwest History* (Norman, OK: University of Oklahoma Press, 1981), 96; Humphreys, 73–92.
39. Gary D. Joiner, *Through the Howling Wilderness: The 1864 Red River Campaign and Union Failure in the West* (Knoxville: University of Tennessee Press, 2006), 4.
40. J. Fair Hardin, "An Outline of Shreveport and Caddo Parish History," *Louisiana Historical Quarterly* 18 (October 1935): 787, 830.
41. Richard Follett, *The Sugar Masters* (Baton Rouge: Louisiana State University Press, 2005), 21, and 31.
42. Documenting Louisiana Sugar, 1845–1917, accessed June 15, 2011, http://www.sussex.ac.uk/louisianasugar/; All numbers come from this source and also the original reports in P.A. Champomier, *Statement of the Sugar Crops of Louisiana* (New Orleans: Cook, Young & Co., 1861), VI.
43. *Ibid.*
44. *Ibid.*

Chapter Two

1. Emory Thomas, *Robert E. Lee: A Biography* (New York: W.W. Norton, 1995), 188; Douglas Southall Freeman, *R. E. Lee: A Biography* vol. I (New York: Scribner, 1935), 431–447; House of Delegates Virginia General Assembly, *Virginia State Capitol Visitor's Guide* (Richmond: House of Delegates Clerk's Office, 2012), 5.
2. *Shreveport Weekly News* April 22, 1861.
3. Thomas W. Cutrer, and T. Michael Parrish, eds. *The Civil War Letters of the Pierson Family* (Baton Rouge: Louisiana State University Press, 1997), 13–14.
4. William Ivy Hair, *The Kingfish and His Realm* (Baton Rouge 1997), Chapter 1.
5. John Sacher, "'Our Interest and Destiny Are the Same': Gov. Thomas Overton Moore and Confederate Loyalty," *Louisiana History* 49 (Summer 2008), 261–286.
6. Cutrer and Parrish, 13–14. All quotations.

7. David Potter, *The Impending Crisis, 1848–1861* (New York: Harper & Row, 1977).
8. John Sacher, *A Perfect War of Politics: Parties, Politicians, and Democracy in Louisiana, 1824–1861* (Baton Rouge: Louisiana State University Press, 2003); William Cooper, *We Have the War Upon Us: The Onset of the Civil War November 1860-April 1861* (New York: Alfred A. Knopf, 2012), 23–24.
9. Sacher, *A Perfect War*, 279–287.
10. Presidential vote totals from *Whig Tribune Almanac* vol. 2 (New York: New York Tribune, 1864), 51–52; Parish precinct returns for Rapides from Alexandria *Constitutional*, November 10, 1860 in Chronicling America, accessed January 9, 2012, http://Chroniclingamerica.Loc.Gov/Lccn/Sn85038570/.
11. *Whig Tribune Almanac*, 51–52.
12. Election returns by precinct in Prudhomme Family Papers, Cammie Henry Special Collections, Northwestern State University. A Creole is a person of non-American ancestry who was born in America; see Gwendolyn Midlo Hall, *Africans in Colonial Louisiana* (Baton Rouge: Louisiana State University Press, 1992), 157. Also see Gary Mills and Elizabeth Mills, *The Forgotten People: Cane River's Creoles of Color*, rev. ed. (Baton Rouge: Louisiana State University Press, 2013); Henry Robertson, *"In the Habit of Acting Together": The Emergence of the Whig Party, 1828–1840* (Lafayette: Center for Louisiana Studies, 2007); Michael Holt, *the Rise and Fall of the American Whig Party: Jacksonian Politics and the Onset of the Civil War* (New York: Oxford University Press, 1999).
13. Thomas O. Moore to States Rights Gist, October 26, 1860 in Executive Correspondence, State Archives; Steven A. Channing, *Crisis of Fear: The Secession in South Carolina* (New York: Simon & Schuster, 1974).
14. Daniel Crofts, *Reluctant Confederates: Upper South Unionists in the Secession Crisis* (Chapel Hill: University of North Carolina Press, 1989), among others. William W. Freehling, *The Road to Disunion: Volume II: Secessionists Triumphant, 1854–1861* (New York: Oxford University Press, 2008), 385.
15. Gary B. Mills, "Alexandria, Louisiana: A Confederate City at War with Itself" in Arthur W. Bergeron, Jr., *The Louisiana Purchase Bicentennial Series in Louisiana History* vol. 5 Part B. (Lafayette: Center for Louisiana Studies, 2004.), 17.
16. Carl Laurent, ed. *George P. Whittington Rapides Parish, Louisiana, a History* (Pineville, LA: Red River X-Press, 2011), 22 and 129.
17. *Ibid.*, 113.
18. W. Darrell Overdyke, *the Know Nothing Party in the South* (Baton Rouge: Louisiana State University Press, 1950); Ryan M. Hall, "A Glorious Assemblage: The Rise of the Know-Nothing Party in Louisiana," MA thesis, Louisiana State University, 2015.

19. *Constitutional,* accessed June 10, 2013, http://chroniclingamerica.loc.gov/lccn/sn85038570/.

20. Walter Prichard, ed., "A Tourist's Description of Louisiana in 1860," *Louisiana Historical Quarterly* 21 (October 1938), 1156. For physical description of Boyce, see Oath of Allegiance, Department of the Gulf Records, RG 393, National Archives. William T. Sherman OR, series 1, vol. 34, pt. 3, 76–77.

21. *Constitutional* August 13, 1860.

22. Laurent, *Whittington,* 130. Louisiana Seminary and Military Academy became Louisiana State University.

23. *Ibid.,* 130–131; Quote in Pritchard, ed., 1156.

24. *American* and *Constitutional* description in Chronicling America, accessed January 9, 2012, http://chroniclingamerica.loc.gov/lccn/sn85038570/.

25. *Constitutional,* November 3, 1860. A mass meeting of Louisiana's Constitutional Union party took place in south Louisiana, John King to John J. Moore September 7, 1860 in Moore Papers, Historic New Orleans Collection.

26. *Ibid.*

27. Robertson, *In the Habit,* Chapter 2.

28. G. Howard Hunter, "Thomas Overton Moore," KnowLA Encyclopedia, accessed April 29, 2015, http://www.knowla.org/entry/937/; *Louisiana Democrat* November 10, 1859;

29. Laurent, 131; Prichard, 1156; Eric H.Walther, *The Fire-Eaters* (Baton Rouge: Louisiana State University Press, 1992).

30. Louis Wigfall to Thomas Manning et. al. September 13, 1860 in Thomas C. Manning Papers, James C. Bolton Library, Louisiana State University at Alexandria.

31. Thomas O. Moore to Manning September 27, 1860, in *Ibid.*

32. Moore, "Special Message of Thomas O. Moore Governor of the State of Louisiana, to the General Assembly" (Baton Rouge: J.M. Taylor, State Printer, 1860), 3.

33. Returns in Charles B. Dew, "Who Won the Secession Election in Louisiana?" *Journal of Southern History* 36 (February 1970): 18–32.

34. *Louisiana Democrat* November 10, 1859 and *Whig Tribune Almanac,* 51–52.

35. Charles P. Roland, "Louisiana and Secession," *Louisiana History* 19 (Fall 1978): 393.

36. *Constitutional,* November 10, 1859, November 10, 1860, and January 12, 1861.

37. Susan Dollar, "The Red River Campaign, Natchitoches Parish Louisiana a Case of Equal Opportunity Destruction" *Louisiana History* 43 (Fall 2002): 427.

38. Sacher, *A Perfect War,* 279–287.

39. Quoted in Wynona Gilmore Mills, "James Govan Tailaferro, 1898–1876 Unionist and Scalawag," MA Thesis, Louisiana State University, 1964, 1–9.

40. Dew, "Who Won the Secession," 18–32.

41. Quoted in Ethel Taylor, "Discontent in Confederate Louisiana," *Louisiana History* 2 (Autumn 1961): 411.

42. All quotes in Stephen Ash, *When the Yankees Came* (Chapel Hill: University of North Carolina Press, 1995), 123. Also see Jefferson Davis Bragg, *Louisiana in the Confederacy* (Baton Rouge: Louisiana State University Press, 1969), 257–258.

43. *Democrat* clipping in Sue Eakin Collection, Louisiana State University at Alexandria.

44. G.M.G. Stafford, *The Wells Family and Allied Families* (Alexandria, LA: Standard Printing Co., 1942).

45. Barnes F. Lathrop, " Disaffection in Louisiana: The Case of William Hyman," *Journal of Southern History* 24 (August 1958): 308–318.

46. Cuthbert Puckett to Abraham Lincoln, November 24, 1863, Lincoln Papers, Library of Congress.

47. Joel Gray Taylor, *Louisiana Reconstructed 1863–1877* (Baton Rouge:, Louisiana State University Press, 1974); Joseph G. Dawson, *Army Generals in Reconstruction: Louisiana, 1862–1877* (Baton Rouge: Louisiana State University Press, 1982); Justin Nystrom, "Reconstruction" in KnowLA Encyclopedia, accessed April 29, 2015, http://www.knowla.org/entry/463/.

48. Lathrop, 308–318. See also the account of Louisiana Unionist Dennis E. Haynes in Arthur W. Bergeron, Jr., ed., *A Thrilling Narrative: The Memoir of a Southern Unionist* (Fayetteville: University of Arkansas Press, 2006).

49. James G. Hollandsworth, Jr. *Pretense of Glory: The Life of General Nathaniel P. Banks* (Baton Rouge: Louisiana State University Press, 1998), 162.

50. Charles Stone to Banks, March 23, 1864 OR, series 1, vol. 34, pt. 1: 179.

51. Banks to Dr. A. P. Dudley February 18, 1864, Department of the Gulf Records Letters Sent, RG 1738, vol. 6.

52. Charles Stone to Banks OR, series 1, Volume 34, part 1, 178–179.

53. St. Louis *Republican* April 24, 1864 and Dave to Ellen, April 1, 1864, Pearce Civil War collections Navarro College, Corsicana, Texas.

54. All quotes, M.R. Ariel to General Nathanial Banks, March 27, 1864, Banks Papers, Library of Congress.

55. G. Howard Hunter, "Unionist Troops in Louisiana" KnowLA Encyclopedia, accessed April 30, 2015, http://www.knowla.org/entry/1425/.

56. *Harper's Weekly* April 30, 1864.

57. Both quotations in "Joint Resolutions Relative to the Illegal Organization of a State Government by the Public Enemy," February 10, 1864 in Rebel Archives, Executive Communications, 1860–1864, Louisiana State Archives.

58. Henry W. Allen, Proclamation, February 13, 1864, *Ibid*.
59. See Johnson, Joiner, and Prushankin.

Chapter Three

1. Thomas W. Cutrer and T. Michael Parrish, eds. *The Civil War Letters of the Pierson Family* (Baton Rouge: Louisiana State University Press, 1997), 5.
2. Randy Decuir, "Civil War in Avoyelles Parish," May 31, 2013, Civil War Sesquicentennial Commemoration, Marksville, LA.
3. John Anderson, ed., *Brokenburn: The Journal of Kate Stone, 1861–1868* (Baton Rouge: Louisiana State University 1995), 119.
4. Both Quotes in Craig A. Bauer, *Creole Genesis* (Lafayette, LA: University of Louisiana at Lafayette Press 2011), 139.
5. First two quotes Robert A. Newell to daughter January 24, 1864, Newell Papers, MSS 653, Louisiana and Lower Mississippi Valley Collection, Hill Library, Louisiana State University, Baton Rouge, LA; Third quote Newell to daughter February 22, 1864 in *Ibid.*; Fourth quote Newell to daughter March n.d. in *Ibid.* and final quotes Sarah Newell to Robert Newell May 22, 1864 in *Ibid.*.
6. *Natchitoches Union* March 27, 1862.
7. Amos Lee Armstrong, *Sabine Parish Louisiana: "Land of Green Gold"* (Shreveport: Jones & Springfellow Printing 1958), 112–113.
8. Stephen Ash, *When the Yankees Came: Conflict and Chaos in the Occupied South, 1861–1865* (Chapel Hill: University of North Carolina Press, 1995).
9. John Reed, "Opelousas the Capital and the Twenty-Seventh Legislature of the State of Louisiana," June 29, 2013 Young-Sanders Center, Franklin LA.
10. Gary D. Joiner, *One Damn Blunder from Beginning to End* (Latham, MD: Rowman & Littlefield, 2003), 17–18.
11. See Donald S. Frazier, *Fire in the Cane Field: The Federal Invasion of Louisiana and Texas, January 1861–January 1863* (Buffalo Gap, TX: State House Press, 2009); Donald S. Frazier, *Thunder Across the Swamp: The Fight for the Lower Mississippi, February–May 1863* (Buffalo Gap, TX: State House Press, 2011).
12. *Natchitoches Union* in P.E. Cloutier Papers, Cammie Henry Special Collections, Watson Library, Northwestern State University, Natchitoches, LA.
13. John Sacher, "'A Very Disagreeable Business'": Confederate Conscription in Louisiana," *Civil War History* 53 (June 2007): 144.
14. *Ibid.* Proclamation of Henry Watkins Allen, May 1864, in Louisiana State Archives, Baton Rouge, LA.
15. Quotations from Moore's address in *Louisiana House of Representatives* (Shreveport, LA: The State, 1864), 117; Also see *Louisiana Democrat* November 2, 1864.
16. Quoted in Sacher, "'A Very," 161.
17. Carl A. Brasseaux, *Acadian to Cajun: Transformation of a People, 1803–1877* (Jackson: University of Mississippi Press, 1992), 71.
18. L. Rives to General Taylor February 19, 1864 Letterbook, Department of the Gulf Records, RG 393, National Archives; William T. Block, "The 'Louisiana Scouts' and Other Parish Jayhawkers," accessed January 26, 2012, www.wtblock.com/wtlockjr/jayhawke.htm.
19. Donald S. Frazier "'Out of Stinking Distance': The Guerilla War in Louisiana" in Daniel Sutherland, ed. *Guerrillas, Unionists, and Violence on the Confederate Home Front* (Fayetteville: University of Arkansas Press, 1999), 170.
20. JE Buford to Thomas Manning Alexandria Jan 18, 1864, Western District of Louisiana Letterbook Trans-Mississippi Confederate Records in Department of the Gulf Records, RG 393, National Archives.
21. Governor Thomas O. Moore Papers typescripts, Cammie Henry Special Collections, Watson Library, Northwestern State University, Natchitoches, LA.
22. *Ibid.*
23. Arthur W. Bergeron, Jr. ed. *A Thrilling Narrative: The Memoir of a Southern Unionist* (Fayetteville: University of Arkansas Press, 2006).
24. *Ibid.*, 8.
25. *Ibid.*, 8–11.
26. *Ibid.*, 59.
27. "Claim 782 Dennis E. Haynes of Winnfield, Winn Parish, State of Louisiana," United States. *Commissioners of Claims. Summary Reports in All Cases Reported to Congress as Disallowed Under the Act of March 3, 1871* (Washington: Government Printing Office, 1876–1881), 477.
28. St. John Lidell, *Lidell's Record* (Baton Rouge: Louisiana State University Press, 1997), 174. W. A Broadwell to General Kirby Smith, March 16, 1864, Confederate States of America Records, 1856–1915, University of Texas at Austin.
29. Richard Taylor, *Destruction and Reconstruction* (Edinbough: William Blackwood & Sons, 1879), 141.
30. Allen, "To the Planters and Slave-Owners of Louisiana" March 22, 1864, Governor's Communications, Rebel archive, State Archives, Baton Rouge, LA.
31. Phanor Prudhomme notes May 30, 1863–March 30, 1864 and G. Baillio, Engineer Department of West Louisiana, to Phanor Prudhomme October 25, 1864 in Prudhomme Family Papers Southern Historical Collection, Watson Library, University of North Carolina, Chapel Hill, NC.
32. AR Haynes, Confederate Claims Commission, to Phanor Prudhomme, July 13, 1864

Chapter Four

and receipts dated July 15, 1864 September 30, 1864 and October 1 and 7, 1864 in *Ibid.*

1. Jefferson Davis Bragg, *Louisiana in the Confederacy* (Baton Rouge: Louisiana State University Press, 1969), 202.
2. Judith F. Gentry, "White Gold: The Confederate Government and Cotton in Louisiana" in Arthur W. Bergeron, Jr., ed., *The Louisiana Purchase Bicentennial Series in Louisiana History* vol. 5 Part B (Lafayette, LA: Center for Louisiana Studies, 2004), 112.
3. *Ibid.*, 115. All quotations.
4. John Winters, *The Civil War in Louisiana* (Baton Rouge: Louisiana State University Press, 1963), 325–326.
5. Bernard F. Schererhorn to wife March 27, 1864 in Schermerhorn Papers Indiana Historical Society, Indianapolis.
6. Ludwell Johnson, *Red River Campaign: Politics and Cotton in the Civil War* (Kent, OH: Kent State University Press, 1993), Chapter 2.
7. James E. Boyle, *Cotton and the New Orleans Cotton Exchange* (Garden City, NY: The Country Life Press, 1934), 155. Johnson, 50.
8. Richard Brady Williams, *Chicago's Battery Boys* (Chapel Hill: University of North Carolina Press, 2005), 210.
9. Chester G. Hearn, *Admiral David Dixon Porter : The Civil War Years* (Annapolis, MD: Naval Institute Press, 1996), 241.
10. Johnson, 71–74.
11. *Harper's Weekly*, April 30, 1864. Johnson, 102–103.
12. Gary D. Joiner, *Lincoln's Brown Water Navy* (Lanham, MD: Rowman & Littlefield, 2007), 147–148.
13. *Ibid.*, 101 n. 2.
14. *Ibid.*
15. Joiner, "Lincoln's," 148.
16. Gentry, 114.
17. Porter testimony in United States, Congress. *Report of the Joint Committee on the Conduct of the War* (Washington: Government Printing Office, 1865), 11.
18. Johnson, 66. Frank Flinn, *Campaigning with Banks in Louisiana '63 and '64 and with Sheridan in the Shenandoah Valley '64 and '65* (Boston: W. B. Clarke, 1889), 96.
19. Lucius F. Hubbard, "Civil War Papers," *Collections of the Minnesota Historical Society* vol. 12 (St. Paul, n.p. 1908), 588.
20. *Ibid.*, 105. James G. Hollandsworth, Jr., *Pretense of Glory: The Life of General Nathaniel P. Banks* (Baton Rouge: Louisiana State University Press, 1998), 157–160.
21. Hollandsworth, 4.
22. General Banks to Henry Halleck, May 4, 1863, OR series 1 vol. 15, part 1: 310; Historian James G. Hollandsworth, Jr. wrote that Banks estimated the value of the cotton and sugar seized in 1863 at 10 million dollars, Hollandsworth, 121.
23. Banks to Halleck, May 4, 1863, OR, series 1 vol. 15, prt 1: 310.
24. Welch to S.B. Holibird, April 12. 1864 in Department of the Gulf, Letters Sent and Received, National Archives, RG 393.4. All quotations. Cotton prices in Boyle, 155. Calhoun had supported the Stephen Douglas ticket in 1860.
25. Tom to Banks, April 5, 1864 in Banks Papers, Library of Congress.
26. Unidentified soldier in Gary D. Joiner, ed. *Little to Eat and Thin Mud to Drink* (Knoxville: University of Tennessee Press 2007), 51.
27. J.E. Sliger, "How General Taylor Fought the Battle of Mansfield, La," *Confederate Veteran* vol. 31 (1923), 457.
28. Poché in Edwin C. Bearss, ed. *A Louisiana Confederate: Diary of Felix Pierre Poché* (Natchitoches: Northwestern State University Press, 1972), 86–87; David Ray to mother March 6, 1864 David Ray Papers University of Texas at Austin.
29. King in Gary Joiner and Marilyn Joiner, eds, *No Pardons to Ask Nor Apologies to Make: The Journal of William Henry King in Gray's 28th Louisiana Infantry Regiment* (Knoxville: University of Tennessee Press, 2006), 148.
30. Petty to Wife March 10, 1864 in Norman D. Brown, *Journey to Pleasant Hill: The Civil War Letters of Captain Elijah P. Petty, Walker's Texas Division, C.S.A.* (San Antonio : University of Texas, Institute of Texan Cultures, 1982), 377.
31. William Broadwell to O. Hinckley, March 9, 1864 Orramel Hinckley and Family Papers, Louisiana and Lower Mississippi River Valley Collection, Hill Library, Louisiana State University.
32. Horace S. Fulkerson, in P.L. Rainwater, ed. "Excerpts from Fulkerson's 'Recollections of the War Between the States,'" *Mississippi Valley Historical Review* vol. 24 (December 1937), 365.
33. Taylor quoted in Hollandsworth, 159. T. Michael Parrish, *Richard Taylor Soldier Prince of Dixie* (Chapel Hill: University of North Carolina Press 1992), 318–319 discusses Taylor's view that burning cotton was better than allowing the trade to continue.
34. General John S. Clark Papers, March 25, 1864, Cayuga Museum of History and Art, Auburn, New York.
35. John H. Bering, and Thomas Montgomery, *History of the Forty-Eighth Ohio Vet. Vol. Inf.* (Hillsboro, OH: Highland News Office, 1880), accessed June 11, 2008, http://www.48ovvi.org/chap15.html.
36. Charles F. Read, "Army Experiences," UC 804, Historic New Orleans Collection.

37. Bering, *History of the Forty-Eighth*, 129.
38. Thomas M. Brennan, *A Planter's Son Goes to War* (Natchitoches: National Park Service, 2012), 14.
39. Poché, 102.

Chapter Five

1. Edwin P. Becton to Mary Becton, January 2, 1864 in Edwin Pinckney Papers, 1862–1870, Dolph Briscoe Center for American History, the University of Texas at Austin.
2. Charles Dwight to Charles P. Stone, January 7, 1864, USCT microfilm reels, National Archives.
3. George L. Andrews to Major General E.A. Hitchcock, February 7, 1864, OR, series 2, vol. 6, prt 1, 924–925.
4. Allen, "Proclamation," February 13, 1864, Governor's Communications, 1860–1864, Rebel Archives, State Archives, Baton Rouge, LA.
5. Thomas J. Durant to Abraham Lincoln, October 1, 1863, Lincoln Papers Library of Congress.
6. Claude H. Nolan, *African-American Southerners in Slavery, Civil War and Reconstruction* (Jefferson, NC: McFarland & Co., 2001), 134.
7. *Ibid.*
8. *Ibid.*
9. Taylor to William B. Franklin, December 5, 1863 in USCT microfilm, RG 94 National Archives.
10. Charles Dwight to Charles P. Stone, January 7, 1864, *Ibid.*
11. Randal B. Gilbert, *A New Look at Camp Ford Tyler Texas* (Tyler, TX: Smith County Historical Society, 2010), 18.
12. Rhett Breerwood, "Camp Parapet: The Union," *New Orleans Historical*, accessed May 13, 2015, http://www.neworleanshistorical.org/items/show/658; Winters, 143.
13. James G. Hollandsworth, Jr., *The Louisiana Native Guards* (Baton Rouge: Louisiana State University Press, 1995), 51; Don S. Frazier, *Fire in the Cane Field: The Federal Invasion of Louisiana and Texas, January 1861–January 1863* (Buffalo Gap, TX: State House Press, 2009), 195–196; For similar conditions in Iberville Parish see Oscar to Gustave Lauve June 26, 1863 Lauve Papers, MSS 893, Louisiana and Lower Mississippi Valley Collection, Hill Library, Louisiana State University.
14. Soldier to Wife April 24, 1863, MSS 51, Historic New Orleans Collection.
15. Ransdell to Moore, May 26, 1863, in G. P. Whittington, "Concerning the Loyalty of Slaves in North Louisiana in 1863," *Louisiana Historical Quarterly* 14 (October 1931): 494–495.
16. *Ibid.*
17. Carol Wells, ed., *War, Reconstruction, and Redemption on Red River: The Memoirs of Dosia Williams Moore* (Ruston: McGinty Press, 1991), 15.
18. Both quotations in Gary D. Joiner, and Marilyn eds., *No Pardons to Ask Nor Apologies to Make the Journal of William Henry King Gray's 28th Louisiana Infantry Regiment* (Knoxville: University of Tennessee Press, 2006) ,160.
19. Amos Lee Armstrong, *Sabine Parish Louisiana "Land of Green Gold"* (Shreveport: Jones & Springfellow Printing, 1958), 120. All quotations.
20. Department of the Gulf, Oaths of Allegiance RG 393, National Archives.
21. Gary D. Joiner, *Mr. Lincoln's Brown Water Navy* (Lanham: Rowman & Littlefield, 2007), 152.
22. Banks to Lincoln February 25, 1864 in Banks Papers Library of Congress.
23. *Ibid.*
24. *Ibid.*
25. Ezra J. Warner, *Generals in Blue* (Baton Rouge: Louisiana State University, 1964), 480. See Also James Morgan, *A Little Short of Boats: The Civil War Battles of Ball's Bluff and Edwards Ferry, October 21–22, 1861* (Eldorado Hills, CA: Savas Beatie, 2011).
26. General John S. Clark Papers, Cayuga Museum of History and Art, Auburn, New York.
27. Banks Papers, Library of Congress.
28. Charles F. Read "Army Experiences," UC MSS 804, Historic New Orleans Collection.
29. *New York Times*, March 14, 1864.
30. James G. Hollandsworth, Jr. *Pretense of Glory: The Life of General Nathaniel P. Banks* (Baton Rouge: Louisiana State University Press), 178.
31. Ezra J. Warner, *Generals in Blue* (Baton Rouge: Louisiana State University Press, 1964), 454.
32. Joiner, *Little to Eat*, 265–280.
33. Banks to Lincoln February 25, 1864, Banks Papers Library of Congress.
34. "List of Prominent Citizens of Alexandria & Vicinity Who Claim Protection from the United States Government, and as Such, Should Be Compelled to Show Their Hand in the Election That Takes Place Tomorrow" April 1, 1864 in Banks Papers, Library of Congress.
35. Alice Scarborough, director of Kent House to the author April 12, 2012. Historic American Survey, Library of Congress has images of all three homes, accessed April 13, 2012, http://www.loc.gov/pictures/collection/hh/.
36. Banks Papers, Library of Congress.
37. Smith, "Defense of the Red River," *Battles and Leaders of the Civil War* (New York: The Century Co., 1884), 369.

38. Steve Mayeaux, *Earthen Walls, Iron Men: Fort DeRussy, Louisiana, and the Defense of Red River* (Knoxville: University of Tennessee Press, 2007), 307 and 316.
39. Joiner, *One Damn Blunder: The Red River Campaign of 1864* (Lanham: Rowman & Littlefield, 2003),, 39.
40. Smith, "Defense," 269.
41. OR series 1, Vol. 34, prt 1, 498. See *Ibid.*, 496–500 for Taylor's report on Henderson Hill. Donald Parker, "Henderson Hill Reconsidered: The Rediscovered Diary and Letters of a 2nd Louisiana Cavalry Officer," April 7, 2011, Civil War Roundtable of Central Louisiana, Alexandria, LA.
42. John S. Clark Papers, Cayuga Museum of History and Art, Auburn, New York.
43. Joiner, *One Damn Blunder,* 54.
44. Lucius F. Hubbard, "Civil War Papers," *Collections of the Minnesota Historical Society* vol. 12 (St. Paul n.p. 1908), 576.
45. Banks to Captain Welsh Quartermaster Corps March 28, 1864, Department of the Gulf Records, RG 393, Volume 7: 100, National Archives. The exact identity of Walker is unknown. There is a John Walker, a barber, married with no kids living in Alexandria according to the 1860 census. He is a good candidate but so is the John Walker living in Winnfield with a wife and kids in 1860 and his occupation is listed as an editor. Either one could have been in Alexandria and provided service or another Walker not identified here. John Walker, accessed June 16, 2013, http://search.ancestry.com/search/db.aspx?dbid=7667.
46. John Wilkins Diary Notebook, Indiana Historical Society, Indianapolis, IN; *New York Times*, March 23, 1864.
47. Keeler, OR series 1, vol. 34, prt 1, 332. Both quotations.
48. Taylor, OR, series 1,vol. 34, prt 1, 315–316, 334–335, 463–464.
49. Charles F. Read, "Army," All quotations.
50. Brent Nosworthy, *The Bloody Crucible of Courage* (New York: Carroll & Graff, 2003), 235–7.
51. *Ibid.*
52. Steven E. Woodworth, *Beneath a Northern Sky: A Short History of the Gettysburg Campaign* (Lanham, MD: Roman & Littlefield, 2008), 21. Also see From the Fields of Gettysburg Blog, Bill Halainen The Long Road to Gettysburg: The Sixth Corps Epic March to Gettysburg, accessed April 14, 2013, http://npsgnmp.wordpress.com/2013/02/22/The-Long-Road-To-Gettysburg-The-Sixth-Corps-Epic-March-To-Gettysburg/
53. Google Maps, accessed July 25, 2012, http://maps.google.com/maps?hl=en&tab=ll. Select the directions tab and enter the two places and drag to move the route through the historic towns that the army marched through. The millage is then produced by google maps. The distances are approximate because roads have changed.
54. Google Maps, accessed July 25, 2012, http://maps.google.com/maps?saddr=Franklin+Louisiana&Daddr=Mansfield+La for the Union, Franklin to Mansfield. For Confederates, Simmsport to Mansfield, is placed in the boxes to render the results.
55. Stephen Dupree, *Campaigning with the 67th Indiana 1864: An Annotated Diary of Service in the Department of the Gulf* (New York: iUniverse, 2006), 50–51; A Wisconsin soldier reported similar distances. See John Demerit Diary April 7, 1864, Manuscripts Collection M1155, Manuscripts Department, Howard-Tilton Memorial Library, Tulane University, New Orleans, Louisiana 70118; Caroline E. Whitcomb, *History of the Second Massachusetts Battery (Nims' Battery of Light Artillery: 1861–1865* (Concord: Rumford Press, 1912), 64, cited 20 to 30 miles a day for that unit.
56. Henry C. Sampson Diary, MSS 258, Historic New Orleans Collection.
57. John Mead Gould, *History of the First—Tenth—Twenty-Ninth Maine Regiment* (Portland: S. Berry, 1871), 410.
58. Henry Augustus Shorey, *The Story of the Maine Fifteenth* (Bridgeton: Press of the Bridgeton News, 1890), 74.
59. Petty in Norman D. Brown, *Journey to Pleasant Hill: The Civil War Letters of Captain Elijah P. Petty, Walker's Texas Division, CSA* (San Antonio: University of Texas, Institute of Texan Cultures, 1982), 379.
60. W. Randolph Howell, "Journal of 'Louisiana Campaign—1864" in W. Randolph Howell Papers, 1861–1879, Dolph Briscoe Center for American History, The University of Texas at Austin.
61. Hensley to wife March 18, 1864, in Pearce Civil War Collections, Navarro College, Corsicana, Texas.

Chapter Six

1. Shakespeare, *Richard III*, accessed April 14, 2012, http://shakespeare.mit.edu/richardiii/full.html.
2. Henry C. Sampson Diary, MSS 258, Historic New Orleans Collection.
3. *Daily True Delta* April 3, 1864.
4. Steven Mayeaux, *Earthen Walls, Iron Men: Fort DeRussy, Louisiana, and the Defense of Red River* (Knoxville: University of Tennessee Press, 2007), 307 and 316.
5. Gary D. Joiner, *Through The Howling Wilderness* (Knoxville, TN: University of Tennessee Press, 2006), 63; John Winters, *The Civil War in Louisiana* (Baton Rouge: Louisiana State University Press, 1963), 330.
6. Jeff Prushankin, *A Crisis in Confederate Command* (Baton Rouge: Louisiana State University Press, 2005), 88.

7. Richard Lowe, *The Texas Overland Expedition of 1863* (Fort Worth: Ryan Place Publishers, 1996).
8. Joiner *One Damn Blunder from Beginning to End* (Lanham, MD: Rowman & Littlefield, 2003), 98.
9. Banks to Lincoln, May 1, 1863 in Lincoln Papers, Library of Congress.
10. Joiner, *One Damn Blunder*, 87–88.
11. Scott Dearman to the author June 5, 2015. Dearman is the manager at the Mansfield State Historic site and has studied the numbers extensively. The discussion that follows comes from his communication with the author.
12. Walter Prichard, ed., "A Tourist's Description of Louisiana in 1860," *Louisiana Historical Quarterly* 21 (October 1938): 1172–1173.
13. R.M. Venable, "Mansfield," map in Jeremy Francis Gilmer Papers, Southern Historical Collection, University of North Carolina, Chapel Hill, North Carolina, shows the farms on the road south of Mansfield.
14. Sarah Gardner Moss Bannerman, *Shreveport Journal*, April 8, 1937.
15. Quoted in Richard Williams, *Chicago's Battery Boys: The Chicago Mercantile Battery in the Civil War's Western Theater* (Eldorado Hills, CA: Savas Beatie, 2005), 229.
16. National Park Service Soldier's and Sailor's Database, accessed June 19, 2013, http://www.nps.gov/civilwar/search-battleunits-detail.htm?battleunitcode=CTX0006BC.
17. Ibid.
18. Charles F. Read, "Army Experiences," UC 804 Historic New Orleans Collection.
19. David M. Ray Papers and John B. Ray Papers, Dolph Briscoe Center for American History, University of Texas, Austin. For their unit and ranks see Texans in the Civil War, accessed July 8, 2012, http://www.texansinthecivilwar.com/16th_cavalry/company_G); John Ray to mother May 24, 1864, in John Ray Papers.
20. Terrence J. Winschel, *The Civil War Diary of a Common Soldier: William Wiley of the 77th Illinois Infantry* (Baton Rouge: Louisiana State University Press, 2001) contains all biographical information on Webb.
21. National Abolitionist Hall of Fame, accessed April 7, 2014, http://www.nationalabolitionhalloffameandmuseum.org/elovejoy.html.
22. Winschel, 207.
23. Ibid., 22.
24. Ibid.,76.
25. Ibid., 101.
26. R.B. Scott, *History of the 67th Indiana Regiment* (Bedford: Herald Book and Job Print 1892), 71.
27. W. H Bentley, *History of the 77th Illinois Volunteer Infantry* (Peoria: E. Hine Printer, 1883), 254.
28. Arthur W. Bergeron, Jr., "A Colonel Gains His Wreath: Henry Gray's Louisiana Brigade at the Battle of Mansfield, April 8, 1864," Theodore P. Savas, David A. Woodbury, and Gary D. Joiner eds., *The Red River Campaign, Union and Confederate Leadership and the War in Louisiana* (Shreveport: Parabellum Press, 2003), 5.
29. Ezra J. Warner, *Generals in Blue* (Baton Rouge: Louisiana State University Press, 1964), 389–390.
30. Hyatt Diary, Louisiana and Lower Mississippi Valley Collection, Hill Library, Louisiana State University.
31. Ibid. All quotations.
32. Charles F. Sherman to father, April 26, 1864, MSS 115, Historic New Orleans Collection. Both quotations.
33. Ibid.
34. Hyatt Diary.
35. Bergeron, 'A Colonel," 17.
36. W. Randolph Howell Diary, Dolph Briscoe Center for American History, University of Texas, Austin.
37. Gary D. Joiner, *Little to Eat Thin Mud to Drink* (Knoxville: University of Tennessee Press, 2007), 55–56.
38. Quote in Clark, 159; Ransom's wound would trouble him for months and while serving in Georgia he contracted another illness and died. No less than General William T. Sherman remembered him twenty years later as a kindred spirit and patriot. *New York Times* July 11, 1884.
39. Williams, *Chicago's* 236.
40. Bentley, *History of the 77th Illinois*, 256.
41. McAlester Hooker to wife, April 14, 1864, The Yesterdays of Hamilton County, Illinois, accessed June 18, 2013, http://www.carolyar.com/illinois/letters/hookerletter.htm.
42. Melville Bennett to F.M. Bennett, June 11, 1864, Ezra Bennett and Family Papers, Sue Eakin Collection. James C. Bolton Library, Louisiana State University, Alexandria.
43. Harris H. Beecher, *Record of the 114th Regiment, N.Y.S.V.*(Norwich: J.F. Hubbard, 1866), 311.
44. Cynthia Dehaven Pitcock and Bill J. Gurley, eds., *I Acted from Principle: The Civil War Diary of Dr. William M. McPheeters, Confederate Surgeon in the Trans Mississippi* (Fayetteville: University of Arkansas Press, 2002), 138.
45. William Arceneaux, *Acadian General Alfred Mouton and the Civil War* (Lafayette: Center for Louisiana Studies, 1981), 128–136.
46. First quotation, W.H. Mathews to wife, n.d. typescript Mansfield State Historic Site library; Williams, *Chicago's*, 255.

Chapter Seven

1. Quoted in Richard Williams, *Chicago's Battery Boys: The Chicago Mercantile Battery*

in the Civil War's Western Theater (Eldorado Hills, CA: Savas Beatie, 2005), 242.

2. Arthur W. Bergeron, Jr., "A Colonel Gains His Wreath: Henry Gray's Louisiana Brigade at the Battle of Mansfield, April 8, 1864," in *The Red River Campaign* (Shreveport, LA: Parabellum Press, 2003), n. 44.

3. Charles F. Read "Army Experiences," UC MSS 804, Historic New Orleans Collection.

4. *Ibid.*

5. John Palmer Blessington, *The Campaigns of Walker's Texas Division* (New York: Lange, Little & Co., 1875), 189. Bergeron, "A Colonel," 21.

6. Abial Edwards to Anna Edwards, April 13, 1864 in Beverly Hayes Kallgren and James L. Crouthamel, eds., *"Dear Friend Anna": The Civil War Letters of a Common Soldier from Maine* (Orono, ME: University of Maine Press, 1992), 86.

7. John Mead Gould, *History of the First—Tenth—Twenty-Ninth Maine Regiment.* (Portland: S. Berry, 1871), 412.

8. Ezra J. Warner, *Generals in Blue* (Baton Rouge: Louisiana State University 1964), 142–143.

9. I drove on LA 175 at the location of the battle of Pleasant Grove twice and using the on-board GPS system aboard a 2008 Chrysler Town and Country Van determined the elevation.

10. Orton S. Clark, *The One Hundred and Sixteenth Regiment of New York State Volunteers* (Buffalo: Printing House of Mathews & Warren, 1868), 156.

11. Henry Augustus Shorey, *The Story of the Maine Fifteenth* (Bridgeton: Press of the Bridgeton News, 1890), 87.

12. Henry N. Fairbanks, "Red River Expedition, 1864" in Military Order of the Loyal Legion of the United States Commandery of the State of Maine, *War Papers* vol. 1 (Portland: Thurston Print, 1898), 183.

13. Quoted in Richard Lowe, *Walker's Texas Division, C.S.A.: Greyhounds of the Trans-Mississippi* (Baton Rouge: Louisiana State University Press, 2004), 196.

14. Gould, 413.

15. Richard B. Irwin, *History of the Nineteenth Army Corps* (Baton Rouge: Elliotts Book Shop, 1985), 309.

16. Henry Martin Benedict, *Memorial of Brevet Major General Lewis Benedict* (Albany: J. Munsell, 1866), 71.

17. New York State Military Museum, accessed May 21, 2013, https://dmna.ny.gov/historic/reghist/civil/infantry/161stinf/161stifmain.htm Mahlon W. Barber Diary, Dolph Briscoe Center for American History, University of Texas at Austin.

18. Roster of 161st Regiment NYSV at Military Museum of New York, accessed July 27, 2012, http://dmna.ny.gov/historic/reghist/civil/rosters/infantry/161st_infantry_CW_roster.pdf; Quote from Irwin, 310.

19. Clark, 156.

20. Gould, 416.

21. Edwards to Anna Edwards, April 13, 1864 in Kallgren, 86.

22. Seip, "The Battle of Mansfield" August 10, 1906 in G.P. Whittington, Louisiana Collection, 976.3 (c27.17) W 626, Howard Tilton Memorial Library, Tulane University, New Orleans, Louisiana, 70118.

23. Frank Flinn, *Campaigning with Banks in Louisiana '63 and '64 and with Sheridan in the Shenandoah Valley '64 and '65* (Boston: W. B. Clarke, 1889), 109.

24. Banks to U.S. Grant OR, series 1, vol. 34, prt. 1: 182; first quote and R. B. Scott, *The History of the 67th Regiment Indiana Infantry Volunteers* (Bedford: 1892), 72 second one.

25. Seip, "The Battle of Mansfield."

26. Abiel Edwards to Anna Edwards, April 13, 1864 in Kallgren, 86.

27. Mattie Davis Luca and Mita Holsapple Hall, *A History of Grayson County, Texas* (Sherman, TX: Scruggs Printing, 1936), 127.

Chapter Eight

1. Hardin, *Northwestern Louisiana: A His. of the Watershed of the Red River, 1714–1937,* vol. 1 (Shreveport: Historical Record Association 1939), 349.

2. Gary D. Joiner, *One Damn Blunder from Beginning to End* (Lanham: Rowman & Littlefield, 2003),107.

3. Stellarium, accessed May 27, 2013, http://www.stellarium.org/. I set the program for the configuration of the night sky at Pleasant Gove on April 8–9, 1864. The Lafayette, LA planetarium also did the same for me on a visit there in spring 2013.

4. Simon Bott Diary, Manuscripts Collection, M1156, Howard-Tilton Memorial Library, Tulane University, New Orleans, Louisiana, 70118.

5. Orton S. Clark, *The One Hundred and Sixteenth Regiment of New York State Volunteers* (Buffalo: Printing House of Mathews & Warren, 1868), 160. Both quotations.

6. John Mead Gould, *History of the First—Tenth—Twenty-Ninth Maine Regiment* (Portland: S. Berry, 1871), 422.

7. Taylor, *Destruction and Reconstruction* (Edinburgh: William Blackwood, 1879), 218.

8. *Boston Herald,* April 23, 1864.

9. William O. Blake, *Pictorial History of the Great Rebellion* (Columbus, OH: Gilmore & Segner Publishers, 1866), 680.

10. John Ray to mother May 24, 1864 in John Ray Papers, Dolph Briscoe Center for American History, University of Texas Austin, TX.

11. *Ibid.*

12. The following account was taken from John Scott, *Story of the 32nd Iowa Infantry* (Nevada, IA: J. Scott 1896); Benjamin F. Gue, *History of Iowa from the Earliest Times to the Beginning of the Twentieth Century* vol. 2 (New York: The Century History Co., 1903), 320–321; William T. Shaw, "The Battle of Pleasant Hill." *The Annals of Iowa* vol.3 (1898), 401–423. Available at: http://ir.uiowa.edu/annals-of-iowa/vol3/iss5/7; Also see "The Battle of Pleasant Hill" *The Annals of Iowa* vol. 7 (1906), 544–547. Available at: http://ir.uiowa.edu/annals-of-iowa/vol7/iss7/12; Henry H. Childers, "Reminiscences of the Battle of Pleasant Hill." *The Annals of Iowa* vol.7 (1906), 505–516, all accessed July 10, 2014, http://ir.uiowa.edu/annals-of-iowa/vol7/iss7/3.

13. William T. Shaw, "The Battle of Pleasant Hill." *The Annals of Iowa* 3 (1898), 408, accessed July 10, 2014, http://ir.uiowa.edu/annals-of-iowa/vol3/iss5/7.

14. Gary D. Joiner, *One Damn Blunder*, 110.

15. Curtis Brooks Morris, *The Life of Edward Clark: A War-Time Governor of Texas* MA Thesis Stephen F. Austin University, 1954, 70–72.

16. Ralph A. Wooster, "CLARK, EDWARD," Handbook of Texas Online, accessed April 9, 2013, http://www.tshaonline.org/handbook/online/articles/fcl04. All biographical information on Clark comes from this source.

17. Edward Clark Papers, Dolph Briscoe Center for American History, University of Texas at Austin.

18. Louis Mitchell, "LUBBOCK, FRANCIS RICHARD," Handbook of Texas Online, accessed April 9, 2013, http://www.tshaonline.org/handbook/online/articles/flu01.

19. Wooster, "Clark, Edward."

20. Morris, 71–72 both quotations.

21. William T. Shaw, "The Battle of Pleasant Hill," 408.

22. All material comes from Morris, 70–72 and Edward Clark Papers, University of Texas at Austin.

23. V.W. Allen quoted in Benjamin Gue, *History of Iowa from the Earliest Times to the Beginning of the Twentieth Century* vol. 2 (New York: The Century History Co. 1903), 320.

24. Richard Lowe, *Walker's Texas Division, C.S.A.* (Baton Rouge: Louisiana State University Press, 2004), 204–211; For mention of the Black soldiers see Henry Marvin Benedict, *Memorial of Brevet Major General Lewis Benedict*. (Albany: J. Munsell, 1866), 78–79; and a contemporary report at http://ironbrigader.com/2014/03/19/colonel-francis-fessendens-report-brigades-action-battles-sabine-cross roads-pleasant-hill/. Their flag with Pleasant Hill on it is found at Battle Flag of the 84th Regiment, USCT (U.S. Colored Troops), accessed June 17, 2014, http://jubiloemancipationcentury.wordpress.com/2011/02/03/battle-flag-of-the-84th-regiment-usct-us-colored-troops.

25. Joiner, *One Damn Blunder*, 109.

26. Lowe, *Walker's*, 208.

27. Taylor, *Destruction and Reconstruction*, 218.

28. Joiner, *One Damn Blunder*, 114.

29. Benedict, 83.

30. *Ibid.*, 37–38.

31. *Ibid.*, 2.

32. *Ibid.* 12.

33. *Ibid.*, 18 first quote and 47 second.

34. *Ibid.*, 49–59.

35. *Ibid.*, 84–85.

36. *Ibid.*, 119.

37. Joiner, *One Damn Blunder*, 114.

38. *Ibid.*

39. Lucius F. Hubbard, "Civil War Papers," *Collections of the Minnesota Historical Society* vol. 12 (St. Paul n.p., 1908), 578.

40. *Boston Herald*, April 23, 1864.

41. Hubbard, 578–579.

42. Clark, 162.

43. Hubbard, 578–579.

44. Cynthia Dehaven Pitcock, and Bill J. Gurley, eds., *I Acted from Principle: The Civil War Diary of Dr. William M. McPheeters, Confederate Surgeon in the Trans-Mississippi* (Fayetteville: University of Arkansas Press, 2002), 139. All quotations.

45. *Boston Herald*, April 23, 1864.

46. G.G. Benedict, *Vermont in the Civil War. a History*. vol. 2 (Burlington: Free Press Association 1888), 706.

47. *Boston Herald*, April 23, 1864.

48. Lauren Cook Burgess, ed., *An Uncommon Soldier* (Pasadena: the Minerva Center, 1994), 71.

49. Gary Joiner, *One Damn Blunder*, 116.

50. Jakob Heinzelmann to Pastor, April 18, 1864 in Walter D. Kamphoefner and Wolfgang Helbich eds. and Susan Carter Vogel, trans. *Germans in the Civil War the Letters They Wrote Home*. (Chapel Hill: University of North Carolina Press, 2006), 182.

51. Harris H. Beecher, *Record of the 114th Regiment, N.Y.S.V.* (Norwich, NY: J.F. Hubbard, 1866), 324.

52. Heinzelmann, 182.

53. *Ibid.*

54. Hubbard, 271.

55. Gustav Keppler to Parents and brothers, April 15, 1864 in Kamphoefner, 187.

56. Poché in Edwin C. Bears, ed., *A Louisiana Confederate: Diary of Felix Pierre Poché* (Natchitoches: Northwestern State University Press, 1972), 111.

57. McPheeters Diary, April 11, 1864, 141.

58. John Scott, *Story of the 32nd Iowa Infantry* (Nevada, IA 1896), 150–151.

59. Norman D. Brown, *Pleasant Hill: The Civil War Letters of Captain Elijah P. Petty,*

Walker's Texas Division, CSA. (San Antonio: University of Texas, Institute of Texan Cultures, 1982), 411; Account of the boys in the *Mansfield Enterprise* May 17, 1977.

60. Amos Lee Armstrong, *Sabine Parish Louisiana "Land of Green Gold"* (Shreveport: Jones & Springfellow Printing, 1958), 164. Photographs of the battlefield in the 1920s are displayed at the Mansfield State Historic Site museum.

61. W.S. Fowler Medical Register, 1863–1865, Dolph Briscoe Center for American History, University of Texas at Austin.

62. Lowe, *Walker's*, 263.

63. John S. McCulloch, "Reminiscences," typescript, Dolph Briscoe Center for American History University of Texas Austin.

64. Quoted in W. H. Lewis, "Mansfield's Newspaper Story: *Desoto Plume*" (Mansfield, LA: Desoto Historical Society 1980), 158. Thanks to Viki Betts for pointing out this quote.

65. *New York Times*, May 12 and 31, 1864.

66. Thomas W. Cutrer, and T. Michael Parrish, eds., *The Civil War Letters of the Pierson Family* (Baton Rouge: Louisiana State University Press, 1997), 232–234.; Ted Tunnell, *Edge of the Sword: The Ordeal of Carpetbagger Marshall H. Twitchell in the Civil War and Reconstruction* (Baton Rouge 2001), Chapter 6 especially explains similar hardened attitudes still strong in the Red River Valley during Reconstruction.

67. Polignac, "General Polignac's Address to His Brigade at Mansfield" newspaper clipping n.d. Collection Folder 32, Camie Henry Special Collections, Watson Library, Northwestern State University.

68. Ibid.

69. Taylor, "Soldiers of the Western Army of Louisiana!" May 23, 1864 in Louisiana Historical Association Collection, M55, Howard-Tilton Memorial Library, Tulane University, New Orleans, Louisiana, 70118.

70. William to Lizzie, April 11th, 1864; Lizzie to William, April 18th, 1864 in Erika L Murr, ed., *A Rebel Wife in Texas the Diary and Letters of Elizabeth Scott Neblett 1852–1864* (Baton Rouge: Louisiana State University, 2001), 376–395.

Chapter Nine

1. Joiner, *One Damn Blunder from Beginning to End* (Lanham: Rowman & Littlefield 2003), 151.

2. Newspaper estimate and Manning quotations in David C, Edmonds, ed. *The Conduct of Federal Troops in Louisiana During the Invasions of 1863 and 1864* (Lafayette: The Acadiana Press, 1988), 181 and 143.

3. C. Peter Ripley, *Slaves and Freedmen in Civil War Louisiana* (Baton Rouge: Louisiana State University Press, 1976), 21.

4. Henry N. Fairbanks, "The Red River Expedition, 1864" in Military Order of the Loyal Legion of the United States. Commandery of the State of Maine, *War Papers* Vol 1 (Portland: Thurston Print, 1898), 185.

5. Both Quotes in Richard Williams, *Chicago's Battery Boys* (Eldorado Hills, CA: Savas Beatie, 2005), 221.

6. Susan Dollar, "The Red River Campaign, Natchitoches Parish Louisiana a Case of Equal Opportunity Destruction *Louisiana History* 43 (Fall 2002), 419; John Demeritt Diary April 1864, Tulane University; One Soldier Remarked That an "Army of Contrabands" were following them between Henderson Hill and Alexandria. See Charles F. Read "Army Experiences," UC MSS 804, Historic New Orleans Collection.

7. Dollar, 430.

8. *Ibid.*, 429.

9. William Dobak, *Freedom by the Sword the U.S. Colored Troops, 1862–1867* (Washington: U.S. Army Center of Military History, 2011), 123. See also OR, series 1, Vol 34: prt 1: 167.

10. About the Battle, accessed June 5, 2013, http://www.friendsofmansfieldbattlefield.org/about-the-battle has the order of battle for both Union and Confederates.

11. John Winters, *The Civil War in Louisiana* (Baton Rouge: Louisiana State University), 333.

12. Special Order 21, Corps d'Afrique April 6, 1864 in 75th USCT Regimental Letter and Order Book, vol. 2, RG 94, National Archives.

13. 1st Infantry, Corps d'Afrique to General Banks, all quotes in Ira Berlin, ed. *Freedom: A Documentary History of Emancipation, 1861–1867* Series II (Cambridge: Cambridge University Press 1982), 416. This unit became the 73rd USCT.

14. General Order 51, April 19, 1864 was issued at Grand Ecore, Louisiana. Department of the Gulf records, RG 393, National Archives, and Banks Papers, Library of Congress.

15. *Harper's Weekly* May 7, 1864.

16. Krause to mother and brothers May 26, 1864 in Walter D. Kamphoefner, and Wolfgang Helbich eds. and trans. Susan Carter Vogel, *Germans in the Civil War the Letters They Wrote Home.* (Chapel Hill: University of North Carolina Press, 2006), 216. For a discussion of the area see Gary D. Joiner, *Through the Howling Wilderness: The 1864 Red River Campaign and Union Failure in the West* (Knoxville: University of Tennessee Press, 2006), 144–147.

17. Jarratt in Joiner, *Little to Eat and Thin Mud to Drink*. (Knoxville: University of Tennessee Press, 2007), 24; for Bee's role see Fredericka Meiners, "Hamilton P. Bee in the Red River Campaign," *Southwestern Historical Quarterly* 78 (July 1974), 21–44.

18. Samuel W. Mitcham, Jr., *Richard Taylor and the Red River Campaign of 1964* (Gretna: Pelican Publishing, 2012), 252.
19. Joiner, *One Damn*, 153.
20. Franklin to Banks, April 29, 1864 OR series 1, vol. 34, prt 1: 262; Joseph T. Woods, *Services of the Ninety-Sixth Ohio Volunteers* (Toledo: Blade Printing, 1874), 74.
21. *Ibid.*, 75.
22. *Ibid.*
23. Homer B. Sprague, *History of the 13th Infantry Regiment of Connecticut Volunteers* (Hartford: Case, Lockwood & Co., 1867), 195.
24. Joiner, *One Damn*, 154–155.
25. *Ibid.*, OR, series 1, vol. 34, prt 1: 34, 190, 432–435; Beebee's citation in William S. Beebee, accessed April 9, 2012, http://www.history.army.mil/html/moh/civwaral.html.
26. Betrayal at Ebenezer Creek, accessed June 13, 2015, http://www.historynet.com/betrayal-at-ebenezer-creek.htm.
27. Donald S. Frazier, and Andrew Hillhouse, eds., and Anne Ball Ryals, trans., *Love and War: The Civil War Letters and Medicinal Book of Augustus V. Ball* (Buffalo Gap, TX: State House Press, 2010), 264.
28. Louis Lehmann to Fredericka Lehmann, April 27, 1864 in Edmund Louis Burnett, *Civil War Letters of Louis Lehmann* (Hillsboro: Hillsboro College, 2011), 152.
29. Ezra Warner, *Generals in Gray* (Baton Rouge: Louisiana State University Press, 1959), 24.
30. Thomas W. Cutrer, "BEE, HAMILTON PRIOLEAU," Handbook of Texas Online, accessed April 3, 2013, http://www.tshaonline.org/handbook/online/articles/fbe24.
31. Harbert Davenport and Craig H. Roell, "GOLIAD MASSACRE," Handbook of Texas Online, accessed April 3, 2013, http://www.tshaonline.org/handbook/online/articles/qeg02.
32. Hamilton Bee Papers, Dolph Briscoe Center for American History, University of Texas at Austin.
33. Charles F. Read "Army Experiences," UC MSS 804, Historic New Orleans Collection.
34. Bee to Richard Taylor, April 10, 1864, OR series 1, vol. 34, prt 1: 608.
35. Quoted in Jeffery S. Prushankin, *A Crisis of Confederate Command: Edmund Kirby Smith, Richard Taylor, and the Army of the Trans-Mississippi* (Baton Rouge: Louisiana State University Press, 2005), 145.
36. Ludwell Johnson, *Red River Campaign: Politics and Cotton in the Civil War* (Baltimore: Johns Hopkins University, 1958), 281. Michael J. Forsyth, *The Red River Campaign of 1864 and the Loss by the Confederacy of the Civil War* (Jefferson, NC: McFarland & Co., 2002), 101; Joiner, *Through the Howling* 182; Glenn Maxwell to the author, 2013.
37. OR series 1, vol. 34, prt 1: 541–543.
38. Taylor to Bee, April 29, 1864, in "Confederate District of West Louisiana Record Book," Louisiana Historical Association Collection, Manuscripts Collection, Howard-Tilton Memorial Library, Tulane University, New Orleans, Louisiana 70118.
39. Quoted in Prushankin, 145–146.
40. All Bee quotations in OR series 1, vol. 34, prt 1: 613–14; and *Ibid.*, 608–609.
41. Smith, "The Defense of the Red River," *Battles and Leaders of the Civil War* vol. 4 (New York: The Century Company, 1884), 373.
42. *Ibid.*, 615.
43. See Bertram Wyatt-Brown, *Southern Honor: Ethics and Behavior in the Old South* (New York: Oxford University Press, 1982).
44. Joiner, *One Damn*, 156–157.
45. Thomas W. Cutrer, "BAYLOR, GEORGE WYTHE," Handbook of Texas Online, accessed July 18, 2012, http://www.tshaonline.org/handbook/online/articles/fbaar.

Chapter Ten

1. Gary D. Joiner, *Mr. Lincoln's Brown Water Navy* (Lanham: Rowman & Littlefield, 2007), 163.
2. Stephen Binns, "Final Farewell: Signing a Yearbook on the Eve of the Civil War," *Smithsonian in the Classroom* (Washington: Smithsonian Institution, 2009), 2–4.
3. *Ibid.*
4. OR, series 1, vol. 34, prt.1: 607.
5. Binns, 3.
6. *Ibid.*
7. OR series 1, vol. 34, prt. 1: 277.
8. Regimental Association, *History of the Forty-Sixth Regiment Indiana Volunteer Infantry* (Logansport, IN: Wilson, Humphreys, & Co, 1888), 92.
9. G. Warren Thomas to the author, May 12, 2013.
10. OR series 1, vol. 34, prt 1: 612.
11. Binns, 3.
12. Louis Lehmann to Friederike Lehmann April 27, 1864, in Walter D. Kamphoefner, and Wolfgang Helbich eds., and Susan Carter Vogel, trans., *Germans in the Civil War: The Letters They Wrote Home* (Chapel Hill: University of North Carolina Press, 2006), 466.
13. John M. Gould, *History of the First-Tenth-Twenty-Ninth Maine Regiment* (Portland, S. Berry 1871), 409.
14. James Allen Hamilton Diary, April 24, 1864, Dolph Briscoe Center for American History, University of Texas at Austin.
15. Gary Mills Collection of Claims, *Philippe Poete V. United States* #399, Cammie G. Henry Research Center, Northwestern State University of Louisiana, Watson Memorial Library.
16. Susan Dollar, "The Red River Campaign, Natchitoches Parish Louisiana a Case

of Equal Opportunity Destruction," *Louisiana History* 43 (Fall 2002): 415.
17. *Ibid.*
18. *Ibid.*
19. *Ibid.*
20. *Ibid.*
21. William H. Bentley, *History of the 77th Illinois Volunteer Infantry* (Peoria: E. Hine Printer, 1883), 247–248. All quotations.
22. Louis Lehmann to Fredericka Lehmann, April 29, 1864, in Burnett, *Civil War Letters*, 154.
23. Americus Peyroux Cartwright to Parents, May 29, 1864, Cartwright Papers, Dolph Briscoe Center for American History, University of Texas Austin.
24. Dollar, 427.
25. Gary B. Mills, *Civil War Claims in the South: An Index of Civil War Damage Claims Filed Before the Southern Claims Commission, 1871–1880* (Laguna Hills, CA: Aegean Park Press), 60.
26. Quoted Richard Williams, *Chicago's Battery Boys* (New York: Savas Beatie, 2005), 218.
27. Sandra Prud'homme Haynie, *Legends of Oakland Plantation* (Shreveport: LaPress Co. Printing, 2001), 52.
28. Mills, *Civil War Claims*, 60, 57, 61.
29. Buck T. Foster, *Sherman's Mississippi Campaign* (Tuscaloosa: University of Alabama Press, 2006), 1–8. James G. Hollandsworth, Jr. "Preparing the Place for Hell: The Burning of Alexandria in 1864," *Louisiana Cultural Visitas* (Spring 2008): 22–29.
30. Joseph Minis to Father and Mother, May 6, [june4?] 1864, at 11th Wisconsin Civil War Regiment, accessed June 6, 2008, http://11wisconsinregiment.soldierstudies.org/?p=37. Original letter is in Wisconsin Historical Society Archives. Transcribed and posted by Christopher Wehner. All quotations.
31. New York Military Museum and Veterans research center newspaper clippings file at New York Military Museum, accessed July 18, 2012, http://dmna.ny.gov/historic/reghist/civil/infantry/161stinf/161stinfcwn.htm.
32. Lucius F. Hubbard, "Civil War Papers," *Collections of the Minnesota Historical Society* vol. 12. (St. Paul, n.p. 1908), 583.
33. Homer B. Spragues, *History of the 13th Infantry Regiment of Connecticut Volunteers* (Hartford: Case, Lockwood & Co., 1867), 190.
34. New York State Military Museum clippings.
35. Sprague, 193.
36. Howell Diary, Howell Papers Dolph Briscoe Center for American History, University of Texas at Austin.
37. CW Boyce Home, accessed December 12, 2012, http://louisdl.louislibraries.org/cdm/singleitem/collection/LHP/id/4037/rec/9; Bettye Dekeyser, December 16, 2012, interview. Mrs. Dekeyser remembered visiting the home and hearing the story form the Boyce sisters prior to levee construction that removed the home to Mayre St. in Alexandria where it still stands, 2013.
38. Michael J. Goc, *Hero of the Red River: The Life and Times of Joseph Bailey* (Friendship, WI: New Past Press, 2007). See archeology report at Bailey's Dam, accessed July 21, 2012, http://www.crt.state.la.us/dataprojects/archaeology/virtualbooks/BAILEYS/BAILEYS.HTM.
39. United States, War Department, *Atlas to Accompany the Official Records of the Union and Confederate Armies* New York: Fairfax Press, 1983).
40. Dr. James David, interview, May 18, 2010.
41. Quote in Frank Moore, *Document No. 2: The Red River Dam. the Rebellion Record: A Diary of American Events* vol. 11 (New York: G.P. Putnam, D. Van Nostrand, 1868), 11: Cotton and rails information found in claims 20259 and 21691 United States. Commissioners of Claims. *Summary Reports in All Cases Reported to Congress as Disallowed Under the Act of March 3, 1871* (Washington: Government Printing Office, 1876–1881).
42. Quoted in Sprague, 206–207.
43. Porter, OR, series 1, vol. 34, prt 1, 221.
44. Lieutenant Edward Cunningham, June 27, 1864 OR, series 1, vol. 46, prt 1, 558.
45. Hollandsworth, 27.
46. Arthur W. Bergeron, Jr., ed., *A Thrilling Narrative: The Memoir of a Southern Unionist* (Fayetteville: University of Arkansas Press, 2006), 61.
47. Charles F. Read "Army Experiences," UC MSS 804, Historic New Orleans Collection. Joiner, *One Damn Blunder*, 169.
48. Father Chad Partain, Catholic Diocese of Alexandria, conversation with the author, 2012.
49. Judge Thomas Yeager, 9th Judicial District Court, to the author, 2004 and 2013.
50. Hollandsworth, 27.
51. Herman C. Hemenway to Editors, May 20, 1864, in C. S. Percival, and E. Percival, eds., *History of Buchanan County, Iowa 1842 to 1881* (Cleveland: W.W. Williams 1881), 205.
52. Gary D. Joiner, and Marilyn Joiner, eds., *No Pardons to Ask Nor Apologies to Make: The Journal of William Henry King in Gray's 28th Louisiana Infantry Regiment* (Knoxville: University of Tennessee Press, 2006), 172. Both quotations.
53. Allen quotation in Sara Dorsey, *Recollections of Henry Watkins Allen* (New York; Doubleday, 1866), 279–280;
54. David C. Edmonds, ed., *The Conduct of Federal Troops in Louisiana During the Invasions of 1863 and 1864 Official Report* (Lafayette, LA: The Acadiana Press, 1988).
55. Louis Lehmann to Friedereike Lehmann May 8, 1864, in Kamphoefner, 467.

56. Grady Mcwhinney, and Perry Jamison, *Attack and Die: Civil War Military Tactics and the Southern Heritage* (Tuscaloosa: University of Alabama Press, 1982).
57. Walter, Prichard, ed. "A Tourist's Description of Louisiana in 1860." *Louisiana Historical Quarterly* 21 (October 1938): 1152.
58. Ibid., 1147.
59. OR, series 1, vol. 34, prt 1: 593.
60. Moritz Maedgen to Captain H.G. Carter June 23, 1864 in Joiner, ed., *Little to Eat*, 151.
61. Report of Faries to J.C. Moncure, May 17, 1864, OR series 1, vol. 34, prt 1: 630.
62. Joiner, *One Damn Blunder*, 170.
63. From Emory's "General Order 48," May 18, 1864, OR, series 1, vol. 34, prt 1: 399.
64. Report of Faries to J.C. Moncure, May 17, 1864, OR series 1, vol. 34, prt 1: 631.
65. Chadwick to General L. Thomas June 13, 1864, USCT Letterbook, RG 93, National Archives. All quotations.
66. Joiner, *One Damn Blunder*, 172.
67. Ibid.
68. Wales W. Wood, *History of the Ninety-Fifth Regiment Illinois Infantry Volunteers* (Chicago: Tribune Company's Book and Job Printing office, 1865), 106.
69. Anne Bailey, *Between the Enemy and Texas: Parsons's Texas Cavalry in the Civil War* (Fort Worth 1989), 187.
70. Ibid.
71. W. Randolph Howell Diary, University of Texas at Austin first two quotes; last quote from Cornelius Corwin Diary, Indiana Historical Society, May 18, 1864.
72. Joiner, *One Damn Blunder*, 171. CWSAC battle summaries for Yellow Bayou, National Park Service, http://www.nps.gov/abpp/battles/la023.htm (April 4, 2013).
73. Steve Mayeaux to the audience at "Civil War in Avoyelles Parish," May 31, 2013. The home no longer stands.
74. Grisamore in Arthur W. Bergeron, Jr., *Reminiscences of Major Silas T. Grisamore, C.S.A.* (Baton Rouge: Louisiana State University Press, 1993), 159.

Conclusion

1. Lucius F. Hubbard, "Civil War Papers," *Collections of the Minnesota Historical Society* vol. 12 (St. Paul, n.p. 1908), 573.
2. These numbers come from adding up the reported losses for the major battles at the CWSAC battle summary site for the National Park Service, accessed April 3, 2013, http://eww.nps.gov/abpp/battles/bystate.htm.
3. OR series 1, vol. 34, prt. 1: 390. For Hunter's career see Ezra Warner, *Generals in Blue* (Baton Rouge: Louisiana State University Press, 1964), 244.
4. Quoted in Gary Joiner, *One Damn Blunder from Beginning to End: The Red River Campaign, 1864* (Lanham: Roman & Littlefield, 2003), xix.
5. Carroll Harris to Valery Harris May 25, 1864, Pearce Civil War Collections, Navarro College, Corsicana, Texas.
6. Warner, *Generals in Blue*, 18.
7. Joiner, *One Damn Blunder*, 161 and 173.
8. *Louisiana Democrat* November 2, 1864.
9. Susan Dollar, "The Red River Campaign, Natchitoches Parish Louisiana a Case of Equal Opportunity Destruction," *Louisiana History* 43 (Fall 2002): 429.
10. St. Louis *Republican* April 24, 1864.
11. J. Gordon to M. L Texada June 5, 1864, Ker Texada Family Papers, Manuscript Collection 545, Manuscripts Department, Howard-Tilton Memorial Library, Tulane University, New Orleans, Louisiana 70118.
12. *Louisiana Democrat* November 2, 1864; Allen to Lewis Texada, May 22, 1864, Texada Papers Louisiana and Lower Mississippi Valley Collection, Hill Library, Louisiana State University.
13. Gary B. Mills, *Civil War Claims in the South: An Index of Civil War Damage Claims. Filed Before the Southern Claims Commission, 1871–1880* (Laguna Hills, CA: Aegean Park Press 1980).
14. United States, Commissioners of Claims, *Summary Reports in All Cases Reported to Congress as Disallowed Under the Act of March 3, 1871* (Washington: Government Printing Office, 1876–1881), claims 9705 and 20259. All quotations.
15. Ibid. Landry Baillio genealogy at Baillio family and Lecour, Leonard, Kirkland, Stafford, accessed June 19, 2015, http://www.genealogy.com/forum/surnames/topics/baillio/10/.
16. United States, *Claims*, Claims 9356 and 13164. C.W. Boyce service record, accessed June 23, 2013, http://www.nps.gov/civilwar/search-soldiers-detail.htm?soldierId=DC02EB84-DC7A-DF11-BF36-B8AC6F5D926A.
17. United States, *Claims*, Claim 680.
18. Ibid.
19. Gary B. Mills, *Alien Neutrality and the Red River Campaign: A Study of Cases Heard Before the International Claims Commissions* in Arthur W. Bergeron, Jr. ed. *the Louisiana Purchase Bicentennial Series in Louisiana History* vol. 5 Part B. (Lafayette: Center for Louisiana Studies, 2004), 159. All information in this paragraph comes from this source and its tables contained in appendices.
20. Ibid.
21. Oaths of Allegiance, Department of the Gulf Records, RG 393, National Archives. I counted those in the box and estimated how many were from the Red River Valley.
22. Wells to General Nathaniel Banks, April 8, 1864, Banks Papers Library of Congress. J.R. Mainor to Thomas O. Moore, July 7, 1864, Moore Papers typescript Northwestern State University.

23. New Orleans *Daily True Delta*, May 5, 1864, and *Mobile Advertiser and Register* May 18, 1864. Thanks to Steve Mayeaux for showing me this account found by the late Dr. Arthur W. Bergeron, Jr.
24. A. P. Field, Charlie Smith, R W. Taliaferro, J. M. Wells, R. King Cutler, R. V. Montague, Luther F. Parker, and M. F Bonzan, to Lincoln, December 14, 1864 Abraham Lincoln Papers, Library of Congress.
25. *Ibid.*
26. *Ibid.*
27. *Ibid.*
28. Arthur W. Bergeron, Jr. ed. *A Thrilling Narrative: The Memoir of a Southern Unionist* (Fayetteville: University of Arkansas Press, 2006), 65–66.
29. Lincoln to Major General Canby, September 21, 1864, in Lincoln Papers, Library of Congress.
30. Jeff Prushankin, *A Crisis in Confederate Command: Edmund Kirby Smith, Richard Taylor, and the Army of the Trans-Mississippi* (Baton Rouge: Louisiana State University Press, 2005), 176–179.
31. T. Michael Parrish, *Richard Taylor Soldier Prince of Dixie* (Chapel Hill: University of North Carolina Press, 1992), 394–396. Ezra Warner *Generals in Gray* (Baton Rouge: Louisiana State University Press, 1959), 300.
32. *Ibid.*, 280.
33. Arthur W. Bergeron, Jr. "Fort Buhlow and Fort Randolph: Confederate Defenses on the Red River," 591–598 and Thomas Howell, "Forts Randolph and Buhlow in the Civil War," in Arthur W. Bergeron, Jr., ed. *Louisiana Bicentennial Series in Louisiana History* vol. 5 Part B (Lafayette, LA: Center for Louisiana Studies, 2004).
34. Arthur W. Bergeron, Jr., *Confederate Mobile* (Baton Rouge: Louisiana State University Press, 2000), 138.
35. Civil War Trust, General Kirby Smith Surrenders the Trans-Mississippi Forces, accessed June 3, 2015, http://www.civilwar.org/education/history/end-of-war/smith-surrenders.html.
36. George C. Rable, *But There Was No Peace: The Role of Violence in the Politics of Reconstruction* (Athens: University of Georgia Press 1984), 132; Nicholas Lemann, *Redemption: The Last Battle of the Civil War* (New York: Farrar, Straus & Giroux, 2006), 76–77; Leeanna Keith, *The Colfax Massacre: The Untold Story of Black Power, White Terror, & the Death of Reconstruction* (New York: Oxford University Press, 2007); Charles Lane, *The Day Freedom Died: The Colfax Massacre, the Supreme Court, and the Betrayal of Reconstruction* (New York: Henry Holt, 2008).

Bibliography

Libraries and Archives

Cayuga Museum of History and Art, Auburn, New York
General John S. Clark Papers.

Historic New Orleans Collection, New Orleans, Louisiana
Charles F. Sherman Civil War Letters, MSS 114
Charles F. Read "Army Experiences," UC MSS 804
General Orders No.—Soldiers of Western Louisiana, MSS 238.50
Governor Henry W. Allen's Address to the Citizens of New Orleans, MSS 474. 3
Henry C. Sampson Diary, MSS 258
John Hickman Ransdell Papers, 1820–1869, MSS 5
John J. Moore Papers, MSS 12
Maris L. Deloach Papers, MSS 370
Thomas Overton Moore Letters, MSS 469
Henry C. Sampson Diary, MSS 258
Union Soldier's Letter, MSS 51

Indiana Historical Society, Indianapolis
Andrew Piatt Civil War Letters
Bernard F. Schermerhorn Papers, 1862–1864
Cornelius Corwin Papers, 1862–1921
David King Diary
John Wilkins Diary Notebook, 1911

Library of Congress
Abraham Lincoln Papers
Nathaniel Banks Papers

Mansfield State Historic Site, Mansfield, LA
W.H. Mathews Letter (typescript)

Navarro College, Corsicana, Texas
Pearce Civil War Collections

National Archives, Washington, D.C.
Department of Gulf Records. RG 93, RG 94, RG 109, RG 393, RG 393.4, RG 1738, RG1788.

Louisiana State Archives, Baton Rouge
Rebel Archives, Letters Received, Executive Department, State of Louisiana, 1860–1865.
Rebel Archives. Proclamations Executive Department, State of Louisiana, 1860–1865

Hill Memorial Library Louisiana State University, Baton Rouge
Arthur W. Hyatt papers, 1861–1895
Charles Oscar Dupuy letter, 1863
David D. Porter letter, 1866
Edward Clifton Wharton Papers, 1819–1947
George B. Marshall Papers, 1807–1900
James G. Taliaferro Family papers, 1787–1934
John Coddington Kinney letters, 1862–1864
J. Fair Hardin collection, 1718–1939
Joseph L. Brent papers, 1869–1940
Josiah Goodwin diaries and research collection, 1862–1864, 1983–1984
J.P. Van Nest letter, 1864
Nathaniel P. Banks letterpress copybook, 1863 Aug. 1–1864
Robert A. Newell Papers, 1841–1887
Robert A. Tyson diary, 1863–1864
Orramel Hinckley and Family Papers, 1811–1897
Phanor Prudhomme family Papers, 1836–1868 and 1804–1940
Lewis Texada and Family papers, 1830–1939
William H. Tamplin Letters, 1862–1865
William S. Beebe papers, 1864

Louisiana State University-Alexandria, James C. Bolton Library
Ezra Bennett and Family Papers
Sue Eakin Collection
Mannning-Compton Family Papers
Charles Mulholland Memorandum Book, Mulholland-Polk Family Papers

Northwestern State University, Watson Memorial Library Camie Henry Special Collections, Natchitoches, Louisiana
Governor Thomas Overton Moore Papers (Typescripts)
P.E. Cloutier Papers
Prudhomme Family Papers

Tulane University, Howard-Tilton Library, Manuscripts Department, New Orleans
Alfred S. Lippman Collection of Civil War Letters, 1848–1866, Manuscripts Collection 993
G.P. Whittington Collection Louisiana Collections, 976.3 (027.1) W626
John Demerit Diary, 1863–1866, Manuscripts Collection, M1155
Ker and Texada families papers, 1813–1922, Manuscripts Collection 545
Louisiana Historical Association Collection, Manuscripts Collection 55
Simon Bott Diary, 1864–1868, Manuscripts Collection M1156

University North Carolina, Watson Library, Chapel Hill
Phanor Prudhomme papers, 1804–1940, Natchitoches Parish, Louisiana

University of Texas at Austin, Dolph Briscoe Center for American History
Americus Peyroux Cartwright Papers, 1853–1865
Confederate States of America Records, 1856–1915
Confederate States of America. Army. Trans-Mississippi Dept. General Orders: Headquarters, 1863–1865
Edward Clark Papers, 1842–1910, 1946
E. Cort Williams. "Recollections of the Red River Expedition: A Paper Read Before the Ohio Commandery" 1886
Edwin Pinckney Papers, 1862–1870
David M. Ray Papers, 1859–1879
Hamilton Bee Papers, 1838–1894

John B. Ray Letters, 1861–1864
James Allen Hamilton Diary, 1861–1864
John S. McCulloch, "Reminiscences of Life in the Army and as a Prisoner of War" (Typescript), 1877.
John Thomas Diaries, 1864–1865
Mahlon W. Barber and Durning C.S. Diary, 1864
Raney Green Jr. Papers, 1862–1865
W. Randolph Howell Papers, 1861–1879.
W.S. Fowler, Medical Register, 1863–1865

Newspapers

Boston Herald (Boston, MA)
Constitutional (Alexandria, LA)
Daily True Delta (New Orleans)
Louisiana Democrat (Alexandria, LA)
Harper's Weekly (New York)
Houston Daily Telegraph (Houston, TX)
Le Courier (New Orleans)
Louisiana Democrat (New Orleans)
New Orleans Bee
New Orleans Times
New York Times
Natchitoches Union
Red River Republican (Alexandria, LA)
Republican (St. Louis)
Shreveport Journal
Shreveport Weekly News
Whig Tribune Almanac

Regimental Histories

Beecher, Harris H. *Record of the 114th Regiment, N.Y.S.V.* Norwich: J.F. Hubbard, 1866.
Benedict, G.G. *Vermont in the Civil War: A History.* vol. 2. Burlington: Free Press Association, 1888.
Bentley, William H. *History of the 77th Illinois Volunteer Infantry.* Peoria: E. Hine Printer, 1883.
Bering, John A. and Thomas Montgomery. *History of the Forty-Eighth Ohio Veterans Volunteer Infantry.* Hillsboro: Highland News Office, 1880. Accessed June 11, 2008. http://www.48ovvi.org/chap15.html
Clark, Orton S. *The One hundred and Sixteenth Regiment of New York State Volunteers.* Buffalo: Printing House of Mathews and Warren, 1868.
Fairbanks, Henry N. "Red River Expedition, 1864" in *Military Order of the Loyal Legion of the United States. Commandery of the State of Maine War Papers.* vol.1. Portland: Thurston Print, 1898.
Gould, John Mead. *History of the First–Tenth—Twenty–Ninth Maine Regiment.* Portland: S. Berry, 1871.
Irwin, Richard. *History of the Nineteenth Army Corps.* Baton Rouge: Elliott's Book Shop, 1985.
Pellet, Ellias P. *History of the 114th Regiment New York State Volunteers.* Norwich, NY: Telegraph and Chronicle Power Press Print, 1866.
Regimental Association. *History of the Forty-Sixth Regiment Indiana Volunteer Infantry.* Logansport, IN: Wilson, Humphreys, and Co, 1888.

Scott, John. *Story of the 32nd Iowa Infantry.* Nevada, IA: J. Scott 1896.
Scott, R.B. *History of the 67th Indiana Regiment.* Bedford: Herald Book and Job Print, 1892.
Shorey, Henry Augustus. *The Story of the Maine Fifteenth.* Bridgeton: Press of the Bridgeton News, 1890.
Sprague, Homer B. *History of the 13th Infantry Regiment of Connecticut Volunteers.* Hartford: Case, Lockwood and Company, 1867.
Wood, Wales W. *History of the Ninety-Fifth Regiment Illinois Infantry Volunteers.* Chicago: Tribune Company's Book and Job Office, 1865.
Woods, Joseph T. *Services of the Ninety-Sixth Ohio Volunteers.* Toledo: Blade Printing, 1874.

Books, Articles and Websites

Allen, V.W. in Benjamin Gue. *History of Iowa from the Earliest Times to the Beginning of the Twentieth Century.* vol. 2. New York: Century History Company, 1903.
Anderson, John, ed. *Brokenburn, The Journal of Kate Stone, 1861–1868.* Baton Rouge: Louisiana State University Press, 1995.
Arceneaux, William. *Acadian General Alfred Mouton and the Civil War.* Lafayette: University of Southwestern Louisiana, 1981.
Armstrong, Amos Lee. *Sabine Parish Louisiana: "Land of Green Gold."* Shreveport: Jones and Springfellow Printing, 1958.
Ash, Stephen V. *When the Yankees Came: Conflict and Chaos in the Occupied South, 1861–1865* Chapel Hill: University of North Carolina Press, 1995.
Bailey, Anne J. *Between The Enemy and Texas: Parsons's Texas Cavalry in the Civil War.* Fort Worth: Texas Christian University Press, 1989.
"The Battle of Pleasant Hill " *The Annals of Iowa.* vol. 7 (1906). Accessed July 10, 2014. http://ir.uiowa.edu/annals-of-iowa/vol7/iss7/12
Bauer, Craig A. *Creole Genesis.* Lafayette: University of Louisiana Press, 2011.
Bearss. Edwin C., ed. *A Louisiana Confederate: Diary of Felix Pierre Poché.* Natchitoches: Northwestern State University Press, 1972.
Benedict, Henry Marvin. *Memorial of Brevet Major General Lewis Benedict.* Albany: J. Munsell, 1866.
Bayou Boeuf History. Accessed April 7, 2014. http://bayouboeuflouisiana.blogspot.com/2013/07/stop-2-lamourie-locks-in-bayou-lamourie.html.
Bergeron, Arthur W., Jr. "A Colonel Gains His Wreath: Henry Gray's Louisiana Brigade at the Battle of Mansfield, April 8, 1864," in Theodore P. Savas, David A. Woodbury, and Gary D. Joiner, eds. *The Red River Campaign: Union and Confederate Leadership and the War in Louisiana.* Shreveport: Parabellum Press, 2003.
____. *Confederate Mobile.* Baton Rouge: Louisiana State University Press, 2000.
____. "Fort Buhlow and Fort Randolph: Confederate Defenses on the Red River." *The Louisiana Purchase Bicentennial Series in Louisiana History.* vol. 5 Part B. Lafayette: Center for Louisiana Studies, 2004.
____. ed. *The Louisiana Purchase Bicentennial Series in Louisiana History* Vol. 5 Part B. Lafayette: Center for Louisiana Studies, 2004.
____. ed. *Reminiscences of Major Silas T. Grisamore, C.S.A.* Baton Rouge: Louisiana State University Press, 1993.
____. ed. *A Thrilling Narrative: The Memoir of a Southern Unionist.* Fayetteville: University of Arkansas Press, 2006.
Berlin, Ira, ed. *Freedom: A Documentary History of Emancipation, 1861–1867.* Series II. Cambridge: Cambridge University Press, 1982.
Betts, Vicki. "Civilian Reaction to the Red River Campaign, 1864, from Natchitoches to Mansfield, Louisiana." Accessed December 12, 2013. http://files.usgwarchives.net/la/state/history/military/wbts/redriver.txt.

Binns, Stephen. "Final Farewell: Signing a Yearbook on the Eve of the Civil War." *Smithsonian in the Classroom.* Washington, D.C.: Smithsonian Institution, 2009.
Blake, William O. *Pictorial History of the Great Rebellion.* Columbus, OH: Gilmore and Segner Publishers, 1866.
Blessington, John Palmer. *The Campaigns of Walker's Texas Division.* New York: Lange, Little and Company, 1875.
Boggs, William R. *Military Reminiscences of General William R. Boggs, C.S.A.* Durham, NC: Seeman Printery, 1913.
Boyle, James E. *Cotton and the New Orleans Cotton Exchange.* Garden City: Country Life Press, 1934.
Bragg, Jefferson Davis. *Louisiana in the Confederacy.* Baton Rouge: Louisiana State University Press, 1941.
Brasseaux, Carl A. *Acadian to Cajun: Transformation of a People, 1803–1877.* Jackson: University of Mississippi Press, 1992.
Brennan, Thomas M. *A Planter's Son Goes to War.* Natchitoches: National Park Service, 2012.
Brooksher, William R. *War Along the Bayous: The 1864 Red River Campaign.* Washington: Brassey's 2001.
Brown, Norman D. *Journey to Pleasant Hill: The Civil War Letters of Captain Elijah P. Petty, Walker's Texas Division, CSA.* San Antonio: University of Texas, Institute of Texan Cultures, 1982.
Buckley, S.B. "Agricultural Resources in Texas," *Debow's Review* vol. 4 (October 1867): 320–334.
Burgess, Lauren Cook, ed. *An Uncommon Soldier.* Pasadena: The Minerva Center, 1994.
Burnett, Edmund Louis. *Civil War Letters of Louis Lehmann.* Hillsboro: Hillsboro Junior College, 2011.
Channing, Steven A. *Crisis of Fear: The Secession in South Carolina.* New York; Simon & Schuster, 1974.
Childers, Henry H. "Reminiscences of the Battle of Pleasant Hill." *The Annals of Iowa* vol. 7 (1906). Accessed July 10, 2014. http://ir.uiowa.edu/annals-of-iowa/vol7/iss7/3.
Cook, Phillip C. "The North Louisiana Upland Frontier: The First Three Decades." B.H. Gilley, ed., *North Louisiana: Essays on the Region and Its History.* Volume 1. Ruston, 1984.
Cooper, William J. *We Have the War Upon Us: The Onset of the Civil War, November 1860-April 1861.* New York: Vintage Books, 2012.
Crofts, Daniel. *Reluctant Confederates: Upper South Unionists in the Secession Crisis.* Chapel Hill: University of North Carolina Press, 1989.
Cutrer Thomas W. and T. Michael Parrish, eds. *The Civil War Letters of the Pierson Family.* Baton Rouge: Louisiana State University Press, 1997.
Davis, William C. *Three Roads to the Alamo.* New York: HarperCollins Books, 1998.
Dawson, Joseph G. *Army Generals and Reconstruction, 1862–1877.* (Baton Rouge: Louisiana State University Press, 1982.
DeBow, J.D. B. *The Seventh Census of the United States: 1850.* Washington, D.C.: Robert Armstrong Public Printer, 1853.
Decuir, Randy. "Civil War in Avoyelles Parish" May 31, 2013, Civil War Sesquicentennial Commemoration, Marksville, LA.
"Defending the Homeland: Union Forces Target Shreveport, Texas and Beyond." Symposium, Shreveport, LA, March 14–16, 2014.
Dew, Charles B. "Who Won the Secession Election in Louisiana." *Journal of Southern History* 36 (February 1970): 18–32.
Dobak, William. *Freedom By the Sword the U.S. Colored Troops, 1862–1867.* Washington: U.S. Army Center of Military History, 2011.

Documenting Louisiana Sugar, 1845–1917. Accessed June 15, 2011, http://www.sussex.ac.uk/louisianasugar/.
Dollar, Susan. "The Red River Campaign, Natchitoches Parish Louisiana a Case of Equal Opportunity Destruction." *Louisiana History* 43 (Fall 2002): 411–432.
Dorsey, Sara A. *Recollections of Henry Watkins Allen*. New York: Doubleday, 1866.
Dupree, Stephen, ed. *Campaigning with the 67th Indiana 1864: An Annotated Diary of Service in the Department of the Gulf*. New York: iUniverse, 2006.
Edmonds, David C., ed. *The Conduct of Federal Troops in Louisiana During the Invasions of 1863 and 1864 Official Report*. Lafayette, LA: The Acadiana Press, 1988.
———. *Yankee Autumn in Acadiana: A Narrative of the Great Texas Overland Expedition Through Southwestern Louisiana, October-December 1863*. (Lafayette: Center for Louisiana Studies, 1979).
Escott, Paul. *After Secession: Jefferson Davis and the Failure of Confederate Nationalism*. Baton Rouge: Louisiana State University, 1978.
Fairbanks, Henry N. "Red River Expedition, 1864" in Military Order of the Loyal Legion of the United States. Commandery of the State of Maine. *War Papers*. Volume 1 Portland: Thurston Print, 1898.
Flinn, Frank. *Campaigning with Banks in Louisiana '63 and '64 and With Sheridan in the Shenandoah Valley '64 and '65*. Boston: W. B. Clarke, 1889.
Follett, Richard. *The Sugar Masters*. Baton Rouge: Louisiana State University Press, 2005.
Foote, Shelby. *The Civil War: A Narrative Red River to Appomattox*. vol 3. New York: Random House, 1974.
Forsyth, Michael J. *The Red River Campaign of 1864 and the loss by the Confederacy of The Civil War*. Jefferson: McFarland Publishing, 2002.
Foster, Buck T. *Sherman's Mississippi Campaign*. Tuscaloosa: University of Alabama Press, 2006.
Frazier, Donald S. *Fire in the Cane Field: The Federal Invasion of Louisiana and Texas, January 1861–January 1863*. Buffalo Gap, TX: State House Press, 2009.
———. "'Out of Stinking Distance': The Guerilla War in Louisiana." in Daniel Sutherland, ed. *Guerrillas, Unionists, and Violence on the Confederate Home Front* (Fayetteville: University of Arkansas Press, 1999), 170
———. *Thunder Across the Swamp: The Fight for the Lower Mississippi, February–May, 1863*. Buffalo Gap, TX: State House Press, 2011.
———. and Andrew Hillhouse, eds. and trans. Anne Ball Ryals, *Love and War: The Civil War Letters and Medicinal Book of Augustus V. Ball*. Buffalo Gap, TX: State House Press, 2010.
Freeman, Douglas Southall. *R. E. Lee: A Biography*. 4 vols. New York: Charles Scribner's and Sons, 1935.
Freehling, William W. *The Road to Disunion: Volume II: Secessionists Triumphant, 1854–1861*. New York: Oxford University Press, 2008.
Gentry, Judith F. "White Gold: The Confederate Government and Cotton in Louisiana" in Arthur W. Bergeron, Jr., ed. *The Louisiana Purchase Bicentennial Series in Louisiana History*. Vol. 5. Lafayette: Center for Louisiana Studies, 2004.
Goc, Michael J. *Hero of the Red River: The Life and Times of Joseph Bailey*. Friendship, WI: New Past Press, 2007.
Gray, Lewis. *History of Agriculture in the Southern United States to 1860*. vol. 1. Gloucester: P. Smith, 1958.
Gue, Benjamin F. *History of Iowa From the Earliest Times to the Beginning of the Twentieth Century*. vol. 2 .New York: The Century History Company, 1903.
Hair, William Ivy. *The Kingfish and His Realm*. Baton Rouge: Louisiana State University Press, 1997.
Halainen, Bill. "The Long Road to Gettysburg: The Sixth Corps Epic March to Get-

tysburg." Accessed April 14, 2013. http://npsgnmp.wordpress.com/2013/02/22/the-long-road-to-gettysburg-the-sixth-corps-epic-march-to-gettysburg.
Hall, Gwendolyn Midlo. *Africans in Colonial Louisiana*. Baton Rouge: Louisiana State University Press, 1992.
Hall, Ryan M. "A Glorious Assemblage: the Rise of the Know-Nothing Party in Louisiana" MA Thesis Louisiana State University, 2015.
Hardin, J. Fair. *Northwestern Louisiana: a History of the Watershed of the Red River, 1714–1937*. vol. 1. Shreveport: Historical Record Association, 1939.
____. "An Outline of Shreveport and Caddo Parish History," *Louisiana Historical Quarterly* 18 (October 1935): 787–830.
Haynie, Sandra Prud'homme. *Legends of Oakland Plantation*. Shreveport: LaPress Co. Printing, 2001.
History of Caddo Parish. Accessed November 14, 2011. http://www.caddohistory.com.
Hearn, Chester G. *Admiral David Dixon Porter: The Civil War Years*. Annapolis, MD: Naval Institute Press, 1996.
____. *The Capture of New Orleans, 1862*. Baton Rouge: Louisiana State University Press, 1995.
Hollandsworth, James G. Jr. *The Louisiana Native Guards*. Baton Rouge: Louisiana State University Press, 1995.
____."Preparing the Place for Hell: The Burning of Alexandria in 1864." *Louisiana Cultural Visitas* (Spring 2008): 22–29.
____. *Pretense of Glory: The Life of General Nathaniel P. Banks*. Baton Rouge: Louisiana State University Press, 1998.
Holt, Michael. *The Rise and Fall of the American Whig Party: Jacksonian Politics and the Onset of the Civil War*. New York: Oxford University Press, 1999.
Howell, Thomas. "Forts Randolph and Buhlow In the Civil War." Arthur W. Bergeron, Jr., Editor. *The Louisiana Purchase Bicentennial Series in Louisiana History*. Volume 5 Part B. Lafayette: Center for Louisiana Studies, 2004.
Hubbard, Lucius F. "Civil War Papers." *Collections of the Minnesota Historical Society*, vol. 12. St. Paul, n.p. 1908.
Humphreys, Hubert Davis. "The 'Great Raft' of the Red River" in B.H. Gilley, ed., *North Louisiana: Essays on the Region and Its History*. Volume 1 Ruston, 1984: 73–92.
Hunter, G. Howard. "Thomas Overton Moore," KnowLA Encyclopedia. Accessed April 29, 2015. http://www.knowla.org/entry/937/.
____. "Unionist Troops in Louisiana" KnowLA Encyclopedia. Accessed April 30, 2015. http://www.knowla.org/entry/1425/.
Joiner, Gary D. *Lincoln's Brown Water Navy*. New York: Roman and Littlefield, 2007.
____. *Little To Eat and Thin Mud to Drink*. Knoxville: University of Tennessee Press, 2007.
____. *One Damn Blunder From Beginning to End: The Red River Campaign of 1864*. Lanham: Scholarly Resources, 2003.
____. *Through The Howling Wilderness: The Red River Campaign and Union Failure in the West*. Knoxville: University of Tennessee Press, 2006.
____. and Marilyn Joiner, eds. *No Pardons to Ask nor Apologies to Make: the Journal of William Henry King in Gray's 28th Louisiana Infantry Regiment*. Knoxville: University of Tennessee Press, 2006.
Johnson Ludwell H. *Red River Campaign, Politics and Cotton in the Civil War*. Baltimore: Johns Hopkins Press, 1958.
Kallgren, Beverly Hayes and James L. Crouthamel, Editors. *"Dear Friend Anna": The Civil War Letters of A Common Soldier From Maine*. Orono, ME: University of Maine Press, 1992.
Kamphoefner, Walter D. and Wolfgang Helbich, eds. and trans. Susan Carter Vogel.

Germans in the Civil War: The Letters They Wrote Home. Chapel Hill: University of North Carolina Press, 2006.

Keith, Leeanna. *The Colfax Massacre: The Untold Story of Black Power, White Terror, & The Death of Reconstruction*. New York: Oxford University Press, 2007.

Kennedy, Joseph C.G. *Agriculture of the United States in 1860*. Washington, D.C.: Government Printing Office, 1864.

____. *Population of the United States In 1860; Compiled from the Original Returns of the U.S. Census*. Washington: Government Printing Office, 1864.

Lane, Charles. *The Day Freedom Died: The Colfax Massacre, the Supreme Court, and the Betrayal of Reconstruction*. New York: Henry Holt, 2008.

Lathrop, Barnes F. "Disaffection in Confederate Louisiana: The Case of William Hyman." *Journal of Southern History* 24 (August 1958): 308–318.

Laurent, Carl N.B. *From this Valley: a History of Alexandria, Pineville, and Rapides, Louisiana*. Alexandria, LA: Red River X-Press, 2004.

____. *The Last Rebel Yell: The Civil War in Central Louisiana*. Pineville, LA: Red River X-Press, 2012.

____. Ed. *George Purnell Whittington: Rapides Parish, Louisiana a History*. Pineville, LA; Red River X-Press, 2011.

Lemann, Nicholas. *Redemption: The Last Battle of the Civil War*. New York: Farrar, Straus & Giroux, 2006.

Lewis, W.H. "Mansfield's Newspaper Story: Desoto Plume" Mansfield, LA: Desoto Historical Society, 1980.

Liddell, St. John Richardson. *Liddell's Record*. Baton Rouge: Louisiana State University Press, 1985.

Louisiana Department of Culture Recreation and Tourism. Archeology Division Accessed July 21, 2012. htttp://www.crt.state.la.us/dataprojects/archaeology/virtualbooks/BAILEYS/BAILEYS.

Lowe, Richard. *The Texas Overland Expedition of 1863*. Fort Worth: Ryan Place Publishers, 1996.

____. *Walker's Texas Division, C.S.A*. Baton Rouge: Louisiana State University Press, 2004.

Luca, Mattie Davis and Mita Holsapple Hall. *A History of Grayson County, Texas*. Sherman, TX: Scruggs, 1936.

Mangham, Dana M. *"Oh, For a Touch of the Vanished Hand": Discovering a Southern Family and the Civil War*. Murfreesboro: Southern Heritage Press, 2000.

Mayeaux, Steven. *Earthen Walls, Iron Men: Fort DeRussy, Louisiana, and the Defense of Red River*. Knoxville: University of Tennessee Press, 2007.

McCall, Edith. *Conquering the Rivers: Henry Miller Shreve and the Navigation of America's Inland Waterways*. Baton Rouge: Louisiana State University Press, 1984.

McWhinney, Grady and Perry Jamison. *Attack and Die: Civil War Military Tactics and the Southern Heritage*. Tuscaloosa: University of Alabama Press, 1982.

Meiners, Fredericka. "Hamilton P. Bee in the Red River Campaign," *Southwestern Historical Quarterly*. 78 (July 1974), 21–44.

Mills, Gary, and Elizabeth Shown Mills, *The Forgotten People: Cane River's Creoles of Color* Revised Edition. Baton Rouge: Louisiana State University Press, 2013.

Mills, Gary B. *Civil War Claims in the South: An Index of Civil War Damage Claims Filed Before the Southern Claims Commission, 1871–1880*. Laguna Hills, CA: Aegean Park Press 1980.

Mills, Wynona Gilmore. "James Govan Taliaferro, 1898–1876 Unionist and Scalawag." MA Thesis Louisiana State University, 1964.

Mitcham, Samuel W. *Richard Taylor and the Red River Campaign of 1864*. Gretna: Pelican Publishing, 2012.

Mitchell, Louis. "LUBBOCK, FRANCIS RICHARD," Handbook of Texas Online. Accessed April 9, 2013. http://www.tshaonline.org/handbook/online/articles/flu01.

Moore, Claude Hunter. *Thomas Overton Moore A Confederate Governor.* Clinton: Commercial Printing Company, 1960.
Moore, Frank. *Document No.2: the Red River Dam. The Rebellion Record: A Diary of American Events.* vol. 11. New York: G.P. Putnam, 1868.
Moore, Thomas O. "Special Message of Thomas O. Moore, Governor of the State of Louisiana, to the General Assembly." Baton Rouge: J. M. Taylor, State Printer, 1860.
Morgan, James. *A Little Short of Boats: The Civil War Battles of Ball's Bluff and Edwards Ferry, October 21–22, 1861.* Eldorado Hills, CA: Savas Beatie, 2011.
Morris, Curtis Brooks. "The Life of Edward Clark: A War-Time Governor of Texas" MA Thesis Stephen F. Austin University, 1954.
Murr, Erika L., Editor. *A Rebel Wife in Texas: The Diary and Letters of Elizabeth Scott Neblett 1852–1864.* Baton Rouge: Louisiana State University Press, 2001.
National Underwater and Marine Agency, Inc. "2006 Magnetometer and Side-Scan Sonar Remote Sensing Survey for: Three Confederate Civil War Submarines, Cross Bayou, LA." Accessed June 17, 2013. http://clivecusslershipwrecks.com/WordPress/NUMA/expeditions/confederate-submarines.
Nolan, Claude H. *African American Southerners in Slavery, Civil War and Reconstruction.* Jefferson, NC: McFarland, 2001.
Norman, Benjamin Moore. *Norman's New Orleans and Environs.* New York: B .M. Norman, 1845.
Northup, Solomon. *Twelve Years A Slave.* Sue Eakin and Joseph Logsdon, eds. Baton Rouge: Louisiana State University Press, 1968.
Nosworthy, Brent. *The Bloody Crucible of Courage.* New York: Carroll and Graf Publishers, 2003.
Nystrom, Justin. "Reconstruction" in KnowLA Encyclopedia. Accessed April 29, 2015. http://www.knowla.org/entry/463/.
Original Red River Sankofa Project. Accessed November 23, 2011. http://www.redriversankofa.org.
Parks, Joseph Howard. *Edmund Kirby Smith, C.S.A.* Baton Rouge: Louisiana State University Press, 1954.
Parrish, T. Michael. *Richard Taylor Soldier Prince of Dixie.* Chapel Hill: University of North Carolina Press, 1992.
Percival, C.S. and E. Percival, eds. *History of Buchanan County, Iowa 1842 to 1881.* Cleveland: Williams Brothers, 1881.
Pitcock, Cynthia Dehaven and Bill J. Gurley, eds. *I Acted From Principle: The Civil War Diary of Dr. William M. McPheeters, Confederate Surgeon in the Trans-Mississippi.* Fayetteville: University of Arkansas Press, 2002.
Potter, David. *The Impending Crisis, 1848–1861.* New York: Harper and Row, 1977.
Prichard, Walter, ed. "A Tourist's Description of Louisiana in 1860." *Louisiana Historical Quarterly* 21 (October 1938): 1110–1214.
Prime, John Andrew. "Shreveport's Civil War Defenses." Accessed March 3, 2013. http://www.home.earthlink.net/~japrime/lagenweb/defenses.htm.
Prushankin, Jeffery S. *A Crisis of Confederate Command: Edmund Kirby Smith, Richard Taylor, and the Army of the Trans-Mississippi.* Baton Rouge: Louisiana State University Press, 2005.
Rable, George C. *But There Was No Peace: The Role of Violence in the Politics of Reconstruction.* Athens: University of Georgia Press 1984.
Rainwater, P.L. ed. "Excerpts From Fulkerson's 'Recollections of the War Between the States." *Mississippi Valley Historical Review* vol. 24 (December 1937): 351–373.
Reed, John Reed. "Opelousas the Capital and the Twenty-Seventh Legislature of the State of Louisiana," June 29, 2013 Young-Sanders Center, Franklin LA.
Richard III. Accessed April 14, 2012. http://shakespeare.mit.edu/richardiii/full.html.
Ripley, C Peter. *Slaves and Freedmen in Civil War Louisiana.* Baton Rouge: Louisiana State University Press, 1976.

Robertson, Henry O. *"In the Habit of Acting Together": The Emergence of the Whig Party in Louisiana, 1828–1840.* Lafayette: Center for Louisiana Studies, 2007.

Roland, Charles P. "Louisiana and Secession," *Louisiana History* 19 (Fall 1978): 389–399.

Royster, Charles. *The Destructive War.* New York: Alfred A. Knopf, 1991.

Sacher, John. "'Our Interest and Destiny Are the Same': Gov. Thomas Overton Moore and Confederate Loyalty." *Louisiana History* 49 (Summer, 2008): 261–286.

_____. *A Perfect War of Politics: Parties, Politicians, and Democracy in Louisiana, 1824–1861.* Baton Rouge: Louisiana State University Press, 2003.

_____. "'A Very Disagreeable Business: Confederate Conscription in Louisiana." *Civil War History* 53 (June 2007): 141–169.

Shaw, William T. "The Battle of Pleasant Hill. "The Annals of Iowa vol.3 (1898), 401–423. Accessed July 10, 2014. Available at: http://ir.uiowa.edu/annals-of-iowa/vol3/iss5/7.

Sliger, J.E. "How General Taylor Fought the Battle of Mansfield, LA." *Confederate Veteran* vol. 31 (1923): 456–458.

Smith, Edmund Kirby. "The Defense of the Red River," *Battles and Leaders of the Civil War* vol. 4. New York: The Century Company, 1884.

Smith, Rebecca W. and Marion Mullins. "The Diary of H.C. Medford, Confederate Soldier, 1864." *The Southwestern Historical Quarterly* (July 1930-April 1931): 106–140.

"Some Large Landholders of Avoyelles, Bossier, Caddo, Desoto, Natchitoches, and Rapides, Parish, 1850" *Louisiana History* Vols. 24, 25, 26, 28 and 29. (Spring 1983, 1984, 1985, 1987 1988).

Spearing, Darwin. *Roadside Geology of Louisiana.* Missoula: Mountain Press Publishing Company, 1995.

Stafford, G.M.G. *The Wells Family and Allied Families.* Alexandria, LA: Standard Printing Co., 1942.

Stuck, Goodloe. *End of the Land: A South Carolina Family on the Louisiana Frontier.* Ruston, LA: McGinty Publications, 1992.

Sutherland, Daniel. *The Emergence of Total War.* Buffalo Gap: State House Press, 1998.

_____.*Guerrillas, Unionists, and Violence on the Confederate Home Front* Fayetteville: University of Arkansas Press, 1999.

_____. *A Savage Conflict: The Decisive Role of Guerrillas in the American Civil War* Chapel Hill: University of North Carolina Press, 2009.

_____. *Seasons of War: The Ordeal of the Confederate Community, 1861–1865* New York: The Free Press, 1995.

Taylor, Ethel. "Discontent in Confederate Louisiana." *Louisiana History* 2 (Autumn 1961): 410–428.

Taylor, Joel Gray. *Louisiana Reconstructed 1863–1877.* Baton Rouge: Louisiana State University Press, 1974.

Taylor, Richard. *Destruction and Reconstruction.* Edinburgh: William Blackwood and Sons, 1879.

Thomas, Emory. *Robert E. Lee: A Biography.* New York: W.W. Norton, 1995.

Tunnell, Ted. *Edge of the Sword: The Ordeal of Carpetbagger Marshall H. Twitchell in the Civil War and Reconstruction.* Baton Rouge: Louisiana State University Press, 2001.

Tyson, Carl Newton. *The Red River in Southwest History.* Norman: University of Oklahoma Press, 1981.

United States. Commissioners of Claims. *Summary Reports in all Cases Reported to Congress as Disallowed Under the Act of March 3, 1871.* Washington: Government Printing Office, 1876–1881.

_____. Congress. *Report of the Joint Committee on the Conduct of the War.* Washington: Government Printing Office, 1865.

____. *Official Records of the Union and Confederate Navies in the War of the Rebellion.* 31 vols. Washington, D.C.: Government Printing Office, 1895–1929.

____. *The War of the Rebellion: A Compilation of the Official Records of the Union and Confederate Armies.* 128 vols. Washington, D.C.: Government Printing Office, 1890–1901.

____. War Department. *Atlas to Accompany the Official Records of the Union and Confederate Armies.* New York: Fairfax Press, 1983.

Virginia General Assembly. *Virginia State Capitol Visitor's Guide.* Richmond: Information & Communications Services (ICS) House of Delegates Clerk's Office, 2012.

Visco, Stephen G. *The Red River Campaign: An Analysis.* Carlisle Barracks: Army Historical Foundation, 2001.

Wall, Bennett. ed. et. al. *Louisiana: A History.* 5th ed. Wheeling, IL: Harlan Davidson, 2008.

Walther, Eric H. *The Fire-Eaters.* Baton Rouge: Louisiana State University Press, 1992.

Warner, Ezra J. *Generals in Blue.* Baton Rouge; Louisiana State University, 1964.

____. *Generals in Gray.* Baton Rouge: Louisiana State University, 1959.

Wells, Carol, ed. *War, Reconstruction, and Redemption on Red River: The Memoirs of Dosia Williams Moore.* Ruston: McGinty Publications, 1991.

Whitcomb, Caroline E. *History of the Second Massachusetts Battery (Nims' Battery of Light Artillery) 1861–1865.* Concord: Rumford Press, 1912.

Whittington, George P. "Concerning the Loyalty of Slaves in North Louisiana in 1863." *Louisiana Historical Quarterly* 14 (October 1931): 494–495.

____. *Rapides Parish, Louisiana, a History: Edited by Carl Laurent.* Alexandria: Red River X-Press, 2014.

Williams, Richard. *Chicago's Battery Boys.* New York: Savas Beatie, 2005.

Winschel, Terrence J. *The Civil War Diary of a Common Soldier: William Wiley of the 77th Illinois Infantry.* Baton Rouge: LSU Press, 2001.

Winters, John. *The Civil War in Louisiana.* Baton Rouge: Louisiana State University Press,1963.

Woodworth, Steven. *Beneath A Northern Sky: A Short History of the Gettysburg Campaign.* Lanham: Rowan and Littlefield, 2008.

Wooster, Ralph A. "CLARK, EDWARD." Handbook of Texas Online. Accessed April 9, 2013. http://www.tshaonline.org/handbook/online/articles/fcl04.

Index

Alexandria 1–4, 12, 15–16, 18, 25, 31, 33–34, 39–40, 43–45, 49–50, 52–53, 66–67, 71–72, 81, 85, 87, 89–92, 96–97, 119, 124, 134, 136–138, 142, 147, 149, 150, 151, 155, 157–158, 160–163, 165, 169, 171–172, 176
Allen, Henry Watkins 17, 53–54, 59, 60, 65, 78, 162, 170
CSS *Arkansas* 21
Armant, Leopold 103, 131
Armstrong, Della 82
artillery 2, 17, 20, 87, 88, 91, 96, 98, 105–108, 109, 118, 125, 135, 141, 163–165, 176
Avoyelles 2, 18, 24–27, 39, 48–49, 55, 59, 61, 77, 85, 137, 163, 170, 173–174

Bailey, Joseph 2–3, 158–160, 165
Bailey's Dam 158–159, 169
Baillio, Landry 171
Ball, Augustus 31, 142
Banks, Nathaniel P. 11–12, 13–14, 51–52, 72–73, 82–88, 97–98, 113, 138, 161, 168–169, 174
Baptist Church (Mansfield) 130
Barber, Mahlon W. 112–115
Baton Rouge 8, 9, 10, 13, 48, 54, 58
Baylor, George 141, 147–148
Bayou Bourbeux 13
Bayou Pierre 19, 24
Bayou Rapides 24, 39, 46, 71, 87, 90, 149, 151, 160
Bee, Hamilton 139, 141–144, 146–148
Beebe, William S. 141
Bell, John 39–44, 46–48
Benedict, Lewis 122–124
Bennett family 30, 106
Bennett Store 130
Birge, William 141
Boggs, William R. 19–20
Booth, John Wilkes 95–96
Boston Herald 118, 125–126

Bowie County (TX) 31, 142
Boyce, Charles 43–44, 88, 157, 171
Breckinridge, John 10, 39–44
Bringier family 56
British Claims Commission 173
Broadwell, William 64, 68

Caddo 24–26, 27, 30, 32, 34, 39, 41, 45, 48, 170
Calhoun, Meredith 43, 74
Calhoun's Landing 74
Cameron, Robert A. 106, 108
Camp Ford (TX) 80
Cane River 24, 42, 110, 133, 136, 138–145, 151–154
Canfield, Mercer 45, 131
Catahoula 48, 61
Catholic Church (Alexandria) 154, 161
Cavalry 2, 7, 57, 76, 85, 87, 90–91, 93, 97, 100, 109, 113, 138, 141, 143, 146, 150, 152, 154, 157, 161, 163–164, 165
USS *Champion No. 3* 135
Chapman's Bayou 111, 114
Chicago Mercantile Battery 105, 107
Churchill, Thomas J. 117, 122, 124, 144
Clark, Edward 119–121
Clark, John S. 82, 84
Cloutierville 41, 42, 48, 138, 152, 155
Conduct of Federal Troops in Louisiana 162
confiscation 16, 64–66
conscription 52, 57, 59–66
Constitutional 44–45
Constitutional Convention 83, 87, 172
Corps d'Afrique 87, 137
Cotton Policy 16, 68, 71–72

David Store 158
Davis, Jefferson 10, 49, 79
Democratic Party 8, 40, 45, 47, 60, 176
Department of the Gulf 9, 11, 13, 14, 51, 68, 82, 87, 88, 90, 124, 136, 169

Index

Desoto 25, 26, 29, 32, 39, 41, 48, 116, 170
Dickey, William 137–138
Dorr, J.W. 32, 44–46
Douglas, Stephen 39–44
Dudley, A.D. 52
Durning Charles S. 113–115
Dwight, Charles C. 77
USS *Eastport* 21

Egg Bend 2
Elgee, John 46, 174
Emory, William 110–112, 116, 140–141, 144, 164
Fessenden, Francis 141
fire 3, 68, 76, 111, 130, 152, 157, 160–163, 166
Fort Buhlow 176
Fort DeRussy 88, 89, 96, 137, 168, 176
Fort Humbug 20
Fort Randolph 176
fortifications 9, 12, 13, 18, 20, 64, 66, 124, 176
Franklin, William 97, 105–106, 116, 140
French Claims Commission 173

Gilmer, James 19
Graham, George Mason 44
Grand Ecore 67, 117, 125, 128, 133, 137, 138, 157
Grant, Ulysses S. 168
greed 3, 69, 70, 76, 162, 170
Green, Tom 2

Halleck, Henry 14
Haynes, Dennis E. 62–64, 161
Henderson's Hill 90, 96, 168
Hinckley, Orramel 75
historiography 3–5
Honeycutt Hill 103, 129
Hubbard, Lucius 19, 90, 125, 127, 157, 168
Hunter, Robert A. 46
Hyatt, Arthur 103–104
Hynson, Robert C. 88

inauguration 83–85
Irish Bend 12

Jackson, "Stonewall" 10, 91, 97, 107, 122, 143
Jayhawkers 3, 57, 61, 62, 63, 70
Joint Committee on the Conduct of the War 169

Kent House 88
King, William Henry 75, 81
Know Nothings 43

USS *Laurel Hill* 74

Lee, Robert E. 37
Levy, William 77, 172
Lincoln, Abraham 8, 14, 39, 42, 46, 70, 73, 78, 80, 83–84, 87, 96–97, 101, 174–175
Lost Cause 176
Louisiana Democrat 45, 49
Loyalty Oath 72

Manning, Thomas C. 46–47, 61, 134, 162
Mansfield 31–35, 93, 96, 98, 99, 127, 130, 132, 127, 130, 132, 176
Mansura 2, 163–164, 173
marching 91–93
Marshall, Henry 29
Martin, "Bloody Bob" 62–63
McNeel, George 150–151
McPheeters, William 125, 128
Meridian Campaign 156
Mississippi River 2, 8, 9, 10–11, 13, 16, 18, 23, 34, 58–59, 67, 70, 75, 77, 80, 83, 92, 136, 147, 165
CSS *Missouri* 20
Moore, Thomas O. 11, 24, 27, 34, 35, 45–46, 49–50, 60, 68, 81, 174
Moss, Sara 98–100
Mouton, Alfred 60, 98–99, 106–107, 131
Mullholland, Charles 27

Natchitoches 7, 8, 19, 24, 25, 26, 28, 29, 33, 39, 41–42, 45, 47, 48, 49, 56, 57, 59, 68, 76, 91, 92, 93, 113, 135, 136, 138, 151, 153, 155, 170
Neblett, Family 132
New Falls City 19
New Orleans 8–11, 14, 19, 25, 32, 35, 43–45, 49–53, 55–58, 67–69, 73–75, 80, 83, 87, 95, 120, 126, 132, 175
Newell family 56–57
Northup, Solomon 27–28

Petty, E.P. 75
Pickett, James 30
Pierson, Davis 37–38
Pierson, Reuben 130–131
Pineville 1, 21, 39, 43, 44, 61, 157, 158, 168, 171, 176
Pleasant Grove 108–109
Pleasant Hill 2, 31–35, 110, 111, 113, 115, 116, 118, 122, 127, 150
Poché, Felix 74, 76, 127–128
Poete, Pierre 152–153
Port Hudson 10, 13, 20, 58, 63, 67, 77, 78, 80, 81, 96, 124, 136, 137, 164
Porter, David Dixon 2, 15, 21, 70, 71, 82, 86, 159, 169
Prize Law 71–72
Prudhomme family 29, 65, 136, 155, 169

Index

Ransdell, John H. 81
Ransom, Thomas E.G. 103, 105
Rapides 24–27, 30, 34, 35, 39, 40, 42, 43, 44, 46, 47, 48, 49, 56, 59, 62, 71, 74, 81, 106, 155, 170, 171, 172–173
Ray, David 75, 100–101, 119
Ray, John 100–101, 118–119
Red River 16, 20, 24, 27, 30, 31, 32, 34, 40, 63, 138
Red River Landing 77
Reed, Charles F. 91, 161
Republican Party 8, 12, 14, 39, 42, 101
Richmond, Enos 172
Richmond, VA 8, 16, 37, 52, 79, 123

Sabine 29, 32, 39, 41, 48, 49, 57, 82, 129, 175
Sabine Pass 13
Sabine River 29
Sasser, Whitty M. 171–172
Scruggs, S.O. 48, 155
secession 5, 37–38, 39, 42–44, 47–49, 120, 171
Seip, Frederic 114
Shaw, William T. 119, 121
Sherman, William T. 12, 44, 156, 168
Shreve, Henry 33–34
Shreveport 2, 15–16, 19–26, 34, 37, 49, 53, 56, 71, 75, 81–82, 96, 139
Simmsport 21, 88, 92–93, 165
Smith, Andrew Jackson 86, 88, 127, 140, 165
Smith, Kirby 4, 16–18, 21, 68, 79, 88, 117, 139, 144, 146, 147, 176–177
Smith, Ralph 30
Smith, William 136–137, 169
Springfield Landing 2, 96
starvation 129, 170, 175
Steele, Frederick 15
Stone, Charles 52, 84
Stone, Kate 55

Taliaferro, James G. 48
Taylor, Richard 2, 4, 10–13, 21, 26, 65, 75, 79–80, 118, 131–132, 142, 146–147;
strategy 18, 88–91, 96–97, 117, 122, 163, 167, 175–176
Texada, Lewis 46, 87–88, 174
Texas 2, 5, 13–14, 21, 23, 31, 34, 62, 67, 93, 120, 143, 150; soldiers from 2, 57, 75, 77, 91, 93, 98, 100, 105, 108, 113, 114, 118, 119–120, 129, 132, 141, 142, 150, 154, 163–164, 166
Tone's Bayou 19, 21
Trans-Mississippi Department 10, 16, 19, 68, 163, 177
Twelve Years a Slave 28

Unionists 3, 5, 43–45, 47, 49–54, 83, 155, 170, 173–175
United States Claims Commission 170–172
United States Colored Troops (USCT) 121, 136–138, 141, 164, 169
United States Treasury Department 72–73

Vicksburg 8, 9, 13, 15, 21, 58, 59, 67, 70, 86, 92, 102, 105, 107, 125
Vincent, William G. 90

wagons 11, 65, 87, 93, 97, 104, 106, 108, 109, 111, 172–173
Walker, John 90, 98–99, 118–119, 120, 146
Washington, D.C. 8, 14, 68, 88, 92, 96, 168
Webb, Lysander 101–103
Welch, Deming N. 73
Wells, James Madison 43, 44, 50–53, 63, 87, 155, 171, 174
Wells, Thomas Jefferson 35, 44–45, 87
Wharton, John 147–148
Whig Party 42–43, 120, 123
Wigfall, Louis 46
Wilson's Farm 98
Winn 38, 39, 48, 49, 61, 130, 170
Withenbury, William 82

Yellow Bayou 2, 163, 165–167

www.ingramcontent.com/pod-product-compliance
Ingram Content Group UK Ltd.
Pitfield, Milton Keynes, MK11 3LW, UK
UKHW042000140426
5217IPUK00015B/897